The
Road
Trip
Book

The
Road Trip
Book

Travel America
Like You've
Always
Dreamed

2nd Edition

Jeremy Krug

Acero Publishing

The Road Trip Book
Travel America Like You've Always Dreamed
2nd Edition

Copyright © 2014 by Jeremy Krug
All rights reserved.

Acero Publishing

ISBN 0-988776-50-2
EAN 978-0-988-77650-0

Printed in the United States of America

917.3 – dc22

All information provided in this publication is provided for information purposes only. Although every reasonable effort has been made to present current and accurate information, the author and publisher make no guar-antees of any kind. Users take the responsibility for verifying all information. The statements and opinions presented in this publication are those of the author and do not constitute legal advice. The author and pub-lisher assume no responsibility or liability for any consequence resulting directly or indirectly for any action or inaction you take based on or made in reliance on the information, services, or material mentioned in this publica-tion. Any Web sites mentioned in this publication are provided as a courtesy. They should not be construed as an endorsement by the author of the content or views of the linked materials. Any trademarks, brand names, or otherwise registered identification markers are used as a courtesy to their services provided and are owned by their respective parties.

Contents

Preface

I'm not afraid to fly. Air travel is the safest mode of transportation, and most of us know that. But over the past two decades, flying has become the most invasive way to travel and arguably the most inconvenient. I can remember plenty of flights that made me wish I'd just stayed home.

For example, there was the flight from Nashville to Atlanta that should have taken 45 minutes, but due to fog actually took five hours, counting delays. I remember a Sunday night red-eye from California to New York, where a middle-aged man sitting behind me spent five hours kicking my seat because he had had a bad weekend. On another flight, my luggage was sent to the wrong continent and didn't get delivered for five days. A short flight I took Christmas night 2010 turned bad when a deicing truck crashed into the wing before takeoff.

Flying usually involves more hassle than it's worth. Dealing with long lines, delays, surly airport personnel, expensive baggage fees, price gouging by the airlines, and draconian security rules that do little to actually improve security make air travel a stressful experience. Although I still fly when I have to or the circumstances require it, I've learned that traveling by road is much more civilized. I get to experience the cities, towns, and countryside I'm passing through – a luxury that air travelers simply don't have. So I've gone back to the road. And when I'm not on the road, I talk about the road on my weekly online radio show, *Road Trip Radio*.

Hosting *Road Trip Radio* every week with my co-host Dave Godar has put me in contact with some of the most interesting people in the world of road travel. There was our chat with Mark Sedenquist, the founder of the RoadTripAmerica.com travel guide and message forum, himself an avid roadtripper who spent most of a decade living on the road. Another week, Ken Smith – one of the authors of RoadsideAmerica.com and an expert on offbeat tourist attractions – talked about the time he accidentally stumbled across a rattlesnake farm in Texas. And who could forget the evening we sat down with Pat Travis, the owner of the Little A'le'inn restaurant in Rachel, Nevada, as she shared her experiences about living just a stone's throw from Area 51!

This book is a compilation of the lessons I've learned from countless road trips and personal experiences, sometimes learned the hard way. I hope that readers can avoid the mistakes I've made along my travels. I hope they'll enjoy their travels by being flexible and willing to discover the unexpected.

And that's the superiority of road travel for those who want to discover what lies along the way. For those who get as excited about the journey as they do about the destination, for those who are ready to expect the unexpected, road trips open a door to endless adventure.

If you've ever wanted to savor the journey, then this book is for you. And if you want to listen to travel talk radio focusing on road trips, head over to www.roadtripradiousa.com and download my show on-demand. Hop in, buckle up, and enjoy the ride!

Part One

Planning a Road Trip

1

Why Take a Road Trip?

If you're reading this book, then you have at least a passing desire to travel the open road. But why do we have this desire to travel, to wander, to absorb everything that surrounds us? Although road trips can be taken in almost any place in the world, they're indelibly etched into the culture of America. Ever since the early days of automobiles, buying a car has been advertised as an almost patriotic way for workers to spend their hard-earned money. Discovering America by car has always been the best and most popular way to explore big cities, small towns, and everything in between.

Some of us take road trips out of necessity. When families move cross-country, they load up all their possessions onto a moving van and drive to their new home. Others take road trips to visit family in distant places. A "trip to Grandma's house" may be a trek unto itself. Families get together for different reasons: weddings, graduations, funerals, reunions. You may find yourself getting into a car and driving to any of these events.

More Options than Flying

The main difference between flying and driving is the freedom to discover places along the way to your destination. Traveling by air, you may be fortunate enough to have a window seat on a sunny day and see the ground from 30,000 feet. But the view from the air simply cannot compare to the sheer majesty of experiencing it from the ground. And when you find an area that you might like to discover a little more, you won't have much success convincing the pilot to land the plane so you can explore.

Driving gives you control of the travel experience. You'll have the freedom to discover an area unplanned; when you see a place that looks interesting or a historical site that catches your eye, you can stop and take a look – something that can't be done with other modes of transportation.

Flying involves the stress of airports, standing in long lines, taking off your shoes, dealing with surly security personnel, waiting in the gate area, paying ever-increasing fees for ever-decreasing service, hoping your luggage ends up in the same place as you do, hoping your flight is not delayed; the list goes on and on. But you get the picture: If you strictly want to get to a specific destination, fly. It will usually get you there faster.

Even that last statement, though, isn't always correct. Short-haul flights often take longer than driving, especially for travelers who don't live near a major airport.

For example, imagine someone who lives in southern Missouri, two hours from the nearest major airport in St. Louis. If this person wants to fly to Chicago, 375 miles away, it's going to require a two-hour drive to the airport, another 20 minutes finding a parking space and taking the shuttle back to the terminal. If this person arrives at the airport two hours before the scheduled flight time – like the airlines say – he or she will spend some time waiting in the gate area before the one hour flight to Chicago. Once the plane lands, it takes yet another hour to get off the plane, get out of the airport, and get somewhere in Chicago. From door to door, our hypothetical air traveler has spent nearly six and a half hours getting to Chicago, a journey that could have probably been driven in six hours.

But isn't it cheaper to fly?

With today's high gas prices, many think that a road trip would cost much more than flying. However, most road trips within 300 miles of your home actually cost less than flying. Take our trip to Chicago, for example. This flight could easily cost $170 round-trip, plus any long-term parking fees at your 'home' airport. Once this person gets to Chicago, they'll need to get to their actual destination. Cab fare or renting a car will add to the expenses significantly. Even with gas at $4.00 a gallon, they could easily make the drive with $160 in gasoline, with a vehicle averaging 20 miles per gallon.

The real benefit to a road trip, though, isn't the cost savings or the time savings, but the experience and adventure of discovering your very own strip of America. On a road trip, you'll discover new sights, sounds, and tastes at your own pace. My favorite road trips are the ones where I'm not tied down to any specific schedule or destination. And that's the charm of this type of travel; you can stop for the night when and where you really want. Later in this book, I will show how it's possible to reserve an inexpensive room, even at the last minute (literally!) while on the road.

Road trips don't have to be expensive. This book will show you how to slash 50% or more from the typical lodging bill. Although eating in local restaurants is a fun way to get to know an area while passing through, it can get quite expensive, especially for a family. I'll share tips that will save money on food – and they don't involve skipping meals! I'll even show you ways to save money on gas while on the road.

Although the typical road trip discussed in this book will last several days, your trip doesn't have to consume that much time, either. Road trips are more about the feeling you get by being free to explore and wander on your own time. It's possible to enjoy a great trip in just one or two days, too. Chapter 5 is devoted to short jaunts that take just a day or two to enjoy and won't consume much more than a tank of gas.

Consider Your Options

A road trip can be a relaxing way to spend a few days of vacation. When you're driving down a lonely stretch of highway surrounded by awe-inspiring scenery, it can be a mind-expanding, nearly euphoric, experience.

Throughout the eastern half of the United States, you'll see much of the natural beauty in the variety of green valleys, rolling hills, rivers, lakes, and rugged mountains. Along the coast, the Atlantic Ocean and nearby beaches will grab your attention. In the Northeast, plan on discovering history scattered through nearly every city, town, and village along your route. Obviously, you could spend days in any major city in this part of the country and still not see all the sights.

But what will *you* choose to do? Will you visit museums, catch a baseball game, go to historic sites, sample the local cuisine?

If you plan to travel through the West, the scenery will be quite different. If you are one of the many Easterners that has never driven cross-country, you may be surprised by the wide-open spaces and long distances involved in driving out West.

There are places in this part of the country where major towns may have just a few thousand people, and those towns may be 80 to 100 miles apart from each other.

Out here, everything just seems bigger. The spaces are bigger, the mountains are bigger, and the states are definitely bigger. In many parts of the West, you can easily drive 500 miles in one direction without ever crossing a state line.

U.S. Highway 50 through northern Nevada, often called the "Loneliest Road in America", crosses nine mountain ranges over its 400-mile trek across the state. Travel this road if you want to experience what 'wide-open spaces' are really about. (See Chapter 19 for more information.) Ribbons of asphalt literally stretch in front of you as far as the eye can see. On a clear day, being able to see mountains 100 miles away is not out of the question.

Highways in the West often stretch as far as the eye can see

If you've never visited the West, you may be a little surprised to see how flat much of this frontier is, with occasional mountains scattered across the distant landscape.

No matter where your journey takes you, always keep an open mind. Plenty of people are mentally opposed to taking road trips. They think that spending a day on the road – or multiple days – would have to be boring. The first thing I tell them is that no road trip *has* to be boring. There's so much to see on the road that even the most mundane of trips can be fun – if you plan ahead.

Keep an Open Mind

I'll be sharing test-tested tips I've learned to keep your trip exciting and fun. Some individuals dread driving through many Plains states such as Kansas, Nebraska, and the Dakotas. However, these states, while relatively small in population, make for some enjoyable driving with plenty of surprising diversions along the way, especially if you're willing to get off the interstate and join two-lane highways. So keep an open mind about your route!

Make no mistake, though: This book is different from other travel books on the market. Although there's an entire section on places to visit, its main purpose is to show readers how to plan a trip, how to enjoy their road trip to the fullest, and how to save money in the process.

As you progress through the chapters, you'll find ways to plan a route that makes sense for you and takes you to places you want to see. Later, you'll read about ways to get your vehicle ready for a long journey. Eventually, we'll discuss ways to enjoy the trip once you're on the road, as well as food and lodging options. And, of course, I've included a comprehensive packing list, tailored to the needs of roadtrippers.

Are you convinced? Are you ready for that road trip you've always wanted to take? Whether your road trip takes you to your destination, or if the road trip *is* your destination, you're sure to discover something unexpected on the open road.

Who Will Go Along?

Once you've decided to take a road trip, then the next step is to decide who will be traveling with you. This step is important because the people you take along often determine what kind of trip you can take and how much you'll enjoy it.

Years ago, a friend of mine took a road trip to Texas, and she invited two friends to join her. Their plan was to leave at about 5:30 on a Saturday morning and drive to their destination in one long day. They had planned their budget and space in the car around three people being on the trip. The morning they were to leave, though, one of her friends showed up at the door, announcing that she'd invited her father to come along.

Needless to say, she was shocked. Instead of a leisurely trip with three friends, the un-invited fourth passenger wanted to control where they stopped, where they ate, and the topic of conversation. The other two spent the last 700 miles (and the next two months!) discussing how they *should have had* a stronger will and refused to take an uninvited person on the trip.

You're Never Alone on the Road

Every day, millions of us take to the road, traveling to places outside our normal routine. During peak holiday travel times, at least 50 million Americans take a road trip of some sort. Even the most isolated of interstate highways have upwards of 5,000 vehicles traveling them each day. Whether your plans call for a short daytrip or a 10,000-mile marathon journey, you're never alone on the road!

Does this experience sound familiar? If it does, you probably learned a valuable lesson: be *extremely selective* of whom you invite on a road trip. If every person in the car doesn't feel comfortable with every other person in the car, somebody's going to be miserable.

Just as importantly, if you're coordinating the trip, make it known to any friends accompanying you that the road trip invitation is *just for them*, and not for *their* friends or family. Besides, a car has limited space, and there's just not that much extra space.

Allow Plenty of Space for Everyone

Let's say that you choose to drive a full-side sedan on a long trip. For a week, three adults can fit comfortably. Four is really starting to push the limit. Although the car technically has six seatbelts, every person will have his or her own luggage and gear. If you add a cooler, a camping tent, or even a couple of pillows, trunk space will fill up very fast.

Remember, you're going to be living out of this car for the next several days, so you'll want to be comfortable and have enough personal space for everybody. Although I have had up to six people in a car on a road trip (four adults and two children), long trips in this type of vehicle are much more comfortable with no more than four people.

If you drive a van or an SUV, you may be able to fit more people, but the same principle applies. Don't take the maximum number of passengers permitted for your vehicle; leave a couple of seats empty for personal belongings and elbow room. You'll be glad you did.

Don't Force Anyone to Go

Lots of people, especially younger peop[le, don't have to be convinced, cajoled, or coerced into taking a road trip. If you're reading this book, you probably *want* to travel. Still, many people simply abhor the idea of spending hours, days, or even weeks in a car driving around the country. They want to get *somewhere* and aren't really concerned about the *ride there*. These people – although not wholly understood by me – are fully entitled to their opinion and shouldn't be forced or convinced to go along. (Truth be told, these people probably don't understand *your* desire to wander around the country in a car for days on end.)

If you suggest the idea of a road trip to a friend, and he or she reacts negatively, don't try to convince him or her otherwise! Taking a 'non-road trip person' along with you could ruin the trip, and more importantly, impair your friendship. Stick to taking those along that really *want* to go. This sounds obvious, but one popular travel guide advises its readers to convince their friends – even the road trip averse – into going along. Not a good idea!

Roadtripping With Friends

When you take friends along on a road trip, discuss expenses *ahead of time*, not as you roll out of the driveway. Later in this book, we'll cover ways to save money, but for now, make sure that everyone in the car knows that they will be expected to cover their equal share of the *group expenses.*

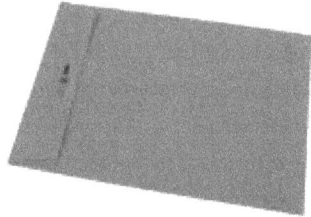

Everyone puts $50 into an envelope for group expenses

Group expenses include gasoline, lodging, tolls, and parking. Consider this method for sharing expenses: at the beginning of the trip, everyone in the car puts $50 cash into an envelope. That envelope will be used only for group expenses. When it runs out, everybody puts in another $50. Any money left over at the end of the trip is divided equally.

This method is one of the easiest for making sure everyone in the car pays their fair share. You might think of a better way. If you pay for gas and lodging with credit cards, it might be just as easy to keep a running total of group expenses in a small notebook. Then, at the end of the trip, each person pays his or her part of the bill, either by cash or check.

Not all expenses are group expenses. Each individual should pay for his or her own food, souvenirs, and admission to attractions. That being said, every person in the car should bring along enough cash or credit to cover these personal expenses.

With several people in the car, it's usually wise to rotate seats occasionally. Unless everyone is satisfied with a specific spot, it may get old being in the back seat for the entire trip. Rotate drivers too, as long as the car's owner allows it. Make sure that each driver has a valid license and feels comfortable driving in unknown territory. Rotating drivers every few hours will let everyone have a better chance to enjoy the scenery and relax on the trip.

For safety's sake, it's best to let the driver control the radio and the temperature in the car. Some people may disagree with me, but the fact is that the driver, by far, is under more stress than anyone else in the vehicle. If the driver is too cold, too warm, or too grumpy, he or she could get drowsy or cause an accident. When the driver chooses a station the rest of the passengers don't like, they need to make use of the audio player on their phone or other electronic device. Don't have one? Get one! We'll talk more about MP3 players and other electronics in Chapter 3. If you're cold, put on a sweatshirt or blanket. If you get too hot, take off a layer of clothing.

When it's time to decide where to eat, why not let everyone have a turn at selecting a place? Everybody has different tastes, and sometimes not everyone will like the restaurant. But that's part of the fun of a road trip – discovering new places and letting everyone have their chance to call the shots.

Letting everyone in the car have a chance to choose also keeps the whole group from eating at the same fast food chain every meal. And seriously, if you feel you have to eat at the same fast food chain every day (or even multiple times a day!), then maybe you'd be better off taking a solo trip.

Roadtripping With Family

Although many teens and twenty-something's dream of taking a cross-country road trip with a group of buddies, most road trips are taken with the family. Mom, Dad, and the kids pile into the car to visit some destination many hours away. Maybe they're visiting Grandma, an aunt, traveling to a wedding, graduation, or possibly even a funeral.

If it's just you and your spouse on this road trip, try not to irritate each other too much. Remember, sometimes people act differently when they sit in a car for many hours at a time. Converse for a while, then listen to music for a while. Even when you're driving, let your spouse stop where she (or he) wants. Look for a shopping center, park, or other attraction to walk around and spend some time. Sometimes, the best souvenirs are purchased, not in tourist traps, but in local stores, or even supermarkets.

Most families take the kids along too. Since young children have a short attention span, they need to be kept occupied. Most young kids won't appreciate scenery as much as adults, so they'll enjoy the trip much more if they get to take a break every hour or two. Whereas most adults can sit in a car for several hours at a time, children need to get out and walk around – or run around – every hour or so.

Young kids like to be entertained. While license plate games and puzzle books do pass the time, many children today don't get very enthused with those kinds of activities. If your kids enjoy playing video games, a portable version and a good set of batteries would be a wise investment. A DVD player or MP3 player will also keep them entertained for relatively little money. Most of these devices have DC vehicle adapters that allow them to be used without constantly recharging batteries.

Although most small children need to be entertained throughout the ride, teenagers can appreciate the trip much more. They might help plan your trip and even document it. Giving teenagers a camera and letting them take pictures will help them look for interesting sights along the way. Many teens are good with maps and can help navigate or suggest places to stop. Let your teens be a part of the trip's success, and they will enjoy it much more.

Some of these tips may work for you, and others may not. You know your children's likes and dislikes better than anyone, so do what works when you take your kids on the road!

Kids like snacks, and those can get expensive if bought exclusively at fast-food restaurants along the road. Stop at a supermarket and buy snacks that you know they'll enjoy. You'll save money and time by avoiding extra fast-food stops.

One more thing: if the kids get tired and want to sleep while you drive, let them. It will give you a chance to relax for a couple hours and enjoy the ride that much more.

Taking Along Your Pet

If you've decided to take your pet along on your road trip, you're not alone. Millions of people do the same thing every year as they drive across the country. Traveling with your pet doesn't have to be difficult.

Of course, some pets travel better than others. Fish or other animals that live underwater don't handle long road trips very well (obviously) and should be left home. Exotic animals such as snakes, monkeys, and certain birds should be left home, too; these animals may even be prohibited from entering certain states without prior authorization or documentation.

For the most part, dogs and cats most commonly go along on road trips; they seem to fare the best on these types of adventures.

Before you take your animal companion on the road, please remember that many public places simply do not welcome pets. Most enclosed public buildings, such as supermarkets, restaurants, and shopping centers expressly prohibit pets, and those prohibitions should be respected. Of course, seeing-eye dogs and other service animals are not pets and are to be welcomed anywhere the public is allowed to enter.

Get Your Pet Ready for the Trip

Getting a pet, especially a dog, used to being in the car for long periods of time takes time and patience. If your dog has never been on a road trip, you'll need to work with him long beforehand to get him accustomed to the car. If you get in the habit of taking short trips to places he likes to go, he will learn to see the car as a fun place to be.

Over time, lengthen the trips somewhat until he is ready for a longer road trip. Very young puppies may have trouble at first, as some tend to get carsick. With puppies you may want to avoid curvy roads and stick to main highways.

The pet needs his own place in the car. Some dogs feel most secure when riding in their carrier; others prefer a blanket in the back seat. Taking a road trip is out of most animals' routines, and many of them act shy, scared, or just different when put into unfamiliar surroundings.

Bringing along some favorite toys can help make your pet feel more comfortable on the road. Animals thrive on routine, and any routines from home that you can bring along will help your pet immensely. Set a fixed feeding time, and stick to it religiously.

Remember that your pet will need as much exercise as when he is at home, maybe even more. After being in the car for a few hours, he'll need to run around and play. Interstate rest areas are perfect for this, and most of them have specified pet exercise areas, well away from the main building. Usually, your pet will have to be kept on a leash in these areas, but they give pets – and their owners – a great opportunity to move around and run while on the road.

If you spend several days on the road, pets will get used to your daily travel routine. Still, you know your pet better than anyone else, and he may still need to stop very often. It's not unusual for animals to need a stop every hour. Most can easily handle two or three hours, though.

At the end of the day, you and your pet will need a place to stay. Many hotels and motels, especially the common chains found at most interstate exits, welcome pets. It may be wise to plan ahead, though, since not all hotels do, and others charge hefty pet fees. Many roadside hotels charge a pet fee of $10 to $30; others charge nothing. Some require a 'pet deposit' to ensure that the room stays in satisfactory condition while your pet is there. Each hotel's website can give specific information about pet policies, deposits, or fees.

Remember, too, that there are other lodging opportunities when you travel with your pet. Campgrounds welcome pets more consistently than hotels, and they almost never charge extra for the privilege. Campgrounds also provide pets a chance to exercise more freely than at a hotel. Whatever you choose, remember that there are plenty of options when traveling with your pet, especially if you plan ahead.

Now that you've decided to take a road trip, and hopefully you know who will be along for the ride, it's time to decide on a place to go, and how to get there. The next chapter will discuss just that: how to choose your route.

2

Charting a Path

By this point, you may be ready to jump out the door, into your car, and onto the road. But don't leave just yet, because planning your trip is part of the fun, too. Maybe you have an idea of where you'd like to go and the sights you want to see. This is the time to start putting ideas to paper, long *before* the trip begins.

Probably the best way to start planning your trip is to acquire a quality print road atlas covering the entire country. Rand McNally's is the best one out there; it's published every year and costs less than ten dollars.

Although Rand McNally is a little slow to include new highways and updates into their maps, their value and overall quality are good enough for most travelers. Each state is mapped separately, and most larger cities have separate, more detailed maps.

Browsing a road atlas for an hour or two can give you an idea of places and attractions you might like to visit. If you want to visit the West, browse those states and look for locations that catch your eye. You may find some places that warrant a multi-day visit, while you might simply pass through other areas, depending on your plans and interests.

If you've never visited the United States before, or if this will be your first trek across the country, you may be surprised at the sheer size of this country. Especially in the West, expect long distances between towns and cities. Many first time roadtrippers from the East want to 'go out West' without knowing what to expect.

For example, just driving across Texas takes a full day – sometimes much more. It's very easy to drive 500 miles within a single state in many parts of the West. By looking at maps, you can start to plot a reasonable route, along with destinations and stops you want to make.

Other Maps You'll Need

Along with a quality print atlas, I recommend enlisting the use of computer mapping software. Many travelers recommend *Microsoft Streets and Trips* or *Delorme Street Atlas USA*. Both of these products have detailed street-level maps, as well as GPS capability. They also include information on hotels, restaurants, gas stations, museums, and other points of interest along the way. You can calculate exact mileage for a route, estimate fuel stops, and even hear turn-by-turn directions if you install the optional GPS receiver and take your laptop along. Many of these programs are useful for planning any type of road trip.

Another option is to make use of one of the many free online mapping services, such as Google Maps, Mapquest, and Yahoo! Maps. Although these services don't have quite as much capability as purchased software, most simple trip planning tasks can be accomplished on these increasingly-robust websites. For example, satellite imagery from Google Maps can be very useful for finding a specific location in a city. Although some software programs have limited satellite image availability, Google Maps and Google Earth provide much more comprehensive satellite and street images.

Members of AAA can order custom-made maps, called Trip-Tiks, for their road trips. Along with these maps, AAA offers guidebooks listing most hotels, popular restaurants, and key attractions for each state. Members receive these trip-planning services free of charge, and they do come in quite handy.

Know Your Own Limitations

When planning a road trip, it's important to be reasonable in the distance you plan to cover. Answer these three questions to see how well you know your limitations on the road:

- How many hours can you drive without a break?
- How many hours do you plan to spend on the road each day?
- How many miles can you drive in one day?

These questions are posed in order of increasing difficulty, and it's important to know the answer to each one before you commit to a long, multi-day road trip. The first question is usually a tough one for new roadtrippers. Honestly, although each person is different, most drivers find they *really* need a stop or some sort of break after three nonstop hours behind the wheel.

To be honest, drivers that stop only every three hours probably have a specific destination, and they need to be there quickly.

Most drivers will stop at least every two hours, sometimes more. Remember, stops have to be made for food, fuel, and restroom, not to mention sightseeing. You'll find that when more passengers are in your group, the more often you'll have to stop.

The second question is more difficult because most of us tend to overestimate our endurance. When I took my first road trip, I assumed I could begin about 4:00 a.m. and drive until about 10 or 11 at night, and that was a solo trip! Needless to say, that didn't happen. That would have made for an 18-hour day. Not only is that unsafe, it nearly guarantees being miserable by evening.

When the plan involves a quick, one-day drive, it's not unreasonable to arrive in one long, 15-hour day. On multi-day trips, though, plan to drive no more than about 10 or 11 hours each day. Although this might not sound like a lot, being on the road much more than 10 hours a day will tire a driver very fast. Even if you have several drivers switching off, you'll need to spend time outside the vehicle to truly enjoy your road trip.

Now, how many miles can you reasonably drive in one day? If your answer is anywhere close to 1000, then you seriously need to rethink your possibilities. Most experienced roadtrippers average about 55 miles per hour over the course of a driving day. In rural areas, this value may be as high as 57 or 58 miles per hour. Now, these average speeds include stops for meals, fuel, and other necessities. Lengthier stops for sightseeing or side trips are not included. This means that a driver who plans to be on the road ten hours a day can cover a little over 550 miles.

I've heard several ambitious drivers tell me they can cover much more than 550 to 600 miles in a day. But remember, although the speed limit may be 70 miles per hour or higher in some places, it is virtually impossible to average that speed over the course of an entire day. Traffic will slow you to much less than a 70 mph average, and work zones will do the same.

Each stop, even for a quick restroom break, will take at least ten minutes. Even motorists who drive well over the speed limit hit the same traffic bottlenecks, take basically the same stops, and pass through the same work zones as other drivers. In other words, no matter how fast you try to drive, you will be hard-pressed to average much more than 57 or 58 miles per hour over the course of a day.

What Would You Like to Experience?

America is full of interesting attractions for every taste. Do you want to explore cities? Or would you rather spend the bulk of your time in rural areas? Perhaps you'll enjoy the treasures available in the increasingly-popular National Park system. Maybe you want to visit the desert. How about a scenic drive or hike through the Rocky Mountains? Maybe you'll search out great museums along your route. Art or history buffs will find enough museums to keep them occupied for any length of time.

Many travelers make food the center of their trip. They literally eat their way across America. Interesting locally-owned eateries invite road travelers with home cooking, friendly service, and regional specialties simply not found in the chain restaurants. Some roadtrippers even plan their meal stops long before making hotel reservations.

You'll find plenty of unusual roadside attractions along the way as you motor across America. From the *Cadillac Ranch* in the Texas panhandle to *Wall Drug* in South Dakota, unusual stops can make for an interesting diversion along the road. Although *The Thing* along I-10 in Arizona may not be as culturally stimulating as visiting an art museum or a national park, roadside oddities might make a trip that much more memorable. Many of these places pre-date the interstate highway system and are destinations unto themselves. Others may just warrant a short stop to look around and see what the fuss is all about.

Whether you plan to make your road trip a quest for culture, a search for tasty food, or simply a hunt for kitschy roadside Americana, make a list of the places you want to visit. Don't be surprised if you have to narrow your destinations by half or more.

How Much Time Is Available?

Great road trips don't require a month on the highway. In fact, Chapter 5 is specifically devoted to shorter trips. Still, you'll need to know how much time is available for your trip. To make sure you have enough time, do the following quick calculation: How far from your starting point is the farthest destination on your list? Take that mileage and divide it by 200. The answer is the *minimum* number of days you will need to make the trip comfortably.

For example, if you live in Houston, and you're planning a road trip to Washington, DC, your destination is about 1400 miles from home. That means you'll need *at least* seven days for this trip. By the way, those seven days count drive time, and some *minimal* sightseeing. Even then, most travelers will want more than that minimum time for their trip. Once you get on the road, you'll find sights worth exploring more closely, and you'll likely want *more* time for your trip, not *less*.

How Fast Do You Have to Get There?

If your road trip is taking you to an important meeting, family event, or other engagement, you may be looking for a more direct route with fewer intermediate stops. Your sightseeing along the road may be limited to a few carefully chosen spots. If time is an issue, stick to the interstate highway system as much as possible.

Although the majority of road trip 'purists' loathe the interstates for their uniformity and lack of character, when you're in a hurry, they can't be beat. However, planning ahead can reveal lots of hidden treasures along your route, even when traveling the interstates.

Due to the high speed involved in driving the interstates, it is *possible* to cover a longer distance in a day. If you ever find yourself in the difficult situation of having to cover 800 or 900 miles in one day – which I don't recommend – the interstates are really the only way to make the trip. It's possible to travel 200 miles or more without stopping, and due to the quality engineering of most interstate highways, they truly are an architectural marvel.

However, interstates, due to their design requirements, tend to showcase less of an area's natural beauty. Since lanes must maintain a certain width and grades can only be so steep, interstate highways tend to look very similar to each other, even in remotely different areas of the country. Also, since these superhighways require more than a 100-foot right-of-way, highway developers tend to find inexpensive, less scenic areas much easier for road building. Mountain highways cost

2-Lane or 4-Lane?

Two-lane roads let you drive closer to the scenery. Most four-lane roads actually take you *around* the scenery. If your schedule allows enough leisure time to explore and enjoy the surroundings a bit more, follow two-lane highways and byways. Many road atlases – such as Rand McNally's national atlas – specifically identify highways known for their scenic nature using green dots. If you're in any of the following three situations, though, seriously consider sticking to the interstates:

1. When driving in bad weather
2. When driving at night
3. When you're short on time

much more to build than flatter roads, so interstates tend to wind *around* the scenery, instead of passing *through* it.

I-80 through Donner Pass in California showcases the region's natural beauty

Although interstates have a reputation for being somewhat boring, a number of them break that stereotype and are scenic roads in their own right. Some of these are discussed specifically later in this book. Interstate 70 through Colorado and Utah, Interstate 64 through West Virginia, and Interstate 80 through eastern California are roads that are worth a look, simply for their natural beauty.

If you don't have any particular place to be, and your road trip *is* the destination, you can take my favorite kind of road trip, which is a slow wander across the land. When time abounds, you'll likely find two-lane roads to be more memorable, where it feels like you're actually closer to the surrounding terrain.

Even in areas where the interstate highway seems bland, veering onto a two-lane highway will often completely change the scenery. For example, many travelers dislike Interstate 70 across Kansas, because it seems empty and flat. If you dislike level land, Kansas may not be for you, but the natural beauty of this state is better appreciated by taking the southern route, U.S. 400. The distance is nearly identical, but the two-lane road will let you soak in the towns, villages, fields, and rolling hills of this region.

True, taking the two-lane road is slower. You may get behind a slow-moving truck, and giant gas stations – or *travel centers*, as they are now called – may be scarcer. But the two-lane roads are where road trip memories are made. So, try to include regional two-lane highways on your trip if time allows.

How Carefully Do You Want to Plan?

Part of the fun of a road trip is the freedom to choose where you want to travel, how much time to spend, and the route to take. Because of that, many roadtrippers start out with only a vague, general sense of where they want to go. They meander across a few states, making stops in places that interest them. They literally decide where to go when they see the road sign. This kind of spontaneity makes for a fun trip, but it works best with just one or two people in the car.

Some of my favorite road trips are those where I got into the car at the beginning of the ride without knowing where I'd end up. When you take that kind of trip, you really *do* feel a sense of adventure as you wander into your very own uncharted territory.

If you choose this spontaneous type of trip, be aware that you may pay more for lodging than you would by reserving ahead. Still, I'll discuss ways later in this book to save money, even on last minute hotel rooms.

If you really want to plan your road trip carefully, be aware that it's possible to plan nearly every detail of your journey, down to the very last fuel stop. Planning ahead can save money, especially when reserving hotel rooms and show tickets. A little planning can help save fuel, especially if you study the map to ensure taking the shortest route.

Most roadside attractions have websites. Those that don't *will* have online reviews on sites such as TripAdvisor.com, so you can decide which places are worth your time. When planning a road trip, try for one or two attractions a day. More than two can be very tiring, especially if you want to advance down the road any significant distance. Making two sightseeing stops in a day, one in the morning and one in the afternoon, helps keep the trip from getting monotonous.

What do you do if there are no attractions along a significant portion of your route? In this case, I recommend making your own attraction. Try discovering the downtown area of a small town. Even the smallest cities are trying to revive their downtown shopping districts. You may discover a quaint antique shop, a local history museum, or an interesting cafe. These are also some of the best places to interact with local residents, who can also give you tips on other places to visit that may not be listed in the guidebooks.

Try planning your route around places you want to visit, and not vice versa. As an example, suppose you want to take a road trip around Arkansas. This state, though small in population, hosts some real natural wonders and interesting tourist attractions. Much of the state can be enjoyed easily in a one-week road trip. List some of the attractions you want to visit:

- Crater of Diamonds State Park
  – dig for your own diamonds
- Hot Springs National Park
- Crystal Bridges Art Museum in Bentonville
- Ozark Mountains, Eureka Springs

Now, maybe these attractions aren't what you would have chosen. Still, these are just examples. Next, make a dot on your map for each attraction you want to visit. Try to have at least one attraction – but not more than two – for each day of your road trip. Now comes the fun part! Use roads to connect the dots on your atlas, trying to include as many scenic roads as you can.

You may want to calculate your daily mileage with a computer program or even with the atlas itself. Try to keep daily mileage less than 600, and certainly well under 500 for a sightseeing trip. In the example I plotted above, you could very well enjoy this road trip for seven days without driving much more than 200 miles in any one day.

As you decide where to finish each day of your road trip, visit an online hotel booking website. Not only can you reserve a room online, you'll be able to compare prices and select the best value for your taste and budget. If you would rather try camping, try an online or print directory of campgrounds. We'll discuss lodging options later in Chapter 11....

If you like to plan ahead, weigh your lodging options carefully. This is one area where some forethought and a few minutes of

I-70 through Glenwood Canyon parallels the beautiful Colorado River

online research can prevent real headaches. Nothing is more disappointing than driving all day with plans to stop for the night in a certain town, only to find that every motel in town is full – or worse, finding that the town has no motels at all!

Look for Variety

When planning a road trip, try taking one route going to your destination and another route returning. The scenery will be different on the return trip, and you will have an opportunity to see places you would have otherwise missed.

If after looking at all the options for road trips, you're still not sure where to begin, keep reading! Later in this book, I'll suggest some different routes you might want to take, such as a trip from one coast to the other, a drive along historic Route 66, or even a drive to the beach.

In fact, you'll find plenty of books that detail routes, stops, and things to see along the way. Visiting the travel section of your favorite bookstore will lead you to numerous books about Route 66, the Lincoln Highway, and other historic roads. Other books highlight America's scenic roads, and at least one magazine is dedicated to two-lane road adventures.

Don't feel like it's necessary to spend lots of money on books to get an idea of possible destinations. Each state's tourism department offers free travel planning guides with much of the information you'll need to plan your journey. See Chapter 23 for a list of websites where many of these guides can be downloaded for free.

Probably one of the best ways to get excited about planning your trip is to get on the road and take a short getaway. After experiencing the road for a day or two, you'll likely want to plan something longer. Use the ideas and resources mentioned in this chapter, and you'll have plenty of tools to make your adventure memorable.

What about your vehicle? How can you get your vehicle ready for this kind of excursion? What if you don't think your car is up to the challenge? The next chapter will address those concerns.

3

Gearing Up for the Road

It's almost time to begin your adventure! However, some advance planning can make your trip even more enjoyable and reduce the risk of a negative situation ruining the experience. Earlier, I discussed the importance of not stuffing too many people into your vehicle on a long trip. But the question remains: What is the ideal vehicle for a road trip?

Although almost any type of vehicle can work wonderfully on a long drive, the *best* vehicle really depends on the driver and the passengers.

Cars

If you plan to take a typical family-sized sedan on your road trip, you're in good company. Since sedans are the most common vehicles on the road today, it's no wonder that they're the most popular type of road trip vehicle, too. If you drive a particular car every day, you'll be more comfortable with it when in unfamiliar surroundings.

Many drivers opt for a full-size sedan on their road trips. They usually get better gas mileage, and handle the road very well. Since just about everyone has their own door, passengers usually feel less cramped in a larger car. If fewer than four people will be on your trip, you'll likely have more than enough room for your gear.

On the other hand, four or more people on a long trip can get cramped pretty fast in a car. Especially if one (or more) of the passengers hasn't packed light, you may find yourself running out of room in the trunk. True, you may physically be able to *fit* all your stuff back there, but *finding* something may be nigh impossible.

Pickup Trucks

Most people don't drive pickup trucks on road trips unless they are traveling alone or with one other person. Although many pickups of yesteryear made for uncomfortable driving and were better suited for hauling wood and working around the farm, today these trucks can be just as comfortable and roomy as larger vehicles.

However, note this rule of thumb: The roomier and more comfortable the interior of the pickup, the worse the gas mileage will be. Many larger pickup trucks are known for pitiful gas mileage, hovering around 15 miles per gallon, sometimes even less. Light trucks, especially the four-cylinder variety, can be quite economical though, with some even getting as high as 30 miles per gallon. These light trucks may not be as roomy or comfortable as their larger counterparts, but it is a give-and-take proposition. Give up some space, improve fuel economy.

Roadtripping by Motorcycle

In good weather, roadtripping on a motorcycle can be one of the best ways to experience the wide-open spaces around you. Although room for luggage will likely be limited, you'll save on fuel and have nearly unlimited travel options. Dozens of riding clubs organize annual road trips along some of the most scenic highways in the country.

Visit www.moto-directory.com/touring.asp for more information on taking a motorcycle trip.

Of course, if you really need to move a larger amount of luggage, maybe because of a long-distance move, a pickup truck could be your best bet. Once again, your priorities dictate which vehicle is the best choice for a long trip.

Vans and Sport Utility Vehicles

Vans, minivans, and sport utility vehicles are also common road trip vehicles. Trips with the family – especially three or more children – will be the most comfortable in these types of vehicles.

When it comes to gas mileage, most minivans outperform full-size vans and SUV's. However, the extra room the other two can offer make them worth your attention. Large families and groups of five adults or more will be most comfortable in an SUV or van, where there's plenty of room for luggage in the back.

Although most vans and SUV's can carry the same number of passengers, be aware that most larger vans may not handle as well as an SUV; sometimes full-size vans feel a little 'top heavy'.

In short, if you're looking for the best gas mileage among larger vehicles, minivans get the nod. However, if you need the maximum amount of space possible, go for a full-size van.

Red Tape

The last few pages have assumed that you will have the luxury of choosing among various vehicles to take your road trip. In reality, though, most of us have only one or two vehicles parked outside our homes, so the choice is simpler.

If you have one vehicle, then the choice is already made for you. Of course, if someone else is going along, perhaps he could offer his car. Still, the fact remains that the 'perfect road trip vehicle for everyone' doesn't exist. After taking your first journey, you'll find things about your vehicle you wish you could change. Those may be features you'll look for in your next car – or even add to your current car when you get home!

No matter what car you drive, though, make sure your legal bases are covered. Check your driver's license to make sure it hasn't expired, and carry it with you at all times while on the road. Make sure your car has current registration and insurance forms in the glove compartment. In fact, put those two documents in an easy-to-access location in the glove compartment. For a few dollars, you can purchase a small vinyl pouch to hold your registration and proof-of-insurance forms. You don't want to get stuck in a situation where you can't find these forms when you need them.

As an added security measure, make a copy of your license and keep it in the glove compartment (or scan it and e-mail it to yourself) with your other important documents. In the event your license is lost or stolen, it may be invaluable for getting a replacement in a hurry.

Don't forget to check your license plate to be sure the registration sticker is current. Also, make sure the entire plate is visible. It is illegal in most places to cover any part of the plate with plastic covers or other decorations.

Will My Car Make the Trip?

If you have any doubt as to whether or not your vehicle is ready for a long trip, you need to stop driving it *immediately*! Take it to a mechanic and get it fixed *today*!

Am I overreacting? Not really. If your car can't be taken on a long trip, then it probably shouldn't be driven on local streets around town. In fact, highway miles driven on a road trip are normally some of the easiest a car will ever experience.

Why do I say this? Well, when driving on the open road, a car uses its brakes very little; most drivers use cruise control instead of keeping their foot on the accelerator. On the other hand, driving on local streets requires constant acceleration, deceleration, braking, and turning. So, if your car is truly safe to be driven around town on a daily basis, it should be fine on a long road trip.

Consider Renting

If you don't have a car or simply don't want to drive your own, you may want to think about renting a car. When renting, you'll have the advantage of not putting extra miles or wear-and-tear on your own vehicle. Still, renting *does* add to the total cost of the trip, and the car you rent may not have all the features you want.

One case in which renting would be the best option, though, is for foreign visitors. If you're from somewhere other than North America, bringing your own car to the United States will be difficult

RV's

Recreational vehicles can eliminate the need to stay in hotels. These rolling homes give their occupants the comforts and conveniences of home, but they come at a steep price. Although simple, towed RV's and pop-up campers can be had for less than $20,000, luxury motorhomes often cost upwards of $100,000. If you can't afford to buy a new motorhome, used RV's are constantly available on the market and often a good deal. If you'd like to experience the RV lifestyle without committing to a long-term investment, though, consider renting. Most RV's can be rented for less than $200 a day, which isn't that expensive if divided among several friends or a large family.

For more information on RV's, see Chapter 6.

and costly. In fact, renting is often the *only* option for European visitors.

Foreigners find it very difficult to purchase a vehicle in the U.S., because registering one here is practically impossible without a permanent U.S. address. In addition, insurance on a purchased vehicle is available only to those with a valid U.S. driver's license. Draconian laws have made it almost impossible for individuals from abroad to obtain a license or register a vehicle without some kind of permanent visa (or work visa, in some instances).

Weeklong rental rates are cheaper than booking a weekend rate under some circumstances, so shop around. Also be aware that adding extra drivers may cause your rental fee to increase significantly. If you're under 25, be prepared to pay much more to rent a car. If you're under 21, you probably won't be able to rent at all.

Should you purchase the 'optional' insurance (sometimes called CDW, for *collision damage waiver*) offered at the counter? It depends. If the insurance on your personal car has full coverage, that coverage *probably* travels with you to a rental car, but check your policy to make sure. If you drive with just liability coverage back home, you may be well-advised to buy the rental insurance.

Sometimes, your credit card will include CDW insurance. Check the fine print of your card's benefits package to see whether you have this coverage. Even if you do, credit card CDW insurance is usually used only as a last resort, after your other options, such as your own auto insurance policy, are exhausted. Once again, a call to your auto insurance agent or to your credit card company will save some anxiety at the rental counter. When in doubt, though, it's better to have too much insurance than not enough.

Make sure your rental car contract includes unlimited mileage. Most do, except for a few places out West. If you need to take the car out of state, make sure your contract allows it. Arrange to drop off your car at the same location where you pick it up, or be prepared to pay an expensive one-way drop-off fee. And of course, return the car with a full tank of gas, because you'll pay outrageous fees if you don't!

Mechanical Preparations

If you decide to take your own car, you'll want to get it serviced before embarking on your journey. Many quick-lube places will service your car in 30 minutes or so for less than $50. If you don't know much about cars, this is probably your best choice. For that small fee, they'll change your oil, top off essential fluids, check your tire pressure, and basically make sure that the car is in good working order. They usually change filters, lamps, and windshield wiper blades for an additional fee.

If you're unsure of a vehicle's mechanical health, it may be wise to take it to a trusted mechanic and ask him to check the car from top to bottom. If he finds any problems with the transmission, motor, or exhaust system, the small price you paid will be well worth it. Even if your car is in perfect shape, it's worth the peace of mind to know that it will be less likely to break down at a bad time. Plus, it's better to discover vehicle problems near home rather than hundreds of miles away.

Even drivers who know little about cars need to be able to check basic items on their vehicles. Arguably, the most important mechanical check a driver should perform is the oil level. When you pop the hood, look for a removable dipstick, probably labeled "Oil Level". Pull out the dipstick, and make sure the level is up to the top of the shaded area near the bottom of the stick. If the level is low, add a little oil at the screw-on engine oil fill.

Know how to check your tire pressure. In fact, check your tire pressure often. On the road, check your tire pressure every third tank of gas, at a minimum. Since underinflated tires reduce gas mileage significantly, keeping tires inflated to the recommended pressure (around 32 pounds per square inch for most tires) will save you money!

Tire pressure gauges cost only a few dollars, so it's wise to keep one in your glove compartment while on the road. If you don't want to check your pressure that often, you can buy special valve caps that change color when your tire pressure falls below a certain level. These caps cost around five dollars and do come in handy!

Another easy inspection every driver should make is to check the wheel alignment. If your car pulls to one side, your wheels may be out of alignment. When you drive down a straight stretch of highway and release the steering wheel for a few seconds, the car should not drift much, barring any heavy winds or highway sloping. If it does, your wheels could need realigning. Wheels that are out of

Essential Tools for Emergencies

- Spare Tire (inflated) and Jack

- Can of Emergency Tire Inflator (Fix-a-Flat or similar)

- Lug Wrench

- Pry Bar or Crowbar

- Hubcap Key (if you have special hubcaps)

- Screwdriver

- Tire Gauge

- Mini Air Compressor (to inflate a tire from your cigarette lighter outlet)

- Jumper Cables

alignment will cause your tires to wear unevenly and very quickly. In extreme cases, a tire may need to be replaced after less than 1000 miles of being driven on unaligned wheels!

When you pack your vehicle, remember to include some basic tools. Although auto supply stores will sell you a 'safety kit' or 'emergency kit', it's easy to assemble your own from items you likely already have. Make sure to include basic items, such as those in the box on this page. The need for most of these emergency items is obvious; don't leave home without them!

If you're planning for emergencies and aren't a mechanical expert, arguably the most important item you can take along is an auto club membership. The most popular one in the United States is AAA, and their basic membership costs about $50 a year.

In an emergency, you get free tow truck service, up to five miles, to the nearest shop to get repairs. If you are locked out of your car, they will send a locksmith to help, free of charge. If you run out of gas, they will send someone with enough gas to get you to the next station – you pay for the gas, though. If your battery fails, they will send someone to give you a jump-start. It's a good deal, especially if you drive an older car.

AAA can also help with trip planning with free travel guides, maps, and personalized TripTik maps. Showing your membership card will also score 10 to 20% discounts at many restaurants, hotels, and other attractions. Many auto insurance companies offer similar roadside assistance packages for about the same price, so shop around and see if an auto club is for you.

Once your car is mechanically ready to go, it's time to start packing! What do you want to take along? Before you start packing clothes and shoes, think about some gadgets that you may want to consider that may make your ride more enjoyable.

Satellite Radio

One of the greatest innovations of the last 20 years for people who spend a lot of time in cars is satellite radio. In the United States, it is now possible to listen to the same station from coast-to-coast without losing the signal for more than a few seconds at a time. Whatever your personal taste, you'll find something on satellite radio you enjoy. Commercial-free music, news, talk radio, play-by-play sports, weather, and even local traffic reports are available on both of the major satellite services.

Both services, XM and Sirius, form one company, Sirius-XM Radio. Both services cost about $17 per month, with discounts for those who commit to yearly subscriptions. Although the audio quality is not as good as listening to a CD, satellite radio is the easiest option for those who want the greatest variety of listening options on the road.

Which service is best for you? Really, it depends on your personal tastes. Offerings on both services are very similar. If you are a sports fan, keep this in mind: the NFL and NASCAR are on Sirius, while XM hosts major league baseball and NHL hockey. Both services feature different college sports conferences throughout the

year, so check with the providers to see which service has your favorite team.

Talk radio and news offerings are similar on both services,
with this exception: Sirius seems to have slightly more non-political
talk stations, while XM has more political talk. Once again, it depends on your preference.

If you're traveling with kids, you might want to remember
this: Many talk shows on SiriusXM are 'satellite-exclusive', which
means that they are not subject to FCC regulations regarding the
use of offensive language. Many of these shows, even those on
'mainstream' talk and political talk channels, throw around foul
language freely.

Again, both services are great, and most travelers will enjoy
either one. Satellite radio may not be for everyone, though. If your
iPhone or CD collection has thousands of songs, and you don't care
for news or talk radio, then skip satellite and stick with your phone
or MP3 player.

GPS Navigation

GPS (Global Positioning System) is a free satellite service operated by the U.S. government that determines your location to
within a few feet. Although the service is free, you do have to buy a
receiver. Receivers range in price from about $50 to over $500, depending on the features and convenience desired in the device.

A simple $100 GPS receiver will plug into your car's 12-volt
power outlet, offer turn-by-turn directions and maps of the continental United States, and direct you to any of thousands of local
attractions and points of interest. More expensive models will pronounce local street names and tell you exactly which lane you need
to be in on a freeway. Some offer traffic reports, too. They can be

mounted directly onto the dashboard or placed temporarily on the inside of your windshield with suction cups.

Many drivers keep a portable GPS unit attached to the windshield all the time when on the road. It's easy enough to enter the next destination into the unit and let it guide you through complex street patterns and unfamiliar areas. Although relying on GPS in rural areas is overkill for most drivers, it's invaluable in cities and even in smaller towns, especially when looking for a specific street address. Usually, when searching for a hotel or attraction, the location will already be programmed into the unit and can be found by searching for "Points of Interest."

In rural areas, most GPS units will direct you to take a four-lane highway or interstate instead of a two-lane road. If you opt for the two-lane highway instead of the four-lane, the unit will try to 'guide' you back to the interstate. If you're confident enough of your whereabouts and get tired of hearing the GPS unit tell you where to go, just turn it off; that's always an option.

If you choose to buy a portable GPS unit, be aware that thieves in some areas have been known to steal them for easy cash. When you park your car for the night, remove the unit from the car, and wipe off the suction cup marks from the windshield. Thieves often look for suction cup marks on a windshield as a sign of expensive portable electronics in the car.

Radar Detector

In the last chapter, I briefly discussed why it doesn't really pay to speed. Any amount of stopping, even if just for using the restroom or refueling, will consume any advantage you may have had speeding on the open road. Add even a small suburban traffic jam or construction zone, and you'll find that speeding doesn't really get you to your destination any faster.

Up until a few years ago, I recommended that motorists on long trips use a radar detector, at the very minimum to be aware of their surroundings and to stay alert. However, that advice is no longer valid. Most highway patrols now make use of 'instant-on' radar and laser speed detection, both of which are near-impossible to sense using a typical radar detector.

As a result of these higher-tech radar systems, your detector is practically useless in most highway situations, and is probably more likely to get you profiled as a speeder and targeted for extra scrutiny by the authorities. My current advice has always been your best bet: skip the radar detector and stick to the speed limit. If you have to speed, don't go faster than the flow of traffic.

If you choose to drive with a radar detector, be aware that in Virginia and the District of Columbia, using a radar detector is illegal. When far from home, fighting a ticket in court is virtually impossible. Being fined several hundred dollars is not the way to enjoy a vacation trip, so be careful and don't speed!

What to Pack?

When it's time to pack the car, a few things are obvious: Take clothes, shoes, and basic toiletries. Take your cell phone, and don't forget the car charger. Before leaving, make sure your wireless plan includes coverage in the areas you plan to visit. If it doesn't, you could be hit with hefty roaming fees. Instead of changing plans just for a road trip, consider buying a cheap, prepaid cellphone. For example, *Net10* provides nationwide prepaid cell service for ten cents a minute, all the time, with no roaming charges anywhere in the continental U.S. The phones are pretty cheap, too, starting at about $20 with no contract required.

After you've packed the basics, it may be a little more difficult to think of other necessities to take along. Always remember to pack light! Even when traveling alone, I try to fit all my belongings into one duffle bag (sometimes two). It makes stopping for the night much easier when you can take just one bag into the hotel, instead of making multiple trips to the car. If several people are traveling with you, the 'one bag' rule makes for an easy way for everyone to manage his or her own luggage.

If you'll be storing luggage in the trunk, or if you'll be separated from your belongings in some other way while on the road, think about taking along a small personal case or messenger bag for your gear. Use this secondary bag to store your phone, headphones, sunglasses, reading material, and camera, along with anything else that really needs to stay at your side throughout the trip.

Speaking of things you'll need to keep at your side, definitely remember to take a camera! Unless you're a photography buff, a simple digital camera (maybe even the one on your phone) should be sufficient to document your travels. Remember to take enough batteries to last your trip, or else bring along a small charger. For most people, a 2-gigabyte memory card will be more than enough to store snapshots from your journey.

Dressing for the Road

When packing clothes, be as comfortable as you can. Sitting in the car for hours at a time means you'll want to wear comfortable pants, although shorts can actually make you feel cold if you're sitting in front of an air conditioner vent. During cold months, I prefer to wear a sweatshirt while driving, and I usually wear t-shirts during the summer.

Even during warmer months, you may want to consider taking along a long-sleeve shirt or sweatshirt if your plans include driving north or west. Locations in the northern and western halves of the nation, as well as any area over 3000 feet in elevation, may experience cool, even cold temperatures at night during the summer.

Personally, for not having planned better, I've ended up shivering while camping in Utah during June, and even in Nevada during July. You've heard it before, but I'm saying it again: Mountain and desert areas *really do* get chilly at night, year round. So take a blanket and appropriate clothing if planning to travel to those areas.

For the car, take along a few pillows. People do nap in the car sometimes, and a comfortable pillow can make a long trip even easier. A small cooler with a few snacks and drinks can help bridge the gap between meal stops.

Even if your plans include staying mostly in hotels at night, consider taking along a tent, especially if there's plenty of room in the vehicle. Camping, even if for just one night, can be fun, memorable, and an easy way to save money while on the road. It's also a great way to enjoy nature on a level you just can't experience from a hotel room.

When preparing for the trip, make sure the car has a durable cup holder. The driver will need to stay focused on the road and probably won't have an extra hand to balance a soda or cup of coffee. If your car doesn't have a cup holder, or if the one if your vehicle is just too flimsy, consider buying a small console for your car that includes a quality cup holder. It's a small expense, but it makes a big difference – especially for the driver.

One last comfort item needs to be mentioned in this chapter. No one likes to spend hours in a dirty car, so buy a small trash can or litter bag for your vehicle. Instead of throwing snack bags and empty cups on the floor, use the trash bag. And try to empty it at least once a day. By keeping the inside of your car relatively clean, it will be that much more enjoyable for traveling. Remember, you will be living out of this vehicle for several days, so try to keep it neat!

Is the car ready to go? Have you packed everything? Now comes the exciting part – let's hit the road!

4

What to See

One of the most exciting parts of a road trip is visiting new places and sights along the way. Some travelers, though, make the mistake of trying to see everything in a large area. They fill an itinerary with so many sightseeing stops each day that they get tired and eventually end up wishing they had stayed home. Remember, the point is to have a good time, not tire yourself out.

Other travelers make the opposite mistake. They get in such a hurry to arrive at a destination that they don't make time to see anything along the way. Again, the point is to *enjoy* the trip. Choose destinations that appeal to you and that will make lasting memories. In this chapter, we'll cover several ideas for stopping points and detours that will make your trip more memorable.

National Parks

The United States operates nearly 60 National Parks, mostly concentrated in the West. The vast majority of these parks are well worth a stop, or even a detour along yoru trip. In fact, it's very possible that your vacation is completely oriented around visiting these parks. Each year, millions of tourists - from the U.S. and abroad - visit them. The Grand Canyon, Yellowstone National Park, Death Valley, Yosemite, and Rocky Mountain National Parks are just a few of these popular destinations.

National Parks offer a wide variety of activities, including camping, hiking, and fishing, not to mention some of the most outstanding natural scenery in the country. Although anyone could take a cursory drive through most of the parks in just a few hours, most people could easily spend a week or more wandering and exploring the parks' treasures.

Most National Parks charge an entrance fee. In most cases, the fee averages a flat $15 to $25 per car. The fee covers the entire car group for multiple entries into the park for up to seven days. If you plan on visiting more than two or three parks, it's a better value to purchase an Annual Park Pass. It entitles you to enter as many National Parks as you like, along with anyone in your vehicle, for an entire year. It costs only $80 and is really quite a steal. Senior citizens (ages 62 and up) get an even better deal, with a lifetime parks pass for just $10. Passes generally don't include fees for ranger tours, and they don't include any camping privileges; they normally cover only admission to the park.

The National Park Service manages an additional 300 sites of historical and geographical importance. Although these other sites aren't officially considered National Parks, they're usually worth a visit if you're passing through the area. Many of these locations offer tours and museums, some of which are as popular as the main National Parks.

The famous Gateway Arch in St. Louis, Padre Island National Seashore in Texas, the Statue of Liberty, the Appalachian Trail, and Alcatraz Island near San Francisco are just a few of these amazing sites worth visiting across the country. No matter where your trip takes you, you're never more than a few hours' drive from one of these historic and interesting sites. If there's an admission fee, it will normally be well worth the price for the experience. Details about all of these sites can be found at the National Park Service's website at www.nps.gov.

Local Farmer's Markets

One of my favorite shopping experiences while on the road is finding a local farmer's market and obtaining fresh, delicious food. Often, these markets are open just a couple days a week. Saturdays, Thursdays, and Mondays seem to be the most common in my experience, but a few communities have them in some form every day, albeit with reduced hours. The highest *quality* produce will be found at the beginning of market hours, but the best *prices* are usually available toward the end, when many vendors would rather sell what's left, instead of carrying it back to the farm. Local produce can make for a great, simple lunch, and it's probably healthier than what you'd find in a restaurant.

Some communities offer more than just a small farmer's market exclusively for fresh produce. Many towns have become well-known for their interesting 'flea markets' or 'trade days'. In addition to finding fresh fruits and vegetables, you're likely to find an assortment of antiques, tools, locally-made arts and crafts, and even live animals for sale. These markets often attract vendors from many miles around, not to mention as many as thousands of customers on holiday weekends during the spring and summer. You never know what treasures you'll find!

Finding these markets can sometimes be a challenge, especially if you're just passing through. On occasion, you'll see an open farmer's market or flea market as you pass through a town. If you're ready to spend a few days in a community, though, it's worth it to stop at a local visitor's center and ask when the farmer's market or flea market is open. Ask a few local residents, too; they're usually happy to share information about their community to visitors.

Serious Shopping

Many travelers look forward to shopping in new surroundings and looking for products and deals that just aren't available back home. You can divide travelers into two groups: those who consider shopping a vital part of traveling, and those with absolutely no desire to set foot into an unknown supermarket or shopping mall. It comes down to personal choice. If some members of your group enjoy shopping and others don't, those non-shoppers may have to spend a couple of hours reading a favorite book on a bench or taking a walk around the surrounding neighborhood.

Locally-owned stores can give you a taste of the local culture, plus you might find something useful that can double as a souvenir of your trip. Take time to linger in local stores, as the owners and clerks that work there are likely to give you useful tips for enjoying the community before you move on.

If you travel for more than an hour or two, you're likely to see large shopping malls or shopping plazas. I've made many stops at malls to take a quick walk or even just to use the restroom. Shopping malls are also great places for people-watching. If your vacation is at any time other than the busy holiday shopping season, it's likely the mall will be nearly empty during the late morning and early afternoon. This is the time to visit when you're traveling. You'll beat the crowds, and it will be much easier to get around if you're looking to do a little shopping (or mall walking).

Museums

When most people think of sights to see when traveling, they often think of a museum. Although most museums are located in larger cities, don't count out smaller towns, too. Nearly every county in America has some type of historical society or art guild that operates one. These spots are excellent places to learn about local history and experience local culture. Many of these small museums double as county visitor centers, and to top it off, admission is usually free!

Larger cities have a wider variety of museums, most of which will likely charge admission. If you're a history buff, look for history museums. Children traveling with you will love children's museums and science museums.

Most visitors are familiar with the huge museums available in large cities such as New York, Washington, and Chicago. However, many treasures are hidden off the beaten path and shouldn't be overlooked.

For example, Charleston, West Virginia, is a relatively small city (population 50,000) not normally known for museums. However, the West Virginia State Museum offers free admission (metered parking for 75 cents an hour) and a decade-by-decade history of the state, as well as a detailed look into the culture of Appalachia that can't be found in many other places. I spent two hours there, and even then I felt rushed.

Las Vegas may be known for casinos, glitz, and glamor, but it's also the home to several interesting museums between the Strip and Downtown. For example, the Las Vegas Natural History Museum offers an enjoyable, quiet diversion from the rest of the city. Old-style dioramas, a modern aquarium exhibit room, treasures from ancient Egypt, and dinosaur fossils can all be found here. This museum is much smaller than science museums in Washington and Chicago, but it makes for an interesting afternoon, especially during the week, when the museum is nearly empty. Admission is $10 for adults, but a 2-for-1 coupon is nearly always available online.

Just about every museum has a website detailing exhibits, admission fees, and parking information. Normally, the "Plan Your Visit" section on a museum's website will tell you everything you need to know.

Beaches

Many families and college students take road trips specifically to get to the beach. Whether it's the week of Spring Break, or a more subdued family vacation, beaches are one of the most popular destinations for road travelers.

Before leaving for the beach, do your research first! If your budget allows for only $100 a night for hotels, and you arrive to find the cheapest room costs $175, your vacation will either be cut short or severely curtailed. If it's *absolutely important* to you that your hotel be a beachfront property, book directly with the hotel and make those arrangements ahead of time. If your priority is booking a cheap room, be ready to walk long distances or drive to the beach, and be aware that parking close to the sand will probably not be free.

Beach trips, to some extent, lend themselves to specialized equipment. You can almost always rent beach chairs, umbrellas, and shelters or palapas for shade. However, if you're on a budget, it may be cheaper to buy camping chairs and a foldable shelter at a sporting goods store before you arrive. Supplies, like towels and bathing suits, will likely be more expensive the closer you get to the beach. Your purchases will come in very handy if you're traveling in a large enough vehicle to hold them, and you plan to stay for more than a day or two (or plan to return next year).

For travels to the beach, don't forget your sunscreen, sunglasses, food, drinks, and a portable barbecue (if allowed) on your shopping list.

When planning to visit the beach, choose your dates carefully! A family with young children will likely want to avoid the month of March, which is traditionally college spring break. Expect large crowds during all holiday periods during the summer, such as Memorial Day and the entire week of July 4th. If you're able to travel during the *two weeks before* Memorial Day or the *two weeks after* Labor Day, you're likely to find excellent weather, lower prices, and much smaller crowds.

Take into account Atlantic hurricane season if you plan to visit during the summer. Hurricanes are generally less likely to ruin your trip in June or early July. Late July and August have a much higher probability of hurricanes. Even if a tropical storm hits along the Gulf, though, your trip won't be ruined if your plans are flexible. If you're able to travel to a different part of the Gulf coast, *several hundred miles away* from the storm, you're likely to have a wonderful time with much smaller crowds. Whatever you do, don't get trapped in a hurricane zone; it could ruin more than just your vacation.

Fall Foliage

Every autumn, thousands of Americans take to the road to admire fall foliage and their brilliant, changing colors. This practice has become known as 'leaf peeping', and brings tourists to communities all over New England. While Vermont, New Hampshire,

Maine, and upstate New York are probably the most famous places for enjoying fall colors, don't count out other parts of the country if a New England vacation is out of your reach.

October is a perfect month for roadtripping through the upper Midwest for checking out the leaves. Iowa, southern and western Wisconsin, and northwestern Illinois provide some stunning vistas, especially in communities near the Mississippi River.

The Rocky Mountain region of Colorado, the Ozarks of Arkansas, as well as the Smoky Mountains in Tennessee and North Carolina are also parts of the country that enjoy beautiful fall colors, but may not be as popular with leaf peepers as the New England states. Be ready to make several stops along the way at scenic overlooks, and don't forget your camera!

Welcome Centers

When crossing into a new state or arriving in a new city, make a stop at the tourist information center. Most states operate welcome centers near their borders along interstate highways, and these are perfect places to gather useful information about tourist attractions in the state.

Take time to talk to the hosts at these centers; they're more than just greeters. They can offer suggestions on where to visit, good places to eat, and even where to spend the night. Since they talk to travelers all day, every day, they know what local attractions are tourist favorites. They may be one of the best sources for up-to-date, specific information about places to visit.

Twenty minutes spent in one of these welcome centers is usually time well invested. Pick up flyers and visitor guides to places you might want to see. Thumb through them, and look for places that you and your traveling companions find interesting. These travel guides make excellent, free souvenirs of your trip.

Mountains

Many people enjoy venturing into mountainous areas to enjoy the wide variety of scenery. If you're not used to mountain driving, make sure you review the tips in Chapter 8, "Behind the Wheel," before you begin your trek into the mountains.

Even if you're not a serious mountain climber, a mountain hike is still within reach. Although the Appalachian Trail measures well over 2,000 miles, end-to-end from Georgia to Maine, even a casual visitor can hike a few miles of the trail. If your travels take you to the Las Vegas area, Valley of Fire State Park makes for a perfect daytrip from the city. It combines the beauty of the desert with the majesty of red rock mountains. Stunning views of rock formations can be enjoyed easily by foot or from the comfort of your car.

Even if you prefer to enjoy the mountains from your vehicle, you still have lots of options. In Colorado, for example, the popular Mount Evans Scenic Byway takes you to the peak of one of the most accessible mountains in the nation over 14,000 feet high. The road, located about an hour west of Denver, is the highest paved road in North America. Over its 15-mile length, plan to see stunning vistas at every turn, not to mention interesting wildlife, like bighorn sheep, mountain goats, and elk. Be aware, though, that many people riding along in the passenger seat describe the journey as one of the scariest drives they've ever experienced -- but well worth it.

Other Outdoor Activities - Hunting, Fishing, Cycling

Outdoorsmen find hunting and fishing great reasons to take to the road and enjoy the great outdoors. If you plan to go hunting out of state, make sure your weapon is registered and that all permits are in order. Apply for hunting licenses as early as possible, well before leaving on your trip (weeks, or even months before, in some cases).

Fishing trips are a little simpler, to some extent, since you likely won't be taking a firearm. Still, make sure you always have a valid fishing license for the state you're visiting. These normally don't need to be purchased in advance of your trip; in most states you can obtain one immediately at any sporting goods store.

Cyclists enjoy taking their bicycles along to enjoy trails in other parts of the country. One of the best ways to experience that variety of surroundings is by bicycle. Be aware, though, that vehicle bike racks are fairly expensive, and it takes time to fasten the bike to the rack, and more time to take it down. If you're a serious cyclist, though, it's worth the effort.

Hunting and cycling are both activities that may dictate the type of vehicle you can take on your trip. Compact cars, for example, simply don't have enough room for a bike rack or for hunting gear -- not to mention hauling back wild game or the big trophy. Vans and SUV's tend to be better suited for cycling, and trucks are the better fit for hunters. However, if you enjoy these particular outdoor activities, you probably already knew that.

It's possible that the activities and sights I've mentioned in this chapter don't appeal to you as much as simply getting out, enjoying the open road, and getting miles behind you. Or you may prefer some other activity that wasn't mentioned in this chapter, such as boating, skiing, or visiting historical sites or wineries. And on other trips, time or circumstances simply don't allow for much sightseeing of any kind.

No matter what plans you have, there are endless combinations of sights to see and attractions to experience on the road. Whether you plan to hit the beach for a few days, pass the hours shopping, or do some strenuous mountain hiking or cycling, make time to enjoy your surroundings and experience the joy of being on the road.

5

One-Tank Road Trips

The last four chapters have discussed strategies to plan a typical road trip. When I say "typical road trip", I'm talking about a trip where a couple spend a week on the road to discover the South. Or the group of four friends who take two weeks to wander around the West. Or the family that's driving up to New England for a few days to admire the autumn leaves.

But a road trip doesn't have to last a week or more. A road trip is more a *state of mind* than a number of miles traveled. Some of the best trips involve getting away for a day or two and exploring places close to home. You can enjoy a great drive in as little as a few hours, and it's not necessary to travel very far, either. And it definitely doesn't have to cost a lot of money. This chapter is devoted to shorter trips that don't require much more than one tank of gas.

The Daytrip

Even if you've never gone on a longer road trip, you probably *have* taken a daytrip – a short road trip where you leave home in the morning and return home that same day. Some travelers take daytrips to a state park, a nice restaurant, or a museum. Most short trips use no more than one tank of gas, making them the most economical road trip you can take.

When taking a daytrip, plan to leave at a reasonable hour. If you need to travel several hours, visit an attraction, or run your errand, and return home the same day, you'll need to leave early.

Whether you plan to venture over 100 miles from home or just plan to explore highways and byways closer to home, daytrips have lots of obvious advantages. Since there's no worrying about lodging, there's very little to pack. Most people can take a daytrip with little notice on a Saturday or day off. And since there's no luggage to take, four adults can fit comfortably in most cars for a daytrip, something that might be tougher on a longer trip. If you've never taken any road trip before, start with a daytrip.

The Overnight Trip

If you want a longer 'getaway' than a daytrip, try for an overnight trip. A typical overnight trip might include leaving in the afternoon, driving a couple of hours, enjoying a leisurely dinner, then driving a little farther before spending the night at a hotel. The next day, you can do some sightseeing, visit a park or museum, and enjoy lunch before driving home that afternoon.

When you decide to take an overnight trip, think about how much of a getaway you want. When you get to your destination, what do you want to do? What museums will you visit? Will you go shopping instead? Or will the hotel itself be your destination? Depending on your budget and plans, you may decide to stay at a different type of hotel than you would on a longer road trip.

If the hotel is really your destination, and you don't have any serious sightseeing plans, think about reserving a room at a high-end hotel (see Chapter 11 for more about that). In many cities and suburban areas, high-end hotels, especially in the off-season, don't cost much more than a room at a roadside chain. And if you're looking for a quick getaway, high-end hotels often include more amenities, such as a workout room, jacuzzi, indoor pool, and more comfortable beds.

For a quick overnight trip, don't plan on driving much more than two or three hours from home. A short overnight road trip can be an easy getaway, especially if time is short.

The Weekend Getaway

For some of us, a quick overnight trip just isn't enough. That's why a weekend getaway may be more attractive, especially if you want to see more than one or two sights in a city. On a weekend road trip, you'll likely have time to spend two nights (maybe three nights, in the case of a holiday weekend) instead of just one, giving you a full day for sightseeing.

A typical weekend getaway starts on a Friday afternoon. Most people will leave after work, drive for a couple hours, have dinner, and then arrive at their hotel in the evening. All day Saturday is available for sightseeing. After another night in the hotel, there's still time left Sunday for more sightseeing before driving home that afternoon or evening.

Most families have done a variation of the weekend getaway. It's perfect for families, because it doesn't usually require taking vacation days from work, and it gives everyone a chance to get away for a couple of days and do something out of the ordinary. And what better way to enjoy a Saturday than a trip to a zoo, park, or museum?

Instead of staying at a hotel, you could even try camping for a night or two, especially if the weather is good and the campsite isn't far from home. If you opt for a hotel, be aware that downtown hotels may be significantly cheaper on the weekend, with rates that even rival roadside chains, especially if booking through an opaque booking site like Priceline or Hotwire. Before deciding to stay downtown though, check into hidden fees, like parking, that could drive up the cost of your stay.

Like the other short road trips mentioned previously, weekend getaways work well for short jaunts – those under three hours or so are best.

If you'd like to try taking a one-tank road trip, but aren't sure where to start, let me share some of America's favorite ones over the next few pages. They're short in distance, but the scenery per mile will be fantastic.

Desert Southwest – Las Vegas NV to Seligman AZ
189 miles – about 4 hours

If you happen to be in the Las Vegas area, try taking a trip out to the surrounding desert south and east of the city. This route passes through some of most scenic and historic desert highways in the nation, not to mention along part of Historic U.S. Route 66.

This route starts by heading south out of Las Vegas on U.S. 93. This highway passes through Boulder City, the famous town built for housing workers on nearby Boulder Dam, today known as Hoover Dam. Built as a company town originally populated purely by male workers, rules were strict. Even today, Boulder City is the only town in Nevada where gambling is expressly prohibited.

Just a few miles down the road is Hoover Dam, one of the greatest engineering marvels of the 20th century. For less than $20, you can explore the grounds of the dam, watch a short film about how it was built, and take a tour of the gigantic power generating facility. If you're willing to pay a little more, your tour will include a walk down into the tunnels and passages underneath the dam. Caution: the tour that goes into the base of the dam is not for the claustrophobic or extremely tall, as the tunnels are fairly low and cramped. Still, it's one of the most interesting tours in the Las Vegas area and an easy 45-minute drive from the Strip.

Looking straight down from the bridge over Hoover Dam

Even if you don't take an official tour of Hoover Dam, you can admire the structure from atop the structure for free, which also carries the bridge across the Colorado River. Crossing the bridge puts you into neighboring Arizona.

Driving south on Highway 93 quickly brings you into the barren Arizona desert, with sweeping mountain vistas in every direction. About halfway to Kingman, you'll see a turnoff for the famous Grand Canyon Skywalk. Located on lands under the sovereignty of the Hualapai Tribe, about 50 miles off the main highway, the Skywalk is a giant glass-bottomed viewing structure fastened to the side of the canyon. You can walk out over the canyon and look straight down into it – definitely not for the faint of heart.

The Skywalk is located on the lesser-known West Rim. If you've never been to the Grand Canyon, or don't anticipate ever going to the main South Rim or North Rim, this is an acceptable experience. However, be aware that the Skywalk experience doesn't come cheap; figure about $80 per person. Plus, you won't be able to take pictures; all cameras and electronic devices are expressly prohibited on the Skywalk.

If you continue south on U.S. 93, you'll soon arrive at the small city of Kingman, an important stop for travelers along Route 66 headed to California. Even today, numerous cheap motels dot the highways going through town. You can stay in some of them for as little as $25 a night; many of them still survive from the days of the old Mother Road.

East of Kingman, skip the I-40 freeway and opt for the two-lane Route 66. You'll see the remnants of towns that were once important stops along the old road, but today are just a shadow of what they used to be: places like Valentine, Truxton, and Peach Springs. As you wind through the desert, you'll be driving on one of the most well-preserved stretches of Route 66 in the country. Look for the old Burma Shave signs along the side of the road, and imagine yourself surrounded by travellers who motored along this very road decades ago.

Eventually, you'll come to the town of Seligman. Once a bustling place, most of the traffic through here disappeared after Route 66 was bypassed by the interstate. An interesting place near here is Grand Canyon Caverns, known to be the largest dry caverns in the country. You can take a tour for about $17, and you can even spend the night in a hotel suite over 200 feet below the surface for $700.

The Million-Dollar Highway
Montrose CO to Durango CO
107 miles – about 3 hours

This route starts about an hour south of Grand Junction, Colorado, along U.S. Route 550. Montrose is a gateway to Black Canyon of the Gunnison National Park, about 30 miles to the northeast. On this relatively short jaunt, though, we'll be driving south from Montrose through the rugged San Juan Mountains to the town of Durango, located not far from the famous Four Corners Monument. This entire route is steeped in history and natural beauty, being one of the most breathtaking – and scariest – highways in the country.

Even the Million Dollar Highway name fosters debate. Some say it was inspired by the 'million-dollar' views found at nearly every turn along the way. Others claim that the name traces its roots to a miner that said he wouldn't take that road 'even for a million dollars.' And still others claim that the original road was built using excess dirt from the local gold and silver mines, dirt that turned out to be worth – you guessed it – a million dollars.

Our trip starts in the town of Montrose, a railroad town that sees more action these days as a recreation center. Montrose is just a few miles away from the Telluride ski area, and during the summer kayakers and nature enthusiasts flock here from all over the world. Although the elevation here is nearly 6,000 feet, it doesn't snow that much, due to the near-desert climate. And when it does snow, it doesn't last long, since the sun shines nearly every day, even during winter.

Heading south from Montrose takes us ever closer to the looming San Juan Mountains ahead of us. As you cross the beautiful Uncompahgre River, you enter the quaint town of Ouray. Known as the Switzerland of America, the town is surrounded on three sides by towering 13,000-foot peaks. Take a good look nearly straight up one of the mountains; you'll see the road you're about to be on. While you're here, check out the downtown area, all of which has been designated as a national historic site; many of the buildings look just as they did in the late 19th century when Ouray was synonymous with gold and silver mining. For the adventurous, the town's free ice climbing park – built from a mile-long stretch of frozen waterfalls – will offer an experience you won't soon forget.

The road heading south out of Ouray winds steeply up the mountain, twisting and turning its way up to Red Mountain Pass, 11,075 feet above sea level. Drive carefully, since there are no guardrails along most of the road, and the dropoffs are steep and unforgiving. You'll want to pull off often and admire the scenery from up here; there's even a campground or two if you want to spend the night.

The Million Dollar Highway near Red Mountain Pass is beautiful but unforgiving

After coming down Red Mountain, you'll pass through the town of Silverton, named for the silver mine that used to be here. Although small, it's worth a stop, if only to look for the relics of the silver mine camp. Continuing south, you'll wind up and down mountains for the next 20 miles, though not quite as treacherous as those you just passed. The last 30 miles to Durango are relatively straight and mark a sharp contrast from the crisp mountain ambience near Ouray. The road to Durango quickly becomes arid and has a completely different feel; as it turns out, Durango is only about 70 miles away from the high desert of Arizona.

Louisiana State Route 23
New Orleans LA to Delta LA
74 miles – about 1 hour, 45 minutes

The Great River Road begins near the source of the Mississippi River at Lake Itasca in Minnesota. Here is where it ends.

One of the busiest shipping routes in the world, the Mississippi River carries goods from middle America to the rest of the world. All those ships pass right along the route you're about to take. The last few miles of the mighty Mississippi are a living exhibit in not only the majesty of nature, but how fragile it can also be. Although most travelers following the Great River Road end their journey in New Orleans, there's much to experience along this part of the route known as Louisiana Highway 23, which – for most of the journey – runs no more than a few hundred yards from the river.

Heading south from Gretna, the highway heads quickly out of the New Orleans metropolitan area. An old, two-lane tunnel takes you under the Intracoastal Waterway and soon, the River appears to your left as you enter the small city of Belle Chasse, the largest town in Plaquemines Parish, generally considered the town in the parish that suffered the least damage during Hurricane Katrina. South of here, as of this writing, towns and villages are still recovering from Katrina, and those that have, keep getting battered by other disasters, such as the 2010 Deepwater Horizon oil disaster and Hurricane Isaac in 2012.

Continuing south, you'll occasionally see ships traveling toward the Gulf. If the angle is just right, it can be an eerie sight, because the road is separated from the river by little more than a levee, and you're driving just a couple of feet above the level of the water. This road is prone to flooding, so keep an eye on the weather before deciding to trek down here.

You'll pass through the tiny towns of Port Sulphur, Buras, and Empire, before eventually reaching the town of Venice. The locals call this the 'end of the world' because you can't drive any further south than this in Louisiana. This area boasts some of the best fishing in the world, and the friendly people and easygoing way of life may make you want to stay a while.

The Scenic Southwest – El Paso TX to Roswell NM
225 miles – about 4 hours

This route will take you through one of the most desolate, yet most impressive parts of the desert Southwest. Leaving El Paso heading east on U.S. Route 62, the modern sprawl of the city gives way to expansive desert. Make sure you get gas before you leave El Paso, because there won't be any full-service towns for another 100 miles.

The flat desert of West Texas eventually gives way to rolling hills. The dry, burnt color of the Texas desert stays constant throughout this part of the journey. Eventually, well off in the disistance you'll see a prominent stony peak looming. You're looking at Guadalupe Peak, the highest point in Texas, rising to an elevation of well over

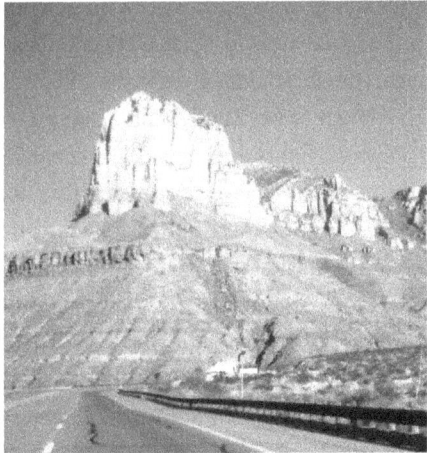

From miles away, Guadalupe Peak looms over the West Texas desert

8,000 feet.

The Guadalupe Mountains rise abruptly from the floor of the Chihuahuan Desert, roughly marking the division between Texas and New Mexico. The summit, part of Guadalupe Mountains National Park, is accessed via a fairly accessible four-mile trail. In the summer, the peak offers a refreshing change from the scorching heat of the desert floor. If you're up for the challenge of hiking to the top of the mountain, it's a great way to spend an afternoon.

When you get to Carlsbad, New Mexico, you're at the gateway to famous Carlsbad Caverns National Park. If you didn't get a chance to hike to the peak above ground earlier, try heading underground into one of the largest cave systems in the world. Tours are available daily, and you'll get a chance to see the Big Room, the third largest cave chamber in North America.

Motoring north out of Carlsbad on U.S. 285, our route winds through the desert of Southeast New Mexico, and we find ourselves in the quirky town of Roswell. Famous for an unusual aircraft that crashed near here in 1947, UFO enthusiasts have flocked here ever since, convinced that aliens visited Roswell and continue to do so.

Much of Roswell is built around UFO and alien themes. The city's street lights are shaped like spaceships, and even some of the local restaurants have statues of aliens and UFO's outside. The Alien Research Center, located downtown, tries to convince visitors about the various conspiracies regarding the 1947 incident. It makes for an interesting visit, even if just for the entertainment factor.

Although Roswell marks the end of this route, you're just a few hours from Santa Fe and Albuquerque via U.S. 285 and Interstate 40. These routes will show you a piece of the desert Southwest that might remind you of times past, especially traveling through the near-abandoned towns of Encino and Vaughn. This is the gateway to the Southwest.

Design Your Own One-Tank Trip

These examples are just a few of the endless options when taking a one-tank road trip. Obviously, several beautiful sections of the country aren't even represented. You may be in New England, famous for the natural color show put on by changing leaves every fall. Or you might be in the Great Plains, where the tranquil beauty of wholesome farmland and grassland stretch for as far as the eye can see. You might be in the South, where history, hospitality, and culture converge. No matter where you happen to be, it's easy to plan a few hours' getaway and still see something new.

One of the great things about one-tank road trips is the ability to explore fascinating places close to home that you've never appreciated before. Rising fuel costs and a struggling economy have led many would-be travelers to settle for a 'staycation'. Instead of just staying home, though, look around your immediate area and explore some highways and byways you've never traveled before.

Get a copy of your state's official transportation map and travel guide (or download one online – see Chapter 23). They're free and they'll help you plan a short road trip near home. Look for scenic byways in your state's travel guide or road map. Often these routes are highlighted with green dots or other markings.

If you're a history buff, look for historical markers. If you enjoy the great outdoors, follow roads that run adjacent to rivers and lakes. By exploring roads in your own part of the country, you're sure to find something new, even if you've lived there your whole life. If you're on a budget or can't afford to take many days off from work, a short trip is the perfect way to get a taste of being on the open road without a big investment of time or money.

Planning a Short Trip

One of the best things about short road trips is that they require little or no advance planning. Especially for a daytrip, it's possible to just jump in the car and take off. Try following a road you've never taken before. Most Americans live within a couple hours of scenic byways, many of which they've never traveled. Avoid the interstates, and favor two-lane roads. Check the weather forecast, and pick a day with good, sunny weather to head out.

Even weekend getaways don't have to be planned far in advance. If the weather will be favorable over a certain weekend, try getting away for a couple of days. With last-minute specials easily available online, it's not necessary to book far ahead of time to get a great deal on a hotel room. Often, the most memorable trips are the unplanned ones, those impromptu journeys where you just get in the car and go.

The sample road trips I've discussed in this chapter are just ideas. These are some of America's favorites, but they're just examples of ways to hit the road when you have little time to spare. Still, your ideal short road trip may be something completely different. No matter what your circumstances are, try taking a short road trip. It really is true: good things often do come in small packages!

6

Extended Road Trips

Some of us dream of traveling the road for months, even for a year or more, wandering the country at leisure to fully experience the extended road trip lifestyle. Although you might think an extended road trip is a dream best saved for retirement, more and more people are learning that living on the road – at least for a while – is a dream within reach. With thorough planning and a carefully planned budget, it's possible to spend an extended time on the road without breaking the bank.

Some people have big ambitions for the places they'd like to see. Many travelers want to visit all 48 of the continental states; others pine for a summer trip to Alaska. Maybe a road trip to Mexico and Central America catches your interest. No matter what travel preference you have, the farthest of destinations require an extended road trip. And extended road trips require extended planning.

First of all, it requires psychological planning. Think about it – will you *really* be able to spend an extended time on the road? Most travelers enjoy getting away, but after about two weeks, they start to miss the stability and routine of being at home. To make sure you can handle a *long* time on the road, try taking a moderately-long trip first, maybe three weeks. How do you feel at the end of those three weeks? Are you ready for more? Or did you really miss home? After three weeks, you'll know if you're ready for something longer.

Before an extended journey, there's even more planning that has to be done back home. Being on the road for a month or more isn't as simple as just taking off and asking a friend to watch the house while you're away. If you prefer trips that require little or no planning, stick to shorter trips. Extended time away from home requires taking care of business first.

Taking Care of Business at Home

You'll need to pay the rent or mortgage if you'll be away for a month or more. Most landlords or rental companies will accept your check early, although they may ask you to postdate your check for bookkeeping purposes. Just ask your landlord or building manager, and likely he or she will be happy to help you.

The landlord may even give you a discount on rent if you'll be away the entire month. Ask about this option that may save you several hundred dollars if it's available.

If you own your home, you'll likely have no problem making your mortgage payment in advance. The mortgage company will gladly accept your checks ahead of time, and you won't even have to postdate them. Just send the appropriate month's payment coupon along with your check, and you should be fine. If you haven't already looked into making online or automatic payments on your mortgage, this is the time to start. By paying your mortgage – and other bills – online, you won't physically need to be home to make payments. You'll conveniently be able to make payments from anywhere in the world.

Other Considerations

Homeowners also need to make sure the lawn is cared for. Hire a lawn care company well in advance of your trip to keep the grass trimmed and weeds pulled. The cost of this service is small compared to the worry of coming home to an overgrown lawn, not to mention possible code violations, citations, and hefty fines. If you ask a friend to take care of your lawn for you, make sure that he or she knows how to use your lawnmower and that there's enough fuel on hand to last your whole trip.

Both renters and homeowners will need someone to check on the home occasionally. Select someone you trust and who won't turn your home into 'party central' while you're away. I know of someone who asked an acquaintance to watch his apartment during an extended trip. Upon his return, he found that nearly every dish in the apartment had been left dirty – but they had all been returned to the cabinets anyway! This 'caretaker' had played a game of darts on the wall; he found darts stuck in the living room wall, the dining room, even in the fish tank! The moral of the story? Don't let just anyone watch your place while you're away; choose someone who's responsible, and preferably older. A trusted coworker or neighbor will often help with this.

If you're going to be gone for a *very* long time, especially from an apartment, it may be wiser to move out, at least temporarily. Landlords usually don't mind if a tenant is gone for a month or two; much longer than that, though, and you may need to give up the apartment and put your belongings in long-term storage. Fortunately, storage units are plentiful and relatively cheap, and they'll cost less than rent. If you're willing to give up an apartment to take an extended trip, putting your possessions in storage will save you serious money.

Remember to stop by the post office to temporarily stop the mail. The post office will hold your mail for up to one month; for longer trips, you'll have to make other arrangements. For trips longer than one month, you'll be better off forwarding your mail to a commercial mailbox service during your absence.

Notice that I mentioned a "commercial mailbox service," not a P.O. Box number. Although a regular post office box works fine when you're maintaining a nearby residence, they don't work very well when you're away. If you need to have a package delivered, only the U.S. postal service will deliver to a post office box. FedEx or U.P.S. won't be able to complete the delivery. Certain applications or other forms will not accept an address with a P.O. Box number.

Commercial mailboxes give you the benefit of an actual street address, so any courier or delivery service will be able to get a package to you. And as long as you keep the mailbox active by paying the annual fee, you can keep having your mail from home forwarded for up to one year. If you'll be away more than a year, change your address with the sender. Mailbox services are actually inexpensive, considering the convenience they offer. Although fees sometimes go on sale, expect to pay about $15 a month for commercial mailbox service.

Paying the Bills

When you're away for two weeks, paying bills is likely the least of your worries; the mail gets picked up at the post office, and the bills get paid when you return. Not so with an extended road trip. It's possible for payment due dates to pass without ever seeing the bill. Making payments and avoiding late fees are more of a challenge when you never know what's owed. That's why it's so important to make careful arrangements well ahead of time for your finances when planning for an extended trip.

Most of my advice for paying bills while away from home can be summed up in two words: *Pay online.* Only a few bills can't be paid this way; and many of those services simply need to be suspended during your absence, anyway. Invest in a computer, tablet, or smartphone with reliable wireless internet capability if you don't already have one; your internet connection can become your biggest asset on the road when it's necessary to communicate with home.

Landline telephone. Many phone companies now offer to bill your credit card directly or deduct the balance due from your checking account. Others let you pay online. If your company still doesn't allow these options, seriously consider having your landline turned off while you'll be away. Home telephones aren't of much use while you're on the road, and you could easily save $100 if you'll be away for more than two months. If you don't want to lose your home phone service, even temporarily, seriously consider changing companies; there's no excuse for any telecom company to refuse online payments these days.

Cell phone. All major cell phone providers accept online payments. If you're not already taking advantage of this service, sign up at least a month before your trip to make sure it works for you. If you don't have a cell phone or use one only in emergencies; seriously consider a prepaid cell phone; some of them, such as Net10, cost as little as 10¢ a minute and never incur roaming charges in the continental United States. Prepaid phones have a significant advantage for the long-term traveler: You'll never miss paying a bill.

Credit card. All major credit cards can be paid online. However, try to log on to your credit card website from your own tablet, laptop, or phone only; some companies require you to re-authenticate your personal data after switching machines. Since paying credit cards online is so easy these days, seriously consider having other bills charged to your card as well. Also, consider charging every road trip expense possible to your card, leaving cash just for emergencies or small, convenience purchases. If your card earns reward points, cash back, or airline miles, your daily expenses may actually help fund your next vacation.

Electricity. If maintaining your residence back home, you won't want to shut the electricity off completely. In fact, it makes sense to keep a few lights controlled by timers for security purposes. Don't shut the heating system off entirely in the winter; your pipes could freeze, causing thousands of dollars in damage to your home. Instead, go into 'low energy' mode: turn the thermostat down to 55 or 60 (in the winter), shut off the hot water heater, and unplug unnecessary electrical devices. In the summer, most homes need very little, if any, air conditioning; consider shutting it off completely.

Many electricity companies are locally owned cooperatives; others are publicly traded corporate entities. In any case, most people don't have a choice as to which electric company they patronize. As a result, you're likely to have fewer payment choices with utility bills. Some electric companies allow you to pay bills online, but many do not.

One option for paying your bill is to estimate the amount of your bill and prepay that amount to the company; this method works best for absences of no more than two months. Beyond two months, it gets very difficult to anticipate the amount of a bill, unless you've enrolled in a saver program that keeps your bill consistent from month to month. Some electric companies that don't accept online payments *do* accept credit card payments. Try calling the billing office and paying over the phone with a credit card. If they don't accept phone payments, you may have to call and ask how much is owed on your account. Then, mail the company a check with your account number written at the bottom.

Water. If you pay a separate water bill, it's unlikely that you'll be able to pay it online. Some water districts even hesitate to accept credit card payments. The best option in this case may be to estimate the water bill to the best of your ability and prepay at least twice the normal amount of your bill. Since you won't be home, your water consumption should be very low, and this amount should cover several months of actual usage. If in doubt, call the water district a couple of months into your trip and ask how much you owe, then send them a check.

Trash pickup. If you pay for your own garbage collection, call the company and put your service on hold if you'll be away for a month or more. There's no reason to pay for a service you won't be using. If they won't put a hold on your service, cancel it. Rehire them – or better yet, find a more flexible company – upon your return. Trash pickup is usually paid in advance, so there shouldn't be late fees to worry about, as long as there's a hold on the service.

Newspaper delivery. Call the newspaper and have them put a vacation hold on your subscription. Otherwise, you may come home to find dozens of newspapers lying on the lawn.

Cable or Satellite television. If you'll be away several months, it may be wise to put your subscription on vacation hold.

Otherwise, most cable and satellite companies allow you to pay online or by electronic check.

Auto insurance. Making sure your auto insurance policy is up-to-date is not only wise, it's required by law. Don't let the policy expire while you're on the road, either. Call your agent and write a check, if necessary, or have the premium deducted directly from your bank account. Most companies now let you print your own proof-of-insurance certificates directly from your online account.

Vehicle registration. Most states allow motorists to renew car registration at least two months before their expiration, sometimes more. If you can't personally go to the D.M.V. to renew, though, most states allow you to renew by mail, sending in a check for the required amount. If you're not sure of the amount owed, call your local Department of Motor Vehicles. If you renew by mail, you will receive the renewal registration form and sticker (or license plate) by mail, as well.

If you're not going to be near your mailbox, it may be necessary to have a friend check your mailbox for you and personally forward the package to you. Vehicle registration is one of the few bills that's best to complete personally. If possible, handle this before leaving home.

Property taxes. If you pay a mortgage, the company should pay property taxes for you out of an escrow account. If you own your home free and clear, though, you'll have to send the check yourself. Most local governments don't take credit cards or online payments, so this is another matter you may have to leave to a trusted friend. Once again, it's best to handle tax payments before you leave; you won't want the county putting a lien on your house while you're away.

Money Matters

Even before you decide that the bills can get paid during your time away, it's important to think about money issues. Do your finances really allow for this kind of trip? And just as importantly, how long can you afford to be away from home? If you're dependent on a regular job, and you feel fortunate to get two weeks vacation each year, taking a month-long road trip may simply be impossible. On the other hand, retired couples with a steady pension income may practically be able to live on the road for months, even years at a time.

Other individuals, though, may be able to manage spending a few months on the road without quitting their jobs. Teachers may be able to arrange being away for a couple of months in the summer; college students may be able to do the same. If you work from home, telecommute, or work over the internet, it may be possible to take your job with you – a working road trip, if you will.

If you don't currently have a 'portable' job, but you want to spend an extended time on the road, seriously consider an online occupation. It may be as simple as selling antiques on Ebay, as complex as being a technical writer or translating text, or somewhere in the middle. 'Working at home' and online jobs are becoming more common, and they're more conducive to living on the road than traditional office jobs.

For those of us who have to work in a fixed location, though, the reality is that work will have to be separate from travel. That means you're going to have to save up to take an extended journey. How much will you need to live on the road? In general, plan on spending at least $2000 a month, in addition to any expenses you have at home. It's possible to live on less than that, but it requires some real scrimping and frugality. And it's very easy to spend *more* than $2000 a month, too, but I'll give a few ideas later for saving money when spending a longer time on the road.

Before you think about spending money, though, make sure you have a place to *get* money. Although locally owned banks usually provide more personal service, they often can't help you avoid ATM fees while traveling. Open an account at a bank with branches across the nation. That way, it will be easier to find a branch where you won't waste money on ATM fees.

At times, it may be impossible to find a bank or ATM where you won't be charged a fee, even with an account at the most common banks in the country. If you must withdraw funds from an ATM where you'll have to pay a fee – usually between two and five dollars – withdraw the maximum daily amount from your account, so you won't have to repeat the process in a few days. Remember, it's possible to cut down on ATM fees by avoiding cash and sticking to debit or credit cards as much as possible.

Should I Buy an RV?

Many long-term travelers decide to buy a recreational vehicle. RV's can range from simple towed pop-ups to rolling luxury behemoths. But is it for you? An RV is a major purchase that could easily cost more than an entire year's worth of living expenses. However, happy RV owners state that it's more than just a purchase; it's an investment in a way of life. In other words, if you've decided to adopt the RV lifestyle and plan to spend weeks or months at a time on the road, and you can afford it, go ahead and purchase an RV.

Keep in mind, though, that the choice of RV's is as nearly extensive as that of passenger vehicles. A simple pop-up camper may be cramped for extended periods, but since it's relatively inexpensive, it may be the perfect choice for the traveler who wants something on a budget. Since pop-ups are towed, their lifespan will likely be longer than the motor towing it. If a larger motorhome needs significant mechanical repairs, the whole trip may have to be put on hold.

Luxury motorhomes are basically small homes on wheels. Driving a beast like this, you may never again miss the comforts of home. Be aware, though, that high-end motorhomes cost as much as $250,000. At this end of the price spectrum, expect satellite TV reception, comfortable furniture, and plenty of space, not to mention numerous other amenities.

If you don't have much experience with RV's, don't buy one until you've driven one and tried one out for a while. It's possible to rent one and experience the RV lifestyle for a few days; you'll have the full support of the rental agency, too, in case of mechanical or other problems. RV's can often be rented for around $200 a day. Renting for a short time can be a wise investment, as it gives the potential owner a good idea how life in an RV would be.

Be aware that most people, even those who plan to spend months on the road, don't need to purchase an RV to get the most out of their time. RV drivers certainly spend less on lodging than other road travelers, and they may also spend less on their total vacation budget than other people – not counting the actual RV purchase itself. Be aware, though, that the fuel economy for most gasoline motorhomes will average six miles per gallon; diesel coaches will be closer to 10 miles per gallon.

Motorhome resale opportunities fluctuate with gas prices and the economic climate; when gas prices are high or the economy is struggling, RV's will be tough to sell. They're wonderful for those

Buying an RV can be a viable option for extended trips.

who will use them and can afford them, but most of us will be just fine with a van or SUV. For one to three people, a car will even suffice for all but the longest of trips.

Special Considerations for the Extended Trip

Long road trips aren't really much different from shorter ones – you'll spend time on the road and likely at various destinations along the way – but there are special considerations that make them a little more challenging. Other than the advance planning discussed earlier in this chapter, think about the following needs on an extended trip.

Laundry. Any vacation longer than a week should include a laundry plan. Since you won't want to wear dirty clothes, nor will you want to haul dozens of different outfits, plan to take enough clothes for a week. At the end of the week, look for a laundromat and take an hour or two to wash clothes. This can even be a welcome diversion just to wait on the dryer and read or listen to music. Some hotels have laundry facilities, but most laundromats are cheaper. If you decide not to bring along detergent or fabric softener, you can buy them at any dollar store. Look online or in the yellow pages to find locations.

Cooler. When on the road for weeks or months at a time, you'll want to have a reliable cooler. Many better coolers are actually small refrigerators that connect to a power outlet in your vehicle.

No matter what bag you choose, be as organized as you can

These will keep you from having to buy ice constantly, especially if you spend a few days camping. Good coolers cost upwards of $50, but they're worth every penny. Coolers work best when full, so don't buy a bigger cooler than you'll reasonably need.

Luggage. Although a duffle bag may do for a shorter trip, longer journeys require more. A three-month journey doesn't require much more luggage than a weeklong jaunt, but after the first week or so, you'll want to know *exactly* where everything is. Suitcases, wheeled bags, and computer cases all have small compartments for those little, easy-to-lose items. Use those compartments! You'll waste valuable time – not to mention fraying your nerves – searching for something important when a little organization would have made it easier to find.

Camping supplies. Even if you plan on staying primarily in hotels, take a tent if you'll be on the road awhile. Staying in hotels can be tiresome after a couple of weeks, and camping can give your trip a needed diversion. It's not necessary to buy the biggest tent on the market, just one that will comfortably sleep the number of people on your trip. Don't forget sleeping bags, pillows, and an air mattress or tent pad. It may sound like a lot of supplies to take, but if you're traveling in an SUV or van, it won't take up that much space. As long as *everyone* remembers to pack light, there will still be plenty of room.

Having a computer often isn't enough. Do you have reliable web access?

Reliable internet access. Internet access has become an integral part of all types of travel, not to mention the fact that the best travel deals are found online. When you're on the road for only a week or two at a time, relying on free public Wi-Fi or hotel internet access will probably be fine. For extended trips, though, it may be wise to investigate something more reliable. Wireless data plans through your cellular provider can keep you online for relatively little money. If you have an iPad, 3 GB of high-speed 4G access costs about $30 a month. This cost may be well worth the investment. (See Chapter 9 for more information about staying connected on the road.)

Mechanical needs. If it's on the road enough, a vehicle will eventually need repairs, or at the very least, preventive maintenance. Every town will have at least one mechanic. If the vehicle was thoroughly inspected before the trip, it's likely you won't have any serious problems. Still, don't be afraid of visiting a mechanic while away from home. If you're reluctant to trust one in a strange town, don't be; just ask around at a local diner or even a laundromat. Local residents will likely recommend someone trustworthy.

Don't forget to get the oil changed every 3000 miles. With quick lube businesses in nearly every town big enough to have a McDonald's, it's easy and quick to get your car serviced – usually in under an hour. Just like back home, they'll change your windshield wiper blades, filters, and top off other necessary fluids if necessary.

Shopping. Plan to visit a supermarket at least once a week. Restaurants are convenient, but they can get expensive and are often unhealthy. Look for supermarket chains that you're familiar with from home; the prices and setup are likely to be similar to what you're used to, saving you both money and time. If you need a specific item, your best bet is to visit a national grocery chain like Kroger, Wal-Mart Supercenter, or Safeway.

Staying Within a Budget

Most people need strict financial discipline to stay on the road for months at a time. All too often, the temptation is just too great, and some travelers end up staying in overpriced hotels or eating overpriced meals, when lower-priced options would have worked just as well.

Your total expenses are the sum of your expenses on the road and the bills that have to be paid back home. The latter set of expenses is fixed; the former set of expenses can be kept low *if* you're willing to follow a few rules.

Budgeting on an extended road trip can be summed up in two simple equations. They are:

Lots of driving + Hotels every night = Lots of money
Less driving + Budget lodging options = Less money

Get the idea? Some expenses can't be reduced much. If the car needs to be repaired, it's an expense that has to be paid. When your clothes get dirty, those around you will *really* appreciate it if you wash your clothes – laundry can't be eliminated to save money. But some expenses really cut into a travel budget more than others. The biggest chunks of a road trip budget are lodging and fuel, and to a lesser extent, food.

Stretching Your Lodging Funds

If you plan to be on the road awhile, you'll have to stretch your lodging budget. Hotel expenses can get out of control very fast, especially with some roadside chains charging upwards of $100 a night for walk-up rates. At that rate, lodging could easily consume half or more of an entire vacation budget! The same thing can be said for gasoline expenses. When prices are high, gas can easily cost $20 just to drive 100 miles in a truck, van, or SUV.

Instead of driving hundreds of miles every day, getting a hotel for the night, eating in a restaurant, then repeating the process the next day, try staying in one place for a few days. Many hotels and motels, especially at the extended stay level, offer weekly rates. By staying put for a week, it's possible to save $100 or more on lodging – plus you'll have more time to explore.

Extended-stay hotels offer another benefit: a full kitchen. With a kitchen, you're never stuck eating fast-food. Stop by a supermarket, and everyone can take turns cooking dinner. This could easily save $100 a week. At the same time, don't get burned out on eating in, either. At least once every other day, plan for a good lunch at a local restaurant with reasonable prices.

Camping provides another opportunity for low-cost lodging. It's worth repeating that state parks, land areas managed by the

Living on the Road for $500 a Week – Plan No. 1

Think it's possible for someone to spend about $500 a week while on an extended road trip? It certainly is, if you're willing to economize and try a budget like this one. The prices are for a single traveler; they'll need to be adjusted for larger groups.

Gasoline – 500 miles total	$ 70
4 Nights in an inexpensive motel	$ 240
3 Nights in a state park campground	$ 60
Groceries	$ 40
4 Restaurant Meals	$ 60
Miscellaneous Expenses	$ 40
Grand Total for the Week	**$ 510**

Army Corps of Engineers, lakes, and national forests are great places to camp, sometimes for as little as $10 a night. If you're looking for a serious deal, try dispersed camping in a national forest, which is absolutely free – of course, you won't have any amenities, either.

Renting a room at a resort or condominium is also a surprising option for budget lodging. Many resorts, especially in the off-season, rent rooms in tourist areas for a fraction of their normal rate. It's possible to spend as little as $350 on a week in one of these resorts, which is really a bargain. Websites such as SkyAuction.com sometimes offer resort rentals like these at the last minute, so check often for the best deals. You may be surprised at the deals available!

Try Something Different!

Spending two months on the road *is* definitely out of the ordinary! Still, being away this long, especially if you're alone or with one other person, can become an isolating experience. So it's important to get out and meet people, talk to others, and enjoy your surroundings. When you eat out, talk to people. Ask about places to visit; often they'll recommend places the guidebook never mentioned.

If you're passing near friends' or relatives' homes, pay them a visit. Spend an afternoon, a day, or a few days, whatever is most appropriate. Take time to meet people and talk to them. You'll probably make new friends.

And even though you're on a road trip, you don't have to travel exclusively by car. If you're on a strict budget, try bus travel. It's safe to say you'll find a wide variety of people on a bus. Even if you decide you hate it, it's an experience you'll never forget.

If you don't want to take a bus, try traveling by passenger rail. Amtrak, America's only nationwide rail system, passes through almost every state and will take you directly to the center of many major cities – no taxi required.

Amtrak is probably one of the best-kept travel secrets in the country, since most Amtrak stations, especially those in smaller towns, offer free long-term parking to train travelers. You can park your car at the Amtrak station, ride the train to the center of a major city, and spend as long as you want. You won't pay for parking, and you won't have to fight city traffic. It's possible to explore most city centers by public transportation and maybe a few taxi rides. Hotel deals, even downtown in major cities are plentiful on sites like Hotwire and Priceline.

I highly recommend traveling by train, especially as a complement to a road trip. On the train, it's hard *not* to meet people. The mood is much more relaxed than on a plane. When passengers get hungry, they can go to the lounge car for snacks, or to the dining car for full restaurant-style meals. If you're willing to splurge, try the train's sleeping accommodations. For as little as $70 it's possible for two people to rent a miniature private room for the night,

Living on the Road for $500 a Week – Plan No. 2

Here's another possibility for living on the road for about $500 a week.

Gasoline – 500 miles total	$ 70
7 Nights in a hotel won on Priceline.com with a successful bid of $35 a night	$ 265
7 Restaurant Meals	$ 90
Groceries	$ 30
Miscellaneous Expenses	$ 40
Grand Total for the Week	**$ 495**

with all meals included; ask the conductor about upgrading to sleeper service if you're interested.

Don't Get Overwhelmed!

Some people start an extended trip with the intention of seeing *everything*. They want to go to every major attraction in the country. They want to visit every state. They want to stop at every kitschy roadside attraction ever built. If that's your intention, you'll probably be disappointed. Most people who live 100 years never see all that.

If you drive all over the country in a zigzag pattern just to say you've set foot in every state, you're shortchanging yourself. Although the car is one of the best ways to get to the places you want to see, most of America can't be experienced from *inside* one. You're going to have to get out and discover what's *outside*; that's what's great about spending time on the road. The journey is about more than miles clocked on an odometer or the exits you've passed. It's about stopping and experiencing what's along the way. So, on an extended road trip, don't get in a hurry. You'll have lots of time to explore and discover, and if you find a place you like, stay longer!

Drive full days only occasionally. On a weeklong trip, it may be easy to drive two or three full days, sometimes more. On a longer trip, though, think in terms of weeks, not days. Instead of spending a day in one spot, plan on spending a week. Then, when it's time to move on, go somewhere else, and spend another week. This style of travel will also give you more of a sense of stability than moving from one place to another nearly every day.

If you've thought about taking to the road for months at a time, you're not alone. Hundreds of thousands of 'snowbirds' do it every year, migrating to places where the sun shines and warm temperatures prevail when it's cold back home. Really, an extended road trip is more about being able to move from one spot to another at will, really experiencing life there. It shouldn't mean nonstop driving or a vacation to go see superficial tourist attractions. It's about finding a place and enjoying it. It's about mingling with the locals. It could even be about finding a new home. Whatever the case, there's no need to fear taking an extended road trip.

7

The Road Trip Packing List

You've planned your route. You know where you want to go. You've picked the sights you'll see, even the places you'll stay along the way. After all this planning, it's time to pack. And really, this is one of the most important parts of planning for a road trip, because how well you pack has much to do with how you'll enjoy your trip – for every unnecessary item you take, it means a little more time loading or unloading luggage and less time enjoying your travels. And think about this: when travelers take more, there's less room left in the car for personal space. When sitting in the car for hours at a time, space becomes important.

Packing light really *is* a virtue. And although it would be a shame to leave something really important at home – like medication, your driver's license, or important documents – most other things are comfort items and can easily be acquired along the way.

So *do* pack light. And if you can, convince everyone else traveling with you to do the same. I've been on enough road trips to know that one inconsiderate person, who thinks he needs to take three large suitcases filled with every important possession and possible clothing item, can spoil the trip for everyone else. Maybe you've been on that trip or traveled with that person. So if you are the 'captain' of the trip or the owner of the car, let everyone know that they need to limit their packing to one suitcase/roller case and one smaller bag.

Really, the 'one suitcase plus a smaller bag rule' is very reasonable. The airlines expect flyers to follow it when carrying luggage onto a plane. If you need more than that, you'll pay extra.

The packing list that follows is rather exhaustive. You may not need everything on this list, but few will need much beyond this list. And unless you're moving cross-country or traveling for several months, it should all fit in a couple of bags, or even just one.

Personal Items

Clothes. We begin with the obvious. Everyone has his or her own fashion preferences, so this area has endless possibilities, but remember to be comfortable. Unless you're planning to attend a business or formal event where dress clothes are expected, leave the suits and dresses at home. Dress clothes generally take up more room than casual clothes. If you expect to enjoy a 'nice' dinner at a formal restaurant, men can take a blazer, and women can pack a dress or skirt. Except in the most unusual of circumstances – making a permanent move, for example – take no more clothes than what you'll need for seven days. After a week, visit a laundromat.

Shoes. Two pairs should be enough for most people: one comfortable pair for the car and another pair for walking or hiking.

Pack a pair of sandals or flip-flops for a trip to the beach or swimming pool.

Towel. Although hotels provide towels for guests, you'll need your own for a camping trip or an emergency spill. In a pinch, it can serve as a makeshift pillow.

Toiletries. This includes your toothbrush, toothpaste, shampoo, mouthwash, deodorant, and shaving products. I like to take travel size packages of most of these products. Small toothpaste tubes can be easily refilled by placing the mouth of the little tube against the mouth of a bigger toothpaste tube. Just squeeze the bigger tube to refill the smaller one. Instead of taking a bulky can of shaving cream, look into a product called *shaving oil* – for a couple of bucks, you can buy a few milliliters, which will last for months – available at many drugstores and even discount stores.

Soap. Great for cleaning small stains from clothes and invaluable at a campsite.

Fingernail clippers. Aside from their obvious purpose, these can be used as makeshift scissors to cut threads or other small objects.

Prescription medications. Take the prescription along, too. Along with these, don't forget any contraceptives or personal hygiene items.

Over-the-counter medications. Prepare a small emergency medication kit that includes your favorite pain reliever, diarrhea relief pills, stomach relief pills, and a few sleeping pills. If you suffer from allergies, include allergy medication, as well.

Brush or comb.

Mirror. Sometimes the rearview mirror just won't do. Look for a basic camping mirror or locker mirror; they cost just a few dollars and are quite durable.

Umbrella. Most of the time, a small emergency umbrella costing one to three dollars will work fine.

Sunglasses and Case. The case will keep the glasses from getting crushed. Also remember to take a few lens cleaning wipes.

> ### Luggage: Wheels or No Wheels?
>
> Today's most popular luggage features a somewhat sturdy frame with wheels attached to the bottom. The metal framework extends, revealing a convenient handle. Are these rolling suitcases best for a road trip, though? Wheeled luggage tends to be heavy, and to be honest, wheels are useful only when rolling your case long distances, such as in an airport. Wheels don't handle too well on city streets or up stairs. Consider, also, that inflexible wheeled luggage gives less usable room in the trunk of the car, especially if four people each plan to take their own case. Consider packing with a large duffle bag; they tend to hold just as much as any wheeled bag – and they usually weigh much less.

Travel mug. Some convenience stores will allow you to refill your own travel mug for a discount. These are also much sturdier than cheap foam or paper cups, which tend to leak or collapse. Remember to wash the mug occasionally!

Calculator. Great for calculating gas mileage or adding up expenses. Buy a solar calculator, so you won't have to worry about batteries. Five dollars or less.

Reading material. For those evenings in the hotel when nothing's on TV, and you just need something to read. Good reading material is a must if you're traveling alone; it will keep your mind occupied while sitting in a restaurant or at other times. Magazines are also ideal; read them, then dispose of them or give them away as you finish. A Kindle or other e-reader works perfectly, too.

Pillow. A pillow from home can make a night's sleep much easier, especially if you'll be away for a while.

Small fleece blanket. A small blanket is perfect for those times when the air conditioner in the car is too cold for your comfort. Don't leave this home in the summertime; you may be surprised how often you'll feel chilly, even in warm weather months.

Earplugs and eye mask. Especially if you need darkness or quiet, these two items will help you get to sleep, even in the noisiest of motels. If you need to take a nap during the day, an eye mask makes it much easier.

Plastic bags. Plastic shopping bags make great litter bags for the car, and you can use them to store dirty clothes until laundry time. Take several of these.

Clothespins. Perfect for closing a bag of chips, hanging clothes to dry at a campsite, or even keeping the curtains closed in a motel room.

Pocket knife. Perfect for cutting, slicing, even peeling an orange.

Hangers. The hotel may not have enough hangers for everyone, so take a couple of your own.

Binoculars. Perfect for enjoying the scenery from the car or on a hike.

Important phone numbers and addresses. If something happens to your cell phone, you'll need to have the most important contact numbers and addresses available in the event of an emergency. Laminate this list and keep it in a safe place, such as a purse or wallet.

Personal checks. If you don't plan to be away for an extended time, two or three checks should be enough. Although most businesses don't accept checks from out of town, you may have to pay a bill or other expense.

Envelopes and postage stamps. If you have to pay a bill by mail when you're away, you'll save time by having a few envelopes and stamps available. Or, you may just want to send someone a card, write a letter, or send a postcard.

Small notebook. For jotting down expenses, places you've been, hotel confirmation numbers, or anything else that may need to be written down.

Spare keys. If traveling with others, let someone else in the group keep the spare keys.

Documents and Red Tape

Driver's license. Very obvious, but you won't want to be stuck without it. Make sure it doesn't expire while you're away.

Current vehicle registration. Keep the original in the vehicle's glove compartment and affix the sticker to the correct spot on the license plate. Once again, make sure it won't expire during the trip.

Proof of insurance. Keep this in your glove compartment, next to the registration information. Laminate both of those forms and paperclip them together.

Passport, birth certificate, and car title. Under most circumstances, necessary only if you'll be leaving the country with your car. See Chapter 22, "South to Mexico."

Copies of all the above documents. Make copies and keep them separate from the originals, preferably in a safe place in your luggage.

Credit card and/or ATM card.

Membership cards. Whether you're a student, a member of AAA, AARP, or a labor union, your membership card may yield valuable discounts. And don't forget your health insurance card.

Communications and Technology

Cell phone. It doubles as a camera, alarm clock, and calculator. And don't forget the car charger!

Laptop or tablet computer. If reliable internet access is a must, make sure your tablet or phone has a robust nationwide data plan. A 3-gigabyte monthly allowance is enough for e-mail, web browsing, and all but the most active video streamers. Otherwise, Wi-Fi should be sufficient for most purposes. If you plan on taking a laptop, and the battery's charge doesn't last as long as it used to, consider buying a new battery before the trip. Of course, don't forget your computer's AC adapter and mouse. Take your machine's recovery disk and copies of any essential software, in case the unthinkable happens, and the hard drive has to be wiped clean for some reason.

Satellite radio or CD collection. Essential for audio entertainment while on the road.

iPod/MP3 player and headphones. For when you don't want to listen to what everyone else is listening to. Consider noise-reducing headphones; they're wonderful at blocking road and engine noise when you want some peace and quiet.

Portable DVD player, movies, and car adapter. Essential when traveling with kids, especially after they've gotten tired of road games and looking at the scenery. Adults may be better off with an iPhone or iPad for watching videos in the car. Still, a portable DVD player can be connected to your hotel TV to watch your favorite movies in the evenings.

Digital camera, rechargeable batteries, and memory card. If your phone's camera isn't sufficient, a simple point-and-shoot model will probably do. If you're a photography buff, a road trip is the perfect chance to capture vistas from around the country.

Battery charger. You may save money by using rechargeable batteries. To save space in your luggage, use the most compact charger you can find.

For the Car

GPS device. The more expensive models pronounce the names of streets and towns, offer traffic reports, give detailed lane guidance, and have larger screens. For most travelers, a simple model should be fine. They can easily be found for less than $100.

DC power inverter. Useful for plugging in a typical electronic device, such as a laptop computer, to a car's DC power outlet. Make sure the rating on the inverter is appropriate for the appliance you plan to run. Blow dryers and microwave ovens were not made to run on these things; keep them for laptop computers and small electrical equipment.

DC power splitter. The phone charger, satellite radio, and GPS all require a 12-volt outlet. Only have one power outlet in your car? Not to worry, because a splitter will convert one outlet into multiple receptacles. Look for one that has three outlets; these usually have an on/off switch and additional safety features.

Toolkit. Most auto supply stores sell an emergency toolkit with basic wrenches and screwdrivers for simple repairs. Just as important are jumper cables and an emergency air compressor. They're essential for jumping the car's battery or inflating a flat tire in an emergency.

Tire gauge. Get in the habit of checking the air pressure in your tires regularly. Well-inflated tires keep your fuel economy at acceptable levels, prevent the tires from wearing out too soon, and make for a smoother ride.

Ice scraper. Even in the summer, frost can form at high altitudes or at northern latitudes. In the winter, you'll likely need to scrape the frost from your windshield in the morning. Cheap scrapers can be found in springtime, when even the best scrapers are often put on clearance for just a few dollars.

Canned tire inflator. If you run over a nail and need to change a flat tire, it's not safe to do it on the shoulder of a busy expressway. You're better off calling for help. If you're in a place where it's safe to do so, a can of tire inflator, such as Fix-a-Flat, will temporarily seal your tire, so it's possible to drive to a repair center instead of having to call a tow truck.

Quart of oil. Check your oil level at least every 1000 miles. If you notice a slow leak or if your car uses more oil than normal, make plans to get it repaired. Until then, add oil yourself and make sure the level stays full.

Liquid rain repellent. This waxy liquid, of which Rain-X is the most common brand, is rubbed onto window glass with a dry cloth. After the glass is treated, rain beads up on the window, drastically improving visibility in poor weather. It's worth it to take a few minutes to treat your windows, before any long trip.

Cooler with snacks and drinks. It's not only convenient to fill a cooler with snacks and drinks, you'll save money, too, by avoiding the drive-thru line every time you get thirsty. Get ice every day or two to keep the drinks cold.

Box of tissues. In addition to their intended use, they can be used as miniature towels. Of course, if you plan on picnicking, take a roll of paper towels, too.

Roll of toilet paper. Not all public restrooms provide toilet paper. So keep a spare roll in the car, and get in the habit of taking a few squares of toilet paper into public restrooms, just in case.

Liquid hand sanitizer. Many public restrooms aren't the cleanest, and sometimes they don't even have proper handwashing facilities. A bottle of liquid hand sanitizer is a must when traveling the (sometimes dirty) road.

Tent. Essential for camping.

Small propane stove. Every discount store with a sporting goods department carries these miniature stoves. They're useful when camping, and even when you're not. It's easier to cook a meal at a park with one of these stoves than to use the park's barbecue pit. Your stove will be cleaner, too.

Flashlight. A good flashlight is useful for finding something you lost under the seat or in the trunk of your car at night. In an emergency, they're invaluable. A small LED flashlight with good batteries will likely serve its purpose through many trips.

Duct tape. We all know duct tape can be used for just about any temporary repair. Keep a small roll in the trunk of your car for emergencies.

Road atlas and other maps. Essential for finding your way. These can be used along with your GPS device.

Guidebooks. Invaluable for finding attractions along the way. Many guidebooks also list inns, hotels, and restaurants. Some even include coupons. Every state has a tourism department that will send you state guidebooks and information free of charge. Most of these can also be picked up at state welcome centers along the interstate. For more information, see Chapter 23, "Road trip Resources."

Coupons for restaurants and attractions. Print coupons from the web for restaurants you may visit along the way. Many attractions also offer online coupons. Keep these in a safe place, such as a dedicated coupon envelope or plastic baggie.

Take What's Important to You

If you take every item on this list, you'll likely have everything you'd possibly need for a typical road trip. However, since every traveler is different, it's best to take this list and create your own personal packing inventory that can be revised and reused over and over again for future travels.

If one of your traveling companions wants to take too much on a trip beyond what's necessary, remind him or her of this fact: Of all the travelers I've met, many of them have told me that they wish they hadn't taken so many things on their trip. I have yet to meet someone who has told me, "I wish I had taken more." It's always the opposite. So pack light, and pack smart.

Part Two

Making
the Best of Your
Road Trip

8

Behind the Wheel

If you've spent a while preparing for your journey, the day before leaving will be hectic. You'll be busy packing your luggage, deciding what to take, what to leave behind, and preparing your vehicle for the trip. The day before leaving on a long road trip, you may even have your own 'routine' for getting ready, both physically and psychologically.

In my case, since I know I'll be sitting in the car for a long time, I try to take a long walk the day before a trip. It's good to exercise, both before and during a road trip.

Another part of my pre-trip routine is preparing a music playlist for the first hour or so of my trip. iPods and other MP3 players make this task simple. Certain songs will put you into the traveling mood, and a string of 20 travel-oriented songs can really get your mind ready for the road ahead.

Getting Onto the Road

After you've packed every last item, checked your car, and prepared your mind and body for the trip, you're ready to go!

If you've filled your gas tank before leaving home, you won't have to buy fuel for several hours. Still, you may need to stop and pick up a few snacks at the store or run an errand before leaving town.

On the open road, make good use of cruise control. Driving long distances is much easier with cruise, and as long as your route has little traffic and the weather is agreeable, cruise control can actually make you a safer driver. By maintaining a constant speed, you're able to focus on obstacles that might be on the highway, not to mention that you can enjoy the scenery that much more.

In the last chapter, I mentioned the wisdom of driving at or near the speed limit. Speeding doesn't usually get you to your destination much faster, and speeders potentially face time-wasting traffic stops or expensive fines. However, some drivers may find themselves in an area with an artificially low speed limit. If you really feel that you need to drive faster than the posted speed limit, try to follow another car, and match that car's speed. Normally, the car at the front of a group of speeding vehicles will be the one that gets stopped by the police. In any case, the lead car will probably see the patrol car first and slow down, giving you the signal to do the same. Remember that most officers will allow you a tolerance of at least five mph over the speed limit. Still, you speed at your own risk; you're always better off sticking to the posted limit.

Don't Be Aggressive

After driving for a few hours, you'll begin to notice how other drivers react to what they experience on the road. Many drivers let

Last-Minute Errands

Before rolling out of the driveway, don't forget these important errands:

- Put a hold on mail and newspaper delivery

- Put lamps on timers – to give the home a 'lived-in' look

- Pay bills ahead of time – to avoid late fees

- Turn thermostat to low-energy mode

- Turn off all appliances, except refrigerator

- Lock all doors and windows

their impatience rule their behavior, and the result is the road rage common on today's highways. Smart drivers won't let rude, impatient behavior on the part of other motorists bother them.

Try to drive courteously, staying in the right lane except to pass on divided highways. Flashing high beams at slower drivers not only shows a lack of patience, it's extremely rude. Slower drivers may be elderly, have mechanical problems, or have some other legitimate reason to drive slower than surrounding traffic.

Tailgating, or following another vehicle too closely, is the leading cause of rear-end collisions. Try to stay at least two seconds behind the car in front of you. In other words, when a car ahead of you passes a fixed object such as an overpass, you should pass the same point no less than two seconds later. Never tailgate another driver, and don't allow other drivers to tailgate you. If another driver is following you too closely, slow down little by little until the car is either able to pass or moves back. Although you may be tempted to slam on your brakes if another car is tailgating you, don't! Doing so could cause a collision.

Watch for Obstacles

On the open road, you will find a surprising number of potentially dangerous obstacles. In rural areas, for example, deer and other animals can cause severe hazards on the highway, especially at night. Hitting a deer can cause thousands of dollars worth of damage to a car, ruining an otherwise well-planned trip.

When driving at night in rural areas, keep an eye out for stray animals, both wild and domestic. Even if deer, elk, or moose are uncommon along your route, hitting a large dog can do nearly as much damage. Many two-lane roads in the West are in open range, so pay special attention to livestock or other large animals. Watch for animals running or standing along the shoulder of the highway. If you see one, *don't swerve*! Instead, slow down and hit your horn a few times to scare the animal away.

In urban areas, obstacles on the road usually consist of traffic jams or emergency vehicles. When you see an emergency vehicle stopped on the side of the road with its lights flashing, move over to the next lane of traffic. All states now require drivers either to move over for emergency vehicles or to slow down drastically.

Another obstacle found mainly during summer months is the construction zone. Remember not to speed in areas where construction workers are present. Most states are getting serious about speeders in work zones. Illinois, for example, now levees $375 fines against work zone speeders for their first offense. Speeders are increasingly being caught with unmarked patrol cars and speed cameras. And motorists in that state who hit a worker, even on accident, will go to jail for 14 years and pay thousands of dollars in fines.

When driving through construction zones, move over to the available lane well ahead of time. If you see a sign instructing vehicles to "Merge Now", merge immediately. Drivers who attempt to pass other vehicles instead of merging could be cited for aggressive driving. Be patient in work zones, and expect delays. You'll be pleasantly surprised if the work zone doesn't slow you down as much as you thought!

Buy Gas Often

Every smart driver knows not to let the gas tank run empty. Common sense, though, can be complicated by unfamiliar surroundings. Drivers who are used to filling up at a favorite corner gas station may be surprised to see 60-mile stretches of highway without any fuel services in many parts of the West.

Most of the time, you'll be fine if you start looking for gas when the tank drops to about ¼ tank. Out West or in especially remote areas, start looking around the ½ tank mark. It's much better to fill up often than to run out in the middle of nowhere.

Start Early, But Not Too Early

The beginning of a road trip is one of the most exciting parts of the adventure. The anticipation of the journey ahead makes the first few hours of every long trip special. A commonly asked question is, "What time of day should we start our trip?" Is it wiser to start early in the morning or later in the day?

Personally, when making a multi-day drive, I prefer to leave in the afternoon on the first day. It helps me sleep easier if I know I won't have to leave at the crack of dawn the following day. Leaving on a late afternoon after work can help you get a head start of a few hours on your journey. I find that starting a road trip with a short driving day gets me used to being behind the wheel, so I'm more adjusted and ready for the longer day to follow.

If you're a morning person, though, you might prefer to hit the road earlier. I've done this many times, too, and beginning a road trip in the early morning can save money, since you're not paying for a hotel room after only a few hours of driving. A word of caution, though: Don't leave too early. Drivers that leave home at 4:00 or 5:00 in the morning tend to get tired very early in the day.

On one trip, I left home just before 4:00 a.m. and ended up having to take a nap by 9:00 in the morning. The reason? I didn't get a good night's sleep before the trip. Leaving too early in the morning can leave you tired and sluggish, even by mid-morning. If you decide to leave in the morning, I don't recommend leaving much earlier than 7:00 a.m. Try to eat a good breakfast before leaving, and remember, it 's extremely tiring to drive more than 10 to 12 hours in a day.

Taking the 'Easy Road'

If you rarely drive for several hours at a time, you may find it difficult to keep your mind occupied while behind the wheel. If you have friends riding along, you'll have plenty of conversation to stay occupied for a while. For those times when everyone else wants to sleep, listen to music, or just enjoy the scenery, make good use of your satellite radio or audiobooks.

If your road trip is for leisure, take advantage of every chance to enjoy scenic overlooks or other natural wonders along the way. Many states deliberately build interstate rest areas in spots known for their natural beauty. Most states also offer welcome centers shortly after crossing the state line along the interstate. Stop at these tourist information centers and pick up a free map and state visitor guide.

Even if you're not spending much time in a particular state, the free resources found at state welcome centers can familiarize you with attractions in the area. They also make great souvenirs of your road trip, and they may even give you ideas for future trips.

You'll probably find that two-lane rural roads offer a more relaxing, scenic drive than most interstate highways. Although there are exceptions, interstates were designed for speed, safety, and efficiency, not for their aesthetic value. Even though the trip along two-lane highways is slower, they make up for it by taking you through quaint places the interstate forgot. They also bring you much closer to the scenery that most interstates only showcase from a distance.

If you're in a hurry, the interstates will normally get you to your destination faster. If you have time, though, include two-lane byways in your travel plans. It may be possible to find non-interstate four-lane highways, which are a happy medium between the interstate and two-lane roads. These 'other' four-lane roads give motorists the chance to pass slower cars, with the advantage of being able to experience communities along the way, almost always with less traffic than the interstate.

Traveling through the rural West is a bit different, though. In several sparesely-populated western states (such as Nevada and Wyoming), just about the only four-lane rural highways you'll find are interstates. Don't worry, though, because the speed limit on two-lane rural highways in these states is usually 65 or 70 miles per hour. Because of this difference, driving through western states like Nevada is almost as fast on a two-lane road as it is on the expressway. Just remember to slow down when passing through small towns along these highways. Although having to brake to 25 miles per hour may seem like a crawl after cruising along at 70 for nearly an hour, small towns out West are usually well patrolled and strictly enforce their speed limits.

Fighting the Boredom

Honestly, even the biggest road trip enthusiasts get tired of driving for long hours each day. That's one reason I wouldn't take a long trip without my satellite radio. Even the radio, though, doesn't always fight the tired feeling that extended driving days can bring. So, it's important to pace yourself. Take breaks often. When you stop to use the restroom during the day, park far from the building and force yourself to walk. Walking will help keep you alert without draining your energy.

When you make a stop, don't just walk. Take some

In the Event of an Accident

If you're involved in an accident, try to steer your vehicle out of traffic and onto the shoulder or another safe place, if possible. Make sure that no one involved in the accident is hurt. Call 911, and don't discuss who's at fault; let the police and insurance companies handle that. Cooperate with all authorities. Of course, keep your insurance information handy. Although minor damage can be repaired, allowing the trip to continue, be aware that if the damage to your vehicle is severe enough, the remainder of the road trip may have to be cancelled.

time to sit on a bench and relax for a few minutes. After sitting in the car for hours on end, though, why would you want to find a bench and sit some more? Mainly because sitting on a bench lets you sit in a different position and stretch your muscles with more flexibility. When in the car, especially if you're the driver, your legs and back are in a set position for hours at a time. Moving around, even if sitting down in a chair or bench, makes a big difference.

How often should you stop? When I drive alone, I stop about every 2 ½ hours. When others ride along, though, I stop more often. On average, I plan for a stop every two hours. And I stop even more often in the morning. On a long drive, it's all about pacing yourself. If you're going to enjoy yourself, you have to *do more than just drive*. Stop as often as you can, even if just to look at the local historical landmarks on the side of the road. Instead of rushing, remember that a road trip is about the journey, not just the destination.

Should I Drive Straight Through?

All too often I talk to roadtrippers that get in too much of a hurry. They assume they can drive 1000 miles in a day. These are the guys that fly down the highway at 90 miles an hour, tailgating and flashing their lights at anybody in front of them. They shouldn't be on the road at all. They're in so much of a hurry that they should have taken a plane instead of hitting the highway.

This type of driver often thinks he can drive straight through the night and get to his destination that much sooner, without having to pay for a hotel. For most drivers, though, driving through the night is not only a draining experience; it's a risky proposition.

I don't recommend driving through the night under most circumstances. Most late-night drivers have already been awake all day. Even if you feel alert, you're probably more tired than you realize. Consider the hazards present on the road during the daytime, and then add wandering wild animals and the fact that hazards are simply harder to see at night. Headlights shining in your eyes tire your vision even faster than usual. Night driving requires a higher state of alertness.

Some stretches of interstate highway have so many crashes resulting from driver fatigue, that a few areas, such as I-95 through central North Carolina, are labeled 'Dead Zones' by safety organizations and state police patrols. I mention I-95 because thousands of people each year drive between South Florida and New York without stopping. If they start driving mid-afternoon, they expect to arrive at about the same hour, the following day. Although many of them make it through the night, fatigue overtakes some in the early hours of the morning, usually between 4 and 8 a.m.

Drowsy drivers cause so many fatalities in the early morning that state troopers are on the lookout for signs of fatigued motorists. If you're tempted to make a thousand-mile drive by running straight through the night, remember that you'll arrive more rested and more relaxed by spending a few bucks on a roadside motel. Remember, it's better to get where you're going a few hours later than not at all.

If You Have to Drive Through the Night

If lack of time or other circumstances force you to drive straight through the night, consider the following suggestions:

1. Never drive alone. If your companion can't help you drive, make sure someone else in the car *will stay awake with you the whole time* to keep you company. If you have other drivers in the car, switch off every hour or two while the other drivers rest their eyes or sleep.

2. Put your radio to use, preferably for talk radio. During the overnight hours, listen to talk radio to stay alert. Relaxing music or rock music will make you sleepy and tire your senses.

3. Make frequent stops. Try to stop every hour to use the restroom, walk around, and stretch. Stopping often will keep you from getting *too* comfortable and dozing off.

4. Stay hydrated. Drinking lots of fluids will help keep you alert. Drink caffeine in moderation; it will keep you awake, but too much of it can make you jittery.

5. Keep the temperature in the car relatively cool, even during cold weather. Turning the heat too high will make you drowsy.

6. Most importantly, if you feel drowsy, don't risk it! Take the next exit, pull off the road, and take a quick nap. A 20-minute nap often makes a world of difference. Not only will you get a little rest, you'll improve your own safety on the road.

Hopefully, your circumstances won't force you to drive through the night. You'll enjoy the trip much more if you limit driving to 10 hours per day. Most motorists would consider 15 hours on the road to be an *extremely* long day. Earlier, I stated that over the course of a driving day, it's reasonable to average between 55 and 57 miles per hour. That means that 550 miles would be a reasonable distance to cover in one day. Driving 15 hours *could* translate to covering as much as 850 miles of interstate driving, but that would be one extremely long day.

So when should you stop for the night? My recommendation is to stop around sunset. Night driving is more stressful (and more hazardous) than daytime driving, so stopping around dusk helps ensure a good night's rest. Driving all day often leaves your arms and legs tense, and it's sometimes more difficult to go to sleep right after stopping for the day. It's best to have two or three hours before bed to unwind, make phone calls, watch TV, and just relax.

Challenging Situations: City Driving

If you're driving in an unfamiliar city, you may find it a real challenge just to find your way. Finding a specific address or location in a city far from home can be more difficult, even with a map, but if you have a GPS unit, the task becomes much easier. Just enter the street address, and the navigation system will give spoken turn-by-turn directions.

Many drivers unfamiliar with a city are unsure of which lane to stay in. If you are navigating along city expressways without much knowledge of the area, my advice is to stay in the center lane. By staying in the center, you will avoid the merging traffic to your right, and you will keep from blocking faster traffic to your left. In addition, by staying near the center, you will never have far to go if you need to change lanes to merge for an exit.

Mountain Driving

If you plan to do any significant amount of east-west driving across the United States, you'll experience a fair share of mountainous terrain. Although mountains usually provide the most beautiful scenery on a road trip, driving across mountain ranges requires some forethought. Don't be afraid, though, because today's vehicles have no trouble maneuvering over mountain highways. Remember, too, that today's mountain roads are safer than ever before, with more lanes, wider shoulders, and safety features that make accidents rare.

When climbing a mountain, be on the lookout for slow moving trucks in the right lane. Interstate highways are limited to 6% grades (occasionally 7%), which make the climb in elevation relatively painless. You won't need four-wheel drive or a special vehicle to cross a mountain range on an interstate highway. When climbing a steep grade on a two-lane road, though, be careful not to pass slow-moving trucks. Those trucks will speed up significantly on the downward slope, and they may not be able to pass you, possibly causing a collision.

Most cars will have no problem with mountain driving. If you are the slightest bit unsure of your vehicle's abilities, though, turn off the air conditioning or defroster. Those features pull power from your engine, so turning them off could give your car some more pep to go up the mountain.

When descending the mountain, start slow. Try not to ride your brake on the way down, but if you feel the need to slow down, tap your brakes gently, especially just before approaching curves. Some larger vehicles may need to shift into a lower gear on the descent, but passenger cars are usually fine in normal gear.

When driving at higher elevations, you'll notice that gasoline has a lower octane rating than what you may be used to. Your engine needs less octane at higher elevations due to the lower concentration of oxygen in the atmosphere higher up. No need to worry, though, since 85-octane gasoline works just as well at higher elevations. Personally, I've seen no decrease in fuel efficiency at higher elevations, even with lower octane gas.

When crossing mountains in wintertime, you may be required by law to carry tire chains. You can buy inexpensive tire chains (or cables) at nearly any auto supply store. Tire chains will include instructions and can be installed in just a few minutes. Before ascending peaks in the Rockies, for example, you will find parking areas labeled "30 minute Chain-Up" especially for this purpose.

Desert Driving

Crossing the desert isn't as big a deal as it used to be, when cars overheated more often and air conditioning was still a novelty.

Today's modern cars will have no problem crossing the desert during hot weather, as long as you keep a few things in mind.

1. Check your fluids. Make sure your antifreeze level is adequate, as well as engine oil and transmission fluid. Most likely the attendant already checked these fluids when your vehicle was serviced before the trip. Still, it doesn't hurt to double check before crossing the desert.

2. Take plenty of water. Well, not really for the car. Intense sunlight and heat can leave *you* dehydrated. Drink plenty of fluids. And yes, in an emergency, water can be used to mix with antifreeze if you need to top off your coolant levels.

3. Stop often. These days, even the most inhospitable desert roads will have rest areas and scenic overlooks. They give the driver a chance to rest and also give your car a few minutes to cool down.

4. Keep an eye on the temperature gauge. If you notice your car starting to overheat, turn off the air conditioner. Turn on the heater instead! By turning on the heater, the engine gets a chance to release whatever heat it's built up. If the vehicle has a tendency to overheat, you may have to drive without air conditioning.

5. Turn your air conditioner to "MAX" or "RECIRC". These settings cool the air already inside your vehicle instead of cooling hotter air from outside. By recirculating the cool air, your engine works less and actually keeps you cooler!

6. Consider crossing the desert in the early morning or late evening. Temperatures are usually the hottest between

10:00 a.m. and 4:00 p.m. By avoiding these hours, you'll not only be more comfortable, your car will work less on your drive across the desert.

Driving in Poor Weather

When most of us think of road trips, leisurely drives in perfect weather come to mind. Most people don't enjoy road trips as much in inclement weather, and for good reason. Poor weather can turn an otherwise fun ride into a dangerous obstacle course.

Most travelers plan their road trips for the spring and summer, when weather is usually the best. However, storms can pop up in any state at any time. Being prepared and aware of your surroundings are the best ways to drive safely in bad weather.

Before leaving on a trip, check the weather ahead of time. The Weather Channel's website (www.weather.com) has an excellent national overview, called "Interstate Forecast". This national map color-codes areas where the most hazardous driving conditions are likely. By pinpointing areas of bad weather, you can plan an alternate route or postpone your trip by a day or two, if necessary.

Much of the time, though, you'll have no choice as to the weather you experience on the road. One of the best ways to prepare for any weather situation is to get your vehicle ready. Keeping an ice scraper, snow brush, and a can of deicer in your car makes sense anytime between October and May. Treating your windshield with a liquid water repellent, such as RainX, greatly enhances your visibility in the rain. And of course, make sure your windshield wipers are in good shape. Have the blades replaced if they're more than a year old.

When driving in the rain, the most important tip I can give you is: Slow down! Drive significantly slower in the rain. In fact, during rainy weather, *the speed limit is usually way too fast.* Keep your headlights on, and even use your hazard flashers if you're driving slower than surrounding traffic. Remember, roads are slickest when rain is just starting to fall. Oil mixing with precipitation can cause very slippery conditions, causing your vehicle to hydroplane. So drive slowly, especially as it begins to rain.

If your road trip brings you to snowy terrain, you'll also need to drive much slower. Don't get in a hurry, and leave much more following distance between you and the next car. Snow and ice reduce your traction, so you'll need much more time to stop. Whatever you do, don't slam on the brakes. If you need to stop in the snow, start tapping the brake gently *long before* you have to stop. At the same time, don't accelerate quickly. Making sudden moves, like slamming on the brakes or jackrabbit starts, will likely make you slide (or worse).

The worst kind of winter weather for drivers is ice. Freezing rain, sleet, and ice storms are rare in America's coldest climates; they're more common across the Central Midwest and South. Ice storms can completely paralyze a region, shutting down schools and businesses for days at a time. The worst ice storms bring down trees and power lines, leaving an entire region in the dark. If a significant winter ice storm occurs, you won't want to be in it. While snow brushes off easily from a car, a half-inch of ice can literally leave you frozen out of your car, and it could take you a while – over an hour – just to open the doors and get the windshield defrosted.

My recommendation is to avoid ice storms if at all possible. This is not the kind of weather that lends itself to a leisurely road trip. If you *must* travel in an ice storm, drive *very* slowly. Don't brake suddenly. In all honesty, if you encounter a major ice storm along a winter road trip, you may be better off just getting a hotel room and enjoying a couple of days indoors.

Enjoy the Road

Hopefully, your road trip won't include any winter weather events or severe thunderstorms. If you're lucky, the worst weather you'll experience will be the glare from the sun. And all you'll need for *that* weather event is a good pair of sunglasses.

When you travel the road, relax and enjoy your surroundings. Savor the freedom of being able to wander scenic country and unknown back roads at your leisure. Don't be afraid of taking that road you've never traveled before. Of course, when traveling, you'll want to keep in touch with friends and family back home. How can you stay connected on the road? That's what the next chapter will cover.

9

Staying Connected

A t one time, staying connected when traveling meant tuning to local AM or FM radio stations and maybe talking with other travelers on a CB radio. Maybe you'd send a few postcards home or make an expensive long-distance call from a pay phone. How times have changed!

Most of us travel with at least a cell phone and the charging cable that accompanies it. Many travelers also carry a laptop or tablet computer, matched with another set of cables. Families with children will also likely pack a DVD player, along with a decent set of movies and yet even more cables. If you haven't noticed, cables play an essential part in keeping your electronic devices connected while on the road. I suggest keeping all your tech cables in one small bag so they don't get separated. If you can, keep each cable on its own spool or clip so they don't get tangled.

Cell Phones

For any type of long-distance road trip, make sure you have nationwide cell coverage. Most cell phone plans are fine in this regard, but there are still a few out there that add expensive roaming charges to the bill if you leave a limited 'local' area.

Check your cell provider's coverage map well before you leave home. Make sure you're not stuck with limited coverage -- or worse yet, no coverage at all -- in areas where you'll be traveling. Generally speaking, Verizon and AT&T offer the best nationwide coverage, with most other carriers lagging behind. While other smaller carriers may be worthwhile choices if staying within major towns and metropolitan areas, many of them leave large patches of rural America -- even along major highways -- with no service whatsoever. If you need reliable coverage when traveling, take this into consideration.

If your cell carrier has inadequate coverage in areas you'll be visiting, seriously consider picking up a cheap prepaid phone for the days you'll be on the road. Net10 cellphones can be purchased at nearly any discount store in the nation; even some corner drugstores carry them. For just a cheap throwaway phone, pay no more than $20. Most of these phones come with 200 or so minutes included; additional prepaid cards can be bought at the rate of 10 cents per minute.

If you plan to use more than about 500 voice minutes away from your carrier's coverage area, think seriously about a StraightTalk phone. These are available at most Wal-Mart stores, starting at a purchase price of about $20. For the cost of a $30 service card, you get 1000 voice minutes and 1000 text messages, enough to get most travelers through several days -- or even an entire month -- on the road. Be aware, though, StraightTalk's coverage is slightly more limited than that of Net10, but still acceptable for most roadtrippers.

Your smartphone data plan should be robust enough to send back several of those wonderful pictures you'll be taking on your trip to friends back home. If yours is limited, seriously consider using only WiFi to send or upload photos; save your bandwidth for other purposes.

Tablet Computing on the Road

Many travelers today have replaced their laptop computer with a tablet for most computing needs, such as an iPad or Android device.   Several features make the tablet computer the ideal tech gadget to take on a road trip:

Universal Wireless Capability. Matched with a cellular wireless plan, a tablet becomes a great way to keep up-to-date on news and weather, check e-mail, and update your Facebook or Twitter accounts with pictures and news of your adventure. Wireless internet is the key to getting full use of most iPad apps.

Small Group Viewing. When latched onto a stand, tablet computers like the iPad turn into a small monitor, perfect if a small group of two or three want to watch a video or movie. Load photos of your trip onto the tablet at the end of the day, and enjoy a group viewing session.

Larger Group Viewing. Add a $40 cable to the iPad to connect it to a larger TV monitor, such as what you might find in a hotel room, and your tablet becomes a portable entertainment system. This cable, available at any electronics warehouse or discount store, makes it possible to play any YouTube, Netflix, or Hulu video stream directly through a larger screen for easier viewing.

Built-In Mapping Software. Although Apple took considerable criticism for its initial Maps release, few can deny the convenience of instant access to maps anywhere with a cellular or WiFi signal. Instead of looking for a random exit and driving around to find a restaurant, store, or hotel, the tablet makes it easy for your copilot to find any place of interest, nearly anywhere in the world, even those that haven't been programmed into your standalone GPS unit.

Apps. Later in this chapter I'll mention several apps that can help in trip planning and guidance. Of course, any app you use on a day-to-day basis can be just as helpful and fun on the road.

Fast Startup. In years past, when I needed to use the laptop to book a hotel or check the weather forecast, it took at least two minutes to boot Windows and open the browser. It usually took at least another minute to find a Wi-Fi signal and get online. Add another minute to actually load the page. A three- to five-minute ordeal can often be reduced to thirty seconds with the fast instant-on capability of today's tablet computers.

Long Battery Life. Today's tablets easily have a battery life of five to ten hours – vastly superior to most laptops. It's annoying and inconvenient to watch a battery go dead just as you're making an important reservation or trying to send a message. Long battery life is a must on the road.

Ways You'll Use a Tablet or Smartphone on a Road trip

To Find a Restaurant. Instead of driving around aimlessly looking for a restaurant or market, one of the passengers can use a smartphone or tablet to find a great place to eat. Just as you can't judge a book by its cover, you can't judge a restaurant by its outward appearance. Check one of the popular restaurant review sites, such as Yelp, TripAdvisor, or UrbanSpoon to make sure you stop somewhere that's worth your time. With your tablet or smartphone, you'll no longer have to limit yourself to billboards, freeway exit signs, or restaurants within view of the interstate.

To Reserve a Place to Stay. Don't call hotel after hotel, asking for the best rate. Most of the best hotel deals are online, even at the last minute. Book online as little as ten minutes before arriving via Priceline, Hotwire, or Kayak. Or use the hotel's own website or app to book directly and get frequent stay points. If booking direct, check hotel reviews online *before* reserving to make sure the hotel has a good reputation.

To Check Gas Prices. We've all filled up the gas tank, only to drive ten minutes down the road and see that it was much cheaper somewhere else. With today's high gas prices, a few cents per gallon savings can add up, especially on a cross-country trip. Use the GasBuddy website or app to look for cheaper gas along the way.

To Keep in Touch. With a tablet or smartphone, it becomes extremely easy to upload trip photos to Facebook or by e-mail, if you prefer. If you have a blog, mobile apps for Blogger and WordPress make it simple and convenient to post trip updates and photos.

To Listen to Music. Most cars today have a convenient iPod dock or auxiliary jack for listening to your favorite tunes on the road. Before hitting the road, consider selecting a playlist with some of your favorite songs. On longer trips, a car charger will keep your music playing as long as you want without ever worrying about a dead battery.

Top Road Trip Apps

Today's smartphones and tablets have nearly endless capabilities for helping to plan your road trip. Here's a list of my favorite road trip apps. All are available on Apple's App Store, and most are also available on Android devices. Most are free.

11. Roadside America. This app will help direct you to the most unusual and quirky roadside attractions in the U.S. and Canada. Published by the avid roadtrippers that author the popular RoadsideAmerica.com website, they've described, rated, and ranked over 10,000 roadside attractions (statues, museums, monuments, kitschy tourist traps, and more) from coast to coast. *$5.99 for the full database, $1.99 for one 'region' of the country.*

10. Speedometer GPS+. If you're riding along on a road trip, this app will make sure you never ever again has to ask, "Where are we?" or "Are we there yet?" Your smartphone or GPS-enabled iPad will be updated with real-time speed and direction. You'll also see your current elevation and map position, along with live tracking to know where you've been. Overall, this is a fun navigation app, with a cockpit-type interface. *$2.99.*

9. Google Earth. The absolute best app for exploring your surroundings from up above. Find nearby businesses, parks, and check out the terrain around you. Google Earth is probably one of the most fascinating apps available, and it makes for an easy -- and educational -- way to pass an hour or so. It works best with a fast internet signal. *Free.*

8. iExit. This app uses your location and direction to find services offered at upcoming interstate exits. Finding a restaurant, hotel, gas station, or rest area is nearly automatic with iExit. The full version allows a copilot or passenger to find services up to 150 freeway exits in advance. The lite version is limited to 10 exits. *Lite version - Free. Full version - $0.99.*

7. Weatherbug. One of the biggest variables on a road trip is the weather. Rain, snow, and severe weather can turn an easy drive into a difficult ordeal. The Weatherbug app gives a live radar track for any location in the United States, so you can see if bad weather is on the way. The app lets you load several cities, so you can check the forecast for the next several days at your destination, as well as the hour-by-hour outlook for your current location. *Free.*

6. Hotwire Hotels. This iPhone app lets you take the big savings and flexibility of the Hotwire hotel discount site on the road. The main advantage of Hotwire over Priceline is being able to specify up to four people in a hotel room. You'll also know what amenities you get -- such as free breakfast and parking -- before you commit. Since there's no bidding with Hotwire, this could be a real timesaver. *Free.*

5. Priceline Negotiator. If you have a co-pilot or passenger who's familiar with bidding on Priceline, you can save some serious money on the road. More information on Priceline bidding can be found in Chapter 12, Saving Money on a Road Trip. This app makes it easy and fun to bid on a hotel, even at the last minute. If you prefer, you can reserve a room the conventional way through the app, too. *Free.*

4. Kayak. If bidding on hotels or other discount methods aren't for you, then look no further then the Kayak app, optimized both for the iPhone and iPad. With this app, you can rank hotels by price and star rating, then check user reviews and photos of the property. If you need to take a flight, this app makes it easy to find the best airfare, allowing you to check prices for flexible travel dates. This is the best non-opaque hotel pricing app on the market. *Free.*

3. GasBuddy.   By default, this app will search for the cheapest gas prices near you. If you prefer, search for a town or city, and the app will find the best prices available. GasBuddy also makes it easy to search for the cheapest gas in a particular state, and the nationwide 'Gas Temperature Map' shows you regions of the country -- right down to the county and zip code -- where gas tends to be cheaper. Log into the app with your GasBuddy account to report gas prices as you travel. *Free.*

2. Waze. With a smartphone or data-equipped tablet, the free Waze app acts as a GPS navigation system with live traffic up-dates. The app gives turn-by-turn directions, but uses other nearby Waze users' data and reports to determine the best route to your destination. With just a couple of touches, users can report traffic jams, debris on the road, construction delays, and speed patrols. *Free.*

1. TripAdvisor. By now, everybody knows that some user reviews on TripAdvisor have to be taken with a grain of salt. Others are just downright phony. But that doesn't stop TripAdvisor from being the best travel review app out there. It's one you need to have loaded on your tablet or smartphone if you plan to do any serious amount of traveling. Although TripAdvisor got its start by letting travelers review hotels, it now hosts reviews and rankings for restaurants and tourist attractions. I've used TripAdvisor to look for dining suggestions in an unfamiliar town and have usually been pleasantly surprised. If you're in a city for a couple of days, search for the top attractions, and you'll find several activities you may have never thought of. *Free*.

Satellite Radio

For unlimited listening options from coast to coast, nothing beats satellite radio. There's one company, SiriusXM, offering two similar -- yet distinct -- subscription services. The XM service offers Major League Baseball, the Oprah & Friends channel, as well as the Opie and Anthony morning show. Sirius hosts the NBA, NFL, and Howard Stern. The music options are nearly identical on the two services, and the talk radio options are also quite similar. Each costs between $10 and $20 a month (depending on the package you choose), with discounts available for longer-term commitments. Occasionally, there are promotions that allow for free trials or discounted radios if you visit the SiriusXM website or call their customer service line.

If you're planning on an extended trip or a solo trip, satellite radio is a great companion. There's always something interesting to listen to, and it can help keep you alert on that long drive.

CB Radio

Since it's heyday in the 1970s, Citizen's Band Radio -- or CB as most people call it -- simply isn't popular as it used to be. Even many commercial drivers use the CB less than in years past, especially since the advent of cell phones and satellite radio. Still, a CB radio can be a useful resource to get real time traffic updates from professional drivers in the field.

Channel 19 gets the most traffic; it's usually called the truckers' channel. If you need help, be courteous and wait for an opening. Passenger cars are usually referred to as 'four-wheelers', whereas professional truck drivers are usually just called 'drivers'. Many 'drivers' are happy to help a 'four-wheeler' who's lost or needs some help.

E-Mail

Staying connected usually means checking your e-mail at some point. It's usually best to use a web-based e-mail program that can be accessed from anywhere. My favorite is Gmail; it does an excellent job of weeding out spam. Gmail – like most web-based e-mail services – can be linked to a smartphone or tablet with little effort. With Gmail, you can integrate documents or other files via Google Docs or just by e-mailing them to yourself and keeping them in the 'cloud'. This primary e-mail address is my lifeline on the road; I check it every day, sometimes several times a day.

I recommend maintaining a second e-mail address for online shopping and less important matters. This mailbox is one that I won't mind getting filled with ads or other 'junk mail.' In my case, this second address is a Yahoo mail account. Hotmail or MSN work fine for this purpose, too. I normally check this address only once a week or so.

Occasionally, you may need to provide an e-mail address to sign up for some sort of promotion or discount. Some websites or online newspapers may require an e-mail address to read certain articles. For these pesky occasions, I provide a 'throwaway' e-mail address from mailinator.com. Messages can be sent to any address @mailinator.com. Go to their website and type in any username you want, no password required.

Of course, you would never want anything private or personal sent to this public e-mail address at Mailinator, but if you just need some sort of confirmation link to activate software or to read an online newspaper, this is the way to do it without cluttering your real inbox. Messages are receive-only; you *can't send* e-mails with Mailinator. Plus, all messages are automatically deleted after about a day.

Modern road trips are very different from even 10 or 20 years ago; our electronic devices travel along with us. But they can be part of the fun! Stay connected on the road, and turn your tablet or smartphone into a useful roadtripping tool!

10

Eating Well on the Road

D riving around an area and exploring its scenery from your car is just one way to enjoy your travels. For most of us, hitting the road is also a great way to enjoy new tastes and favorite foods. Eating on a road trip is more than just a way to stay nourished; it's recreation unto itself.

In this chapter, we'll discuss the vast array of dining options you have on the road. Whether you're eating healthy, want to pig out at buffets, or just want to sample local cuisine, there's something for everyone.

Packing Your Own Food

One of the best ways to save money on food is to take your own. When preparing your own meals, you have the option of purchasing the food you want at your local supermarket. You'll get to shop around for the best prices and be in control of your own nutrition.

If you decide to take along prepared meals from home, remember that you probably won't want to eat every meal out of a cooler, unless you're seriously strapped for cash. When you get tired of self-prepared meals, remember that low-cost restaurants are in abundance these days, and they provide a nice break from eating out of the cooler.

You'll want to invest in a quality cooler that's the right size for your needs. Notice the word *invest*. That means you'll have to pay for quality when buying a cooler. Cheap foam coolers can be had for as little as two dollars, but you'll wish you had paid more when it topples, and ten pounds of melting ice are now saturating your car's interior.

If you're traveling solo, a small cooler will work fine. For my solo road trips, I take a small cooler that's about 12 inches in length. Larger groups will clearly need a larger cooler. My favorite cooler is designed to store beverages in ice, but it has a small plastic shelf that keeps sandwiches elevated above the ice. These types of coolers keep drinks ice cold without making the rest of your food soggy.

It's much easier to carry cans of beverages instead of larger 2-liter bottles. Although 2-liter bottles are cheaper per serving than cans, pouring a bottle into a cup in a moving car can cause a sticky spill. Think seriously, though, about carrying drinks with little or no sugar. Riding in a car doesn't burn many calories, and you may start to feel jittery if you drink nothing but soft drinks all day. Consider buying juice and bottled water instead of just soda.

When preparing meals to take on the road, don't just limit yourself to sandwiches. Sandwiches do tend to get soggy or stale after the first day, and you'll want a greater variety, too. Consider taking cheese and crackers, fresh fruit, potato chips, fresh vegetables with dressing, salads, and beef jerky. Many of these foods, when sealed and kept in a cooler, will last several days.

Salads, sliced fruit, and vegetables will stay freshest in a cooler if you store them in plastic zippered bags. Buy several of the one-gallon variety, and you'll be able to store as much fresh fruit and vegetables as you want.

Shopping for Groceries

If you're concerned with food spoilage, you might want to consider stopping at local grocery stores or supermarkets along your route. You'll be ensured fresh food every day, and buying local helps support the communities you pass through. Shopping local is also a great way to talk to people and get tips on area attractions.

If you get tired of eating food you've prepared yourself, try stopping at a local supermarket's delicatessen for a prepared sandwich or salad. Most supermarkets sell simple prepared meals for much less than you'd spend in a restaurant. For five dollars, you can buy a fresh, tasty meal.

If you pass parks or other roadside stops, you might want to consider having a barbecue. Most parks provide barbecue pits; you provide the charcoal, lighter fluid, match, and the food. A spur-of-the-moment barbecue is a fun way to relax after spending the day on the road. You'll have to take your own seasonings and sauce, but if you like to barbecue, enjoying one away from home is a great way to unwind.

Most people, though, aren't going to want to haul a big bag of charcoal, seasonings, and raw meat in the trunks of their cars. If you'd still like to enjoy a picnic on the road without the hassle of having to cook it yourself, try stopping by a local supermarket and picking up a roast chicken, along with your favorite side dish. A

```
╭─────────────────────────────╮
│  FOOD - EXIT 190            │
├──────────┬──────────┬───────┤
│ FAST     │ FAST     │ Fast  │
│ FOOD     │ FOOD     │ Food  │
├──────────┼──────────┼───────┤
│ MORE     │ Even More│ Greasy│
│ FAST     │ Fast Food│ Food  │
│ FOOD     │          │ Served│
│          │          │ Fast  │
╰──────────┴──────────┴───────╯
```

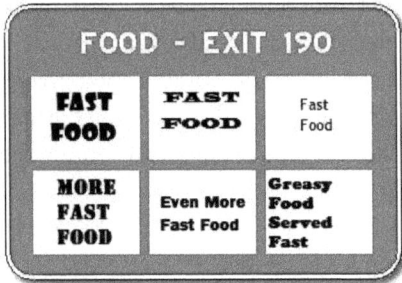

Indulging in too much fast food now may cause problems down the road

simple picnic is an easy and memorable way to eat while on a road trip.

Quick Meals

Most roadtrippers are in a hurry when they stop to eat. That's probably why so many of us choose fast food restaurants when on the road. They're familiar places, they're quick, they're convenient, and they're usually cheap. Still, eat fast food in moderation when traveling. The high fat, high calorie, low nutritional value of many fast foods can keep you from feeling your best, especially when sitting in the car for hours at a time. And remember that you're on the road to discover something new, not to eat the same burger you had for lunch last Tuesday.

Many fast food restaurants, especially at lunchtime, can be so busy that the crowd detracts from the experience. If there's a line, you may find that eating fast food may actually take just as long as a sit-down meal. And watch those prices! Many of the *combos*, *value meals*, or *specials* at that fast food place are just as expensive – if not more so – than a filling plate lunch at a sit-down restaurant. The service will probably be better at the latter establishment, too.

If you really need to get a quick meal, and the fast food place is the restaurant of choice (or necessity), try to eat as healthy as you can. A big cheeseburger may have more fat than you should eat *all day*. Choose a salad instead, and go easy on the dressing. Remember, regular salad dressing may easily have ten times the calories of *the entire salad.* If you really want a burger, a plain hamburger is healthier than one that's loaded with cheese and special sauce.

When looking for variety on the road, and you need it in a hurry, consider stopping at a buffet. Most buffets can get you to a table and to your meal within a few minutes of arriving. The variety of buffet-style restaurants is much greater than just a few years ago, too. Although most feature Chinese food or typical American food, some also offer seafood or ethnic foods not commonly found at this

Roadside Restaurants Worth a Visit

The following restaurants are all located along Historic Route 66. You'll find other great places to eat in your travels, but these three diners are some of the most famous.

Cozy Dog Drive In – The famous restaurant known for its special deep-fried corn dog. This place has been open since the 50's and the recipe hasn't changed a bit. Along Historic Route 66 in Springfield, Illinois.

The Big Texan Steak Ranch – Known for the 72-ounce steak, free if you can eat it in an hour. The food and ambience will give you a taste of Texas beef country, even if you're just passing through. They make use of every Texas stereotype ever created, but it's still a fun place to visit. Located along Route 66 – I-40 as it's called today – in Amarillo, Texas.

66 Diner – Located in Albuquerque, New Mexico, along Historic Route 66 – Central Avenue – this classic diner is a good place to try old-fashioned American food cooked the New Mexico way. Hot chilies are ground into the meat to give the burgers an extra kick. And the ambience makes it feel like you've gone back to the 50's.

price point. And speaking of price, most buffets provide a full meal at a very reasonable price, usually in the 10-to-12 dollar range.

As every road traveler knows, buffets are easy to find. They're often advertised on billboards miles ahead. Most of us are familiar with the common buffet chains: Hometown Buffet, Old Country Buffet, Ryan's, Golden Corral, Sirloin Stockade. Some of the best buffets I've tried, though, are of the non-chain, local variety. So if you're thinking of stopping at a smorgasbord, don't be afraid to try a place you've never heard of before. Stop by the restaurant, and ask to see the buffet before you commit. A reputable restaurant will allow you to look before you decide. Check to see if the place looks clean. If it's not what you're looking for, just say "Thank you" and leave. You'll find something better down the road.

If you decide to try a buffet, remember a word of warning: Don't eat too much! Unless you really plan to do some serious exercising, you'll be sitting in the car for hours, and you won't be burning many calories. Many cheaper buffets feature items chocked full of bread and carbohydrates. Although they'll fill your stomach fast, they may make you regret eating so much. So go easy on the heavy foods!

Full-Service Restaurants

If you're not in the mood for a buffet, but don't want fast food, either, you'll find a plethora of choices available on the road. Local diners and other family-style restaurants welcome travelers, and you'll probably find these restaurants a good option at mealtime.

Plenty of mid-range casual dining chains have dotted cities, suburbia, and even rural America over the last 20 years or so. At most of these spots, you'll pay over ten dollars for even the simplest of meals, if you include a drink and tip. However, these chains, which include restaurants such as Applebee's, Rafferty's, Olive Garden, Cracker Barrel, Chili's, and T.G.I. Friday's, still have deals, and you're likely to get a reasonable, predictable experience when dining there. However, much like the fast food industry, these restaurants thrive on consistency, so the location in Miami is likely to have the same menu, food, and even décor as the location in Boise.

Think about the purpose of your trip. If you're just traveling to get somewhere in a reasonable amount of time, the chain restaurants will give you what you want at a reasonable price. If you're driving to really experience different parts of the country, you'll probably be missing out on local cuisine and homemade specialties by visiting the chains exclusively.

Although I enjoy going to the chain restaurants, especially if there's a special deal, the experience is practically identical no matter where you go. Visit locally owned restaurants and diners when possible. Let your meal choice be influenced by your location; you'll get a better feel for where you are, and the meal will be more memorable.

For example, when in the South, try southern cuisine. Eat Cajun food in Louisiana. Eat Chicago style pizza in, you guessed it... Chicago. Have a cheesesteak in Philly. Eat seafood on the coast. You get the idea. Meals like these are often cheaper than the chain restaurants. Even if the food isn't exactly what you were expecting, the meal will be a lot more memorable than just a stop at another fast food place.

Be Flexible at Mealtime

If you really want to eat fast food at every meal, to the tune of a now-famous documentary, you can do that. If your budget dictates that you have to subsist on cereal and baloney sandwiches out of a cooler, then you're free to do that, too.

One area in which flexibility pays off, though, is the time you choose to eat. The same restaurant that was filled to capacity at noon may be practically empty two hours later. You may have to wait an hour to get a table for dinner at 7:00, but you might walk right to one at 5:00. Since you probably don't want to spend your precious vacation time waiting in a restaurant lobby, try stopping for meals at off-peak hours. You'll likely get more attentive service mid-afternoon, and prices are often lower, too.

Staying Healthy

Anyone who has traveled extensively knows that you're more susceptible to acute illness and general malaise when away from home. The combination of different foods, different drinking water, and a general change of routine can be a shock to your body. The foods you eat really *do* have an impact on how you feel. That's why you should be careful to stay healthy and eat healthy while on the road.

Although you'll want to try new foods, not all of them will necessarily be good for you. That's okay, but remember that *whatever you eat, do so in moderation.* If you treat your road trip as a vacation, then don't stress about eating a few tasty, high-fat foods here and there. At the same time, eating foods that are *extremely* out of the ordinary for you, especially when spending hours seated in the car, can make you feel lethargic, achy, or even nauseous.

Of course, there are several things you can do to eat better and maintain your general well-being while on a road trip. Consider drinking bottled water if you're sensitive to tap water, and drink lots of it. Drinking plenty of fluids will keep you from getting dehydrated. If it's a good idea for your daily routine, it's an even better idea to drink plenty of water while away from home.

If you plan to eat seafood, stick with the kind that's been cooked thoroughly. Fish, shrimp, and crab legs are normally pretty safe. Seafood or shellfish that's undercooked or raw, such as oysters, may be best to avoid, especially if you happen to be far from the coast. In that situation, your meal might not be very fresh. Avoid heavy seafood meals after 8 p.m. Your body requires extra time to digest these meals, and going to bed less than two hours after this kind of meal may make you sick.

When on the road, pack a few Pepto-Bismol tablets (they're not as messy as the liquid form) and a few antacid tablets. If your meal doesn't agree with you a few hours down the road, at least you'll have a quick treatment.

Food that's Good. . . for You

Most food at roadside restaurants is sold based on convenience. It's quick to prepare, quick to serve, and usually quick to eat. Although it may taste good, it might not be quite as good from a nutritional standpoint. Many restaurants load their food with fat and grease. A few still use the dreaded *trans* fat, the type that should really be avoided completely.

If you're on a diet, or you just want to eat better on the road, you have plenty of options – and they don't involve eating a salad three times a day, either. These days, most national chain restaurants readily provide nutrition information for all their items. If you don't see this information when you go in, ask your server. Many restaurants, especially at the mid-level casual dining chains, identify low-fat dishes on the menu with some kind of mark, making it easy to identify food that's good for you.

Local, non-chain restaurants and diners may not have as many health-conscious options. Even at these places, look for the words *grilled* and *fresh* on the menu; they often identify meals prepared with your health needs in mind. When in doubt, ask your server. It's their job to describe the menu if you need help. Your server can suggest low-fat items or other foods that meet your dietary restrictions. Remember, an otherwise unhealthy meal may suddenly become a better choice once you hold the gravy, special sauce, or dressing.

Eating can be as much a part of the road trip experience as the destination you choose or the sights you see along the way. If you end up at a restaurant you regret later, don't stress over it too much. Take it with a grain of salt – no pun intended – and just consider it part of the ride. It's part of the experience, and you'll probably laugh about it in a few days. Try to pick eateries that you don't get to visit in your own neighborhood, and don't be afraid to try something different.

11

Where to Stay

If your road trip lasts more than one day, you're going to need a place to sleep. Unless your plan is to bunk with friends or relatives, you'll likely stay in hotels. This chapter is designed to help you find the best lodging for your circumstances – and budget – and get the best deal in the process.

Nearly every hotel booking engine has a separate way of classifying hotels according to amenities, price, or some other specification. I have my own way of classifying hotels, too, but there are no stars, no thumbs up, and no dollar signs used in my rankings. It's much simpler than that. Here are my four classes of hotels.

High-End Hotels

These hotels are the most elegant and most expensive. They include everything from a typical Hilton all the way up to the Ritz-

Carlton. They also include most full-service hotels such as Marriott, Hyatt, Sheraton, Radisson, and Crowne Plaza. These hotels almost always charge at least $100 a night, and in city centers, they can cost up to four times that.

Although these hotels bill themselves as full-service, be aware that at this level, you *will* pay extra for that service. Breakfast will cost extra, you will often pay extra for parking, and you will likely even pay extra for Wi-Fi internet service.

High-end hotels are perfect for families on vacation. They're well designed to suit the needs of business travelers, too. At this class of hotel, full-service business centers and even convention facilities are common. Many guests at high-end hotels are traveling on someone else's dime, though, so they don't mind the $10 parking charge, the $10 internet fee, or even the $15 breakfast. (By the way, those charges are *per-day*, and they *are* typical.)

What you need to know is that high-end hotels are better suited as *destination* hotels, not designed for stopping alongside the interstate to catch a few winks before continuing along the highway. Nothing against these hotels; they're just meant for a different purpose.

Roadside Chains

These hotels are the typical chains you find at interstate exits, and the price should be less than $100 per night. The number of hotels at this level are too numerous to list entirely, but some familiar names include Best Western, Super 8, Comfort Inn, Microtel, Hampton Inn, Fairfield Inn, Baymont Inn, La Quinta, and Days Inn. There's a more complete list in the "Road Trip Resources" chapter at the end of this book.

I'm using the word *hotels* mainly for convenience. Technically, a *hotel* is a lodging establishment with interior corridors, whereas a *motel*, short for *motor hotel*, has exterior corridors. In other words, at a motel, the door to your room will open directly to the great outdoors. At a hotel, though, the door will open into a hallway. The chains listed above are a mix of hotels and motels, and many of these chains actually have some hotel locations, with motel locations in other cities. The La Quinta brand, for example, operates most of their locations as motels, with other newer properties as hotels.

Many travelers prefer the added security of the hotel setup. At a motel, any stranger can knock on your door. At a hotel, though, visitors have to get past the front desk first. Hotel-type properties tend to have cleaner carpets in the rooms, simply because guests have to walk farther to access them.

Roadside chains always welcome roadtrippers. In fact, highway travelers are the bread and butter of these hotels. They will almost always be full near the holidays and on weekends.

Hotels at this level usually offer the best bang for the buck. Your rate will nearly always include free parking, free Wi-Fi, free local phone calls, and some type of free breakfast. Whether it's called a continental breakfast, a deluxe breakfast, or something else, it's worth it to have the most important meal of the day included in the price of your room, especially with a group of three or four.

Most roadside chains offer at least a minimal discount, 10 to 15 percent, to guests who present a AAA or AARP card at check-in. Be aware, though, that this discount is off the *rack rate*, or most expensive rate, so you may be able to secure a better deal elsewhere.

What roadside chains do well is offer a predictable, reasonable level of quality at a fair price. The President probably won't be staying there when he's in town, but you're likely to be quite comfortable at a roadside chain hotel. The rooms are often identical in design to those at high-end hotels, and you may find that some properties actually give you *more* room.

Do any of the roadside chains stand out from the others? In my opinion, yes. Since nearly all of these properties now offer Wi-Fi, free local calls, and free parking, the chains differentiate themselves in terms of room quality and breakfast quality.

Fairfield Inns, Hampton Inns, Holiday Inn Express, and Wingate Hotels seem to offer excellent quality across their brand. I've had the fewest problems with housekeeping issues and general cleanliness at these hotels. However, they also tend to be among the most expensive, with rates hovering around the $100 mark. And their breakfasts offer quite a variety, with both hot and cold items on the buffet. In fact, one of the best hotel breakfasts I've ever had was at a Holiday Inn Express in Mexico. Breakfast was served daily in the hotel's grand atrium, complete with servers bringing drinks and clearing dishes. The buffet was complete with both Mexican and American breakfast items, tropical and traditional juices, fruits, vegetables, and meat items, completely free for hotel guests.

Not all hotels offer this level of service or variety on their continental breakfasts. I've stayed at a few motels that promise a continental breakfast but deliver only a paltry selection of donuts and coffee. Better hotels at this level will offer an inviting breakfast room, instead of just a couple of tables strewn about the lobby.

Most of my hotel stays on road trips are at roadside chains. They usually offer a predictable product because they have a corporate image to maintain. If you're not sure about a particular property, search for it at travel review websites like tripadvisor.com. Although one or two bad reviews shouldn't bother you, any property whose negative reviews outnumber their positive ones should raise eyebrows.

Independent Motels

By independent motels, I'm referring to those motels you see on the side of the road, usually in small towns, that advertise those really cheap rates on billboards alongside the highway. Often, they're locally owned and operated, sometimes run by a family, with help from a few other employees.

Although independent motels don't belong to any corporate chain, they may be operated by a local business in conjunction with a restaurant or even another motel. The decorations may be dated, but the price usually can't be beat. And you're likely to find many of the same amenities here as you will at roadside chains.

Most independent motels charge less than $60 a night. Motels at this level throughout the South and Southwest may charge as little as $30 a night during the winter or midweek for single occupancy.

Many travelers avoid independent motels, because there's a risk in staying there. Since they have no corporate reputation supporting them, they have to attract customers with lower prices; hence, the highway billboard advertisement is necessary for these motels.

The quality at non-chain motels varies wildly. You may find one that's as nice as any chain motel, if not nicer. But there are plenty of bad apples out there, too. If you stop at an independent motel and aren't sure about the quality, ask to see one of the rooms first. A reputable motel won't have a problem showing you the product *before* you commit.

Since the cost is less at independent motels, the amenities will likely be fewer, too. You'll probably have to forget about a free breakfast, and the furnishings may not be as new or as good as at a chain property. You may find that the rooms are a little worn; maybe the towels are thinner and the walls still have 80's-style paneling. Although more and more motels offer Wi-Fi, you should never have to pay for it at this level of motel. And if the manager tries to charge you for parking at one of these places, it's a good sign you should just walk away and look for something else down the road.

Most independent motels are now listed on review sites like TripAdvisor, so before you commit to staying, it's possible to determine what other guests have had to say.

Extended Stay Properties

Twenty years ago, extended stay hotels were virtually unheard of. Today, they're popping up increasingly in suburban areas where individuals often need to stay on business for weeks at a time. Sometimes, these hotels are found at interstate exits, but more commonly they're located near business campuses and even residential areas.

The concept of the extended stay hotel is markedly different from the other three categories; that's why I think they warrant a separate listing. Extended stay properties give you a room with a small living area and kitchen, complete with utensils, pots, and pans. It's basically a studio apartment, except in a hotel environment. Housekeeping service is usually provided only once a week. If you're staying for less than a week, you'll be expected to take out your own trash, make your own bed, and wash your own dishes.

Extended stay properties have amenities that are different from most other hotels. Although you'll probably get free local phone calls, you *may* have to pay for the Wi-Fi. Room rates, though, are usually quite reasonable, with typical rates well under $80 a night.

Although most extended stay properties don't offer a free continental breakfast, you do get your own kitchen to prepare any meal you want. This can be handy, especially if you need to prepare lunch for the next day. The fridge is normally full-size, so it's easy to keep drinks or other perishables cool overnight.

The furnishings at most extended-stay hotels are basic but functional. Expect one bed in the room; extra bedding usually costs extra. Expect a very simple check-in area with limited hours. The front desk may close as early as 8:00 p.m. with little recourse if you arrive late. Under the best of circumstances, a security guard may be able to let you into your room if you have a reservation.

During the week, parking areas at extended stay properties may be lined with pickup trucks and other heavy-duty vehicles. Construction workers and other laborers often stay at these places when on an extended assignment. You may find that guests treat these properties just like their own homes; they'll wash clothes, have a barbecue in the lawn, or even sit in front of their door and drink beer.

Extended stay hotels can provide a good value, especially on the weekends, but be aware that the ambience may make some travelers nervous. I've been to some extended stay properties that felt more like a run-down apartment complex; others have a more upscale feel. Use your best judgment to decide whether this class of lodging is for you. When in doubt, use websites such as Tripadvisor.com to evaluate a specific property.

What Amenities Do You Want?

Almost every hotel or motel can be classified into one of the four groups just described. Some hotels, though, straddle two of the levels. Courtyard by Marriott, for example, is not exactly a roadside chain. Because it caters more to business travelers, Courtyards tend to provide the amenities business travelers need (free Wi-Fi, comfortable desk and office chair, business center, meeting rooms), but

High-End Hotels
Indoor Pool, Whirlpool, and Workout Area

Roadside Chains
Free Breakfast and Wireless Internet

Independent Motels
Really Low Prices

Extended Stay
Kitchen Facilities

you'll have to pay over 13 bucks for breakfast, something leisure road-trippers usually try to avoid. Most Holiday Inn hotels (not to be confused with Holiday Inn Express) are similar. Although they usually provide free Wi-Fi, some Holiday Inn's still charge for local calls, and they usually charge for breakfast, too.

Think about the amenities that are important to you before making a reservation or booking a room. Do you *have* to have breakfast included with your room? Is free wireless internet a must? Or would you forgo one or more other amenities to have a nice workout room and pool? Maybe you really need a kitchen in your room. Each of the four levels of lodging has features that the others usually don't. At the top of this page, I've listed the most distinctive amenity at each level of lodging.

Depending on the kind of traveler you are, a different level of service may appeal to you. Be flexible, and you'll find plenty of places along your route that will fit your preferences.

To Reserve or Not to Reserve?

Many travelers like the security of knowing where they'll be spending the night several days ahead of time, so they reserve their rooms, either by phone or online, before leaving home. However, if you're on a long trip, you might not know exactly where you'll end up each day. Many people like the freedom of being able to travel until they decide to stop for the night. Be warned, though; you *may* pay more looking for a room late in the evening.

If you decide to reserve a room a few days in advance, make sure that the rate you accept is cancelable. If not, your plans may change, and you'll still be stuck with a charge for a room you never used. When in doubt, ask. Often, the absolute cheapest rates a hotel offers are non-cancelable or non-refundable. Some of the deals with online booking engines, like Expedia or Orbitz, are prepaid or non-cancelable. If you choose to accept these rates, your plans become set in stone.

Some of the best rates, though, can actually be had by *not* reserving ahead of time. If you've stopped at an interstate rest area or a large gas station, you've probably seen small brochures filled with hotel coupons. Those coupons usually offer the lowest rate provided directly by the hotel. Even if you decide not to use the coupons, these brochures can give you a feel for the hotels and rates available in an area.

One word of caution when using these coupons, though. Most of them have restrictions on when they can be redeemed. For example, one roadside chain hotel may advertise a rate of $59.99 in the coupon book. Read the fine print, though, and you may see that that rate is good Sunday through Thursday only; weekends are $10 extra. The rate may also state "1-2 people", which means that if you bring a third person into the room, you'll pay $10 more. So a Friday night stay with three people now becomes $80 before tax. The rate may still be decent, but nothing special. The lesson? Read the fine print, and be aware of any restrictions *before* you use the coupon.

The coupons are also void if the hotel happens to be more than about 85% full that night. If the parking lot is full when you arrive, it's likely that the rate won't be honored, if there's a room available at all.

Most brochure coupons have blackout dates, too. The fine print will often read "Not valid during holidays or special events." If there's a convention in town that week, the hotel can refuse to honor the rate. And what constitutes a holiday? Christmas is obviously a holiday, but what about Columbus Day? And how about President's Day?

The point is this: the hotels will honor their coupons when they want to. If you've been driving all day, you won't want to navigate through an unfamiliar city looking for a place to stay, only to be told they're not accepting the coupon. Call ahead! Use the phone number printed on the coupon. You don't have to make a reservation, just ask if they're accepting the coupon rate of X dollars tonight. You'll save time and get some peace of mind knowing that the hotel you want is offering a good rate.

Getting the Best Rate Without Coupons

Even if you don't have a coupon brochure, you're likely to get a discount at a hotel by simply asking for one. If you choose this route, though, be aware that you could actually pay *more* by waiting until the night of the stay to ask for a discount, unless you are armed with information.

1. Midweek is cheaper. Most roadside chain hotels offer lower rates midweek, Sunday through Thursday. Be prepared to pay more on the weekends. An exception to this rule would be high-end hotels, especially those that cater to business travelers. Those hotels, particularly those in downtown areas, usually have better rates on the weekend.

2. Check out the parking lot. When you drive up to a hotel in the evening, take a quick drive around the parking lot. If it looks full, the hotel likely has few vacancies, and you'll likely pay more. When the hotel is near its maximum occupancy, there's less room for negotiation. If you're looking for a deal and the parking lot is full, it may be worth it to try the next hotel, or even the next town.

3. Travel in the off-season. In most of the country, hotel rooms are cheaper in the fall and winter, when fewer people are on the road. Some holidays, though, are major travel times, so prices will be higher then, too. Plan for hotels to be nearly full in the days leading up to Christmas, Thanksgiving, New Year's, Fourth of July, and Labor Day. In traditional vacation areas, like much of Florida, there's not much of an off-season, since people tend to go there year-round.

4. Try not to pay rack rate. The rack rate is the highest price a hotel charges for a room on a given night. The only thing you really need to know about rack rate is that *you don't want to pay it*! Most hotels offer discounts of at least 10% for members of AAA and senior citizens. If you ask and are friendly, many desk clerks will give you a small discount just for asking. Discounts usually *are* available, even when the rack rate is high.

5. Stay in the suburbs. If you plan to spend the night in a major metropolitan area, be aware that suburban hotels are usually much cheaper than hotels in the city center. In addition, suburban hotels rarely charge for parking, while downtown hotels may charge as much as $40 per night for this privilege. A suburban hotel may be going for $79, while the exact same hotel chain may be charging twice that price for a similar room downtown.

6. Be prepared to walk away. If you don't like the rate, that is. When you're looking for a deal, you may have to try two or three different hotels to find what you want. If you've been driving all day, you'll be tired. So don't attempt to go bargain hunting for a hotel room much after 8:00 p.m. In fact, start looking much earlier. The earlier in the day you start looking, the less chance you have of giving in to an expensive rate simply because you're too tired to keep driving.

7. Get away from the interstate. Hotels within sight of an interstate exit often attract more traffic and can afford to charge guests more. Properties a little farther off the expressway, especially those in towns not served by the interstate at all, are likely to charge much less.

Online Deals

These days, most savvy travelers book their hotel rooms online. Websites such as Travelocity, Expedia, Orbitz, Hotels.com, Hotwire, and Priceline make it easy to compare prices and amenities for different hotels. If you've used these booking engines, you know that all you need is a city and a date, and it's easy to find dozens of hotels that meet your criteria.

Some of these sites have sales and coupons that can save you even more money. Each of the major booking engines has a weekly e-mail newsletter. Sign up for it, and you'll receive notification of major sales or special deals on hotels, as well as other travel products. In the next chapter, we'll go into detail on how to save serious money by booking hotels online, especially at the last minute.

Alternatives to Hotels and Motels: Campgrounds

Hotels are good at providing a predictable level of comfort when you need it. Sometimes you need – or want – something different. Part of being on the road is discovering new places and surroundings. And what better way to relax and enjoy your surroundings than to go camping?

It's easy to find campgrounds. They're advertised in most states on interstate exit service signs, and print directories can be found in the travel section of most libraries and bookstores. Today, most campgrounds have an online presence, too. You'll find lists and reviews of campgrounds readily available on the web, complete with directions and pricing information.

Even if you plan to spend most of your nights in hotels and motels along the way, it's well worth it to consider camping, at least for one night. Not only will you save some money, you'll get to enjoy the outdoors and get some exercise.

If you plan to go camping while on the road, you'll need a tent. Sporting goods stores and even discount chains carry plenty of tents. Make sure that your tent will hold as many people as there are traveling with you. Beware, though: most tents, when occupied by the number of adults specified on the label, make for a *very* tight squeeze. For example, I have a tent that states '3-4 adults' on the label. This tent measures about eight feet by six feet, and I'm not sure that four adults could actually fit in that tent; *two* adults can sleep comfortably in it. Keep this in mind when tent shopping. When in doubt, get a tent that's a little bigger than you think you'll need. It's always better to have too much room than not enough.

If you're traveling in a smaller car, is it still possible to go camping? Definitely! Camping out of a smaller car may be a tight squeeze, though, especially with more than two or three travelers. Tents and other camping gear *do* take up space in the trunk, so vans or SUV's may be better choices. For one or two people, though, there's plenty of space for basic camping gear in all but the smallest of cars.

Camping Gear

What other camping gear should you take along? You'll need a sleeping bag or some other type of bedding. Be aware that most places do get a little cool at night, except in the warmest nights of summer, so consider taking a blanket, even in early summer. Lying directly on the ground with little or no padding will be very uncomfortable after the first 30 minutes. So spend a few dollars on a good camping pad or air mattress; your back will thank you. And don't forget to take a comfortable pillow.

Most tents are easy to set up, and one or two people should be able to handle the job in about 20 minutes. Practice putting it up in the backyard at home, well before your trip. It can be frustrating trying to read tent instructions in an unfamiliar location, especially when it's about to get dark. By practicing with your tent ahead of time, you'll set up camp faster, leaving more time to enjoy your evening.

Speaking of putting up your tent in time, be aware of the time you'll be stopping for the night. If you plan on camping, you can't afford to drive until 8:00 p.m. if sunset is at 8:30. Make plans to stop at least *two hours* before nightfall; otherwise, you'll be setting up camp in the dark. Keep an eye on the local weather forecast, too. If it calls for anything more than light rain, you might want to re-think camping, at least *that* day. Otherwise, you'll need extra time in the morning to let your tent fabric dry before repacking.

Where should you plan to camp? Fortunately, there are plenty of options. Commercial campgrounds, such as K.O.A., are a great choice if you've never been camping before. You'll pay more at these campgrounds, sometimes as much as $40 a night, but often much less. For your money, though, you'll get much more. Commercial campgrounds are equipped with full electric hookups, so you won't be isolated from civilization. Many also feature swimming pools, hiking trails, game rooms, general stores, and even wireless internet.

Beyond the amenities, though, commercial campgrounds usually have a full-time staff whose job it is to assist guests and maintain security onsite. Since these places are private property, only paying guests are allowed to enter.

On the other hand, public campgrounds are very common in rural areas and offer some amenities, too, though not quite as extensive as most commercial grounds. State and national parks have reasonable prices, usually under $30 a night. Be aware that many of the more popular national parks – such as Yellowstone and Yosemite – get *very* busy in the summer months, and you'd be well advised to reserve your campsite months ahead.

Sleeping on a Couch?

If you're low on cash, but would rather not sleep in your car, have a look at CouchSurfing's website, found at www.couchsurfing.com. Hundreds of thousands of hosts from around the world have opened up their homes to travelers at no charge. All they ask in return is that you fill out a profile and offer to host travelers, as well.

The system is actually quite safe, as there's a 'vouching' system, similar to Ebay's feedback system. Those who've successfully hosted travelers earn a higher score and are considered to be 'safer' bets than newbies to the site. If you're not sure about the concept, take a look around the website; it may be a great way to make friends on the road!

Most public campgrounds have a ranger or host who will collect your camping fee and provide help in emergencies. Otherwise, you normally won't find swimming pools or Wi-Fi on these facilities. You'll usually have access to an electric hookup and bathhouse at your site, but other than that, you'll be 'roughing it'.

If you want even more of a wilderness experience, try camping in national forests. Campgrounds in most national forests charge about $15 a night. The campsites will be simpler, and you might not have an electric hookup. The bathhouse may not be very inviting, and it may not offer complete shower facilities. Instead of a paying a full-time ranger, you might put your camping fee into an 'honor box' upon entering the campground. If you're on a very tight budget, you can't beat the price of national forests.

Another secret about national forests: they allow *dispersed camping*, and you don't even have to pay. In other words, unless you see a sign that specifically prohibits camping, you're normally allowed to camp anywhere in a national forest outside the 'official' campground, completely free of charge. It's the best camping deal out there, and most people don't know about it. Of course, you won't have a bathroom, electricity, or running water, but you'll get a lot closer to nature. If you choose the dispersed camping option, though, remember to clean up after yourself! You're expected to take *all* trash when you leave your site and *completely* extinguish any fire you may start.

Hostels: Yet Another Option

Visitors from Europe often ask about hostels when visiting the U.S.A. The fact is, hostels just aren't that common in the United States, and most Americans have never stayed in one. If you look for them, though, you'll find a few hostels scattered around, usually in larger cities.

If you've never heard of a hostel, it's basically a communal hotel. In most hostels, up to eight guests – often strangers – share a room filled with twin beds. Hostels usually offer a modest living area and internet access, too. Obviously, they're great places to meet fellow travelers, and they're most popular with travelers under 30. Essentially though, you're paying for a bed and a place to sleep.

Many hostels also offer more private accommodations as well. They have a few 'suites' that mimic regular hotel rooms designed for couples and small groups traveling together. These mini-suites usually start at around $60 a night. If you don't mind sleeping in the communal area, expect to pay around $20 to $30 *per person*.

My recommendation? If you're a young, solo traveler who wants to meet new people, go ahead and give the hostel a try. However, if the idea of sleeping around strangers makes you nervous, they might not be for you. If your car group includes three or more people – or even as few as two – you'll likely pay *more* at a hostel than you would at an independent motel (sometimes even a roadside chain). Although there aren't many hostels in the United States, many travelers and backpackers swear by them.

What About Sleeping in Your Car?

Although this is clearly not the best option for road travelers, the fact is that many people have done this at one time or another. In fact, sleeping in the car is quite popular. Just stop by nearly any interstate rest area between the hours of midnight and 4 a.m., and you're likely to see several vehicles parked. The people inside are probably trying to get a few hours sleep before moving on. Sleeping in the car is arguably the most uncomfortable, worst way to get rest while on the road. But I know people do it, so let me offer my advice on how to do it safely.

The car *is* the cheapest place to sleep when on a road trip – absolutely free. Is it legal, though? Yes. It is completely legal to sleep in your car. As long as the car is yours, you're free to eat in it, sleep in it, and so forth. Really, the more important part is making sure your car is *parked* legally. In a few states, it is illegal to park overnight at a rest area. In every state, it is illegal to trespass, or to park your car on someone else's private property without their permission. So where should you park, if you decide to sleep in your car? More about that later. . . .

The big question is: Is it *safe* to sleep in your car? The answer is: it depends. It's a lot safer to find an exit and sleep in your car than it is to drive drowsy. Most highway patrolmen would agree. They'd rather see a motorist sleeping for a few hours in a car than seeing him crash into a tree because he fell asleep at the wheel.

If you need to pull off the highway and sleep for a few hours, most highway rest areas are safe. Those that aren't will be heavily patrolled by law enforcement. In most states away from the two coasts, it is perfectly legal to park at a rest area. Check the signage; if overnight parking is prohibited, it will be stated prominently. Remember to lock your doors, leave the windows cracked, with the keys in a handy place in case you need to leave quickly.

After being at the rest area for a few minutes, try to gauge the mood. If you get a bad feeling or see anyone suspicious, you can always drive away. That's one advantage sleeping in your car *does* have; you can get away quickly if you sense trouble, something you can't do in a hotel room or campground. Remember, though, sleeping at a rest area is not something I recommend; it's simply a last resort if you need to catch a few hours' sleep before moving on.

If overnight parking is prohibited at rest areas in your area, where can you park? Often, truck stops or large 24-hour gas stations permit drivers to park for a few hours and rest. Since these are on private property, ask permission before doing so. It may be harder to rest well at these places due to truck noise and bright lights, but they generally are safe.

It's been said that large Wal-Mart parking lots permit overnight parking. Sometimes up to a dozen RV's can be found in a Wal-Mart parking lot on a summer night. Most Wal-Mart stores allow this practice, but it's best to ask a manager or customer service before doing this; some local ordinances prohibit overnight parking on large lots within the city limits. Some travelers prefer hospital parking lots, but the same advice applies: Don't draw attention to yourself; be inconspicuous.

The few times I've had to sleep in my car for a few hours, I've found a quiet country road – plentiful and easy to find in the midsection of the country – and parked there. Look for a lightly traveled gravel road, pull far to the side so cars can pass, and park for the night. You probably won't be bothered; if anyone knocks on your window, they're likely to ask if you need some help.

Be aware of places you definitely *shouldn't* park to sleep. Never park on the shoulder of an interstate highway – or any other major highway – to sleep. And never park in someone's driveway overnight; you're likely to be asked to leave, or in the worst case, you could be fined or taken to jail for trespassing. Try to avoid businesses that normally have empty parking lots at night; a stray car on the lot could arouse suspicions.

If you sleep in your car on a road trip, do so out of necessity only. The rest you get in the back seat won't leave you well rested and cheery the next morning. If you're in a sedan, only one or two people can comfortably rest overnight after reclining the seats. Maybe three or four people, at the very most, could sleep in a larger SUV or van. But remember, sleeping in your car is not the way to enjoy a trip. If you have to sleep this way one night, opt for a motel room or campground the following night. Remember, sleeping in the car is a last resort, something to hold you over until you can get some *real* rest, not something you'll want to do all the time.

Overnight Stays Are Part of the Fun

No matter where you choose to spend the night, make it part of the fun. When you stop for the evening, get out and explore your surroundings. Don't stop so late at night that you're completely drained of energy. And be open to options, like camping or hostels, that allow you to meet people and try something different.

Now that you're well on the way to your destination, you've probably spent quite a bit of money. How can you save some of that hard-earned cash while on the road? Read on, road warriors! That's what the next chapter is about.

12

Saving Money on a Road Trip

oad trips can get expensive. Really expensive. In fact, let's pause for a minute and think about all the plans we've talked about making. Spending nights in hotels, paying for gas, buying tents, eating out – all these activities cost money. In fact, on a road trip you can easily spend $200 *per day*. Yours doesn't have to be that expensive, though. This chapter will offer you 40 suggestions to save money at every step along the way.

Saving on Gasoline

1. Pay attention to gas prices, and fill up where it's cheaper. This bit of advice seems like common sense, but you'd be surprised how often people don't even pay attention to the price of gas. Since every gas station in a town might be charging a different price for essentially the same product, it pays to keep an eye out for spots where gas is cheaper. If gas is more expensive in one town, it may be several cents less a few miles down the road. Watch your gas gauge, though! Don't let yourself run out of gas trying to find a better price.

2. Look for gas stations away from interstate exits. Gas stations adjacent to the freeway exit tend to charge more because road travelers usually don't stray from the interstate much more than a third of a mile. If you take an exit near a town, try driving toward the business district. You're sure to find gas stations, likely with less traffic and lower prices.

3. Get a gas discount card. If you have a favorite gas station chain, sign up for its charge card. Pay it off every month, and you'll save up to 10% on your gasoline purchases, both on your trip and after returning home. Nearly every major fuel chain offers a credit card, and applications are often available right at the pump.

4. Use the internet to look for cheaper gas. The best place to explore gas prices online is GasBuddy.com. Here you'll find which areas and even individual stations that offer a lower price. Since gas stations change their prices daily, focus on the 'Gas Price Temperature Map', which gives an idea of states and counties where gas is cheaper – and places where it's more expensive, too. Determine which areas offer the best gas prices and plan your fuel stops accordingly.

5. Check your air filter, change your oil, and make sure your car is tuned up. A dirty air filter decreases fuel economy. Likewise, old, misfiring spark plugs will lower gas mileage. And get your oil changed before a road trip, since dirty oil also af-

fects fuel use. These three minor maintenance repairs may improve
your fuel economy 10% or more.

6. Inflate your tires properly. You already know this, but
it's worth repeating. Underinflated tires may waste 10% or more of
the gasoline in your tank. Follow the instructions in your vehicle's
owner manual, but keep in mind that
most car tires need to be inflated to at
least 32 psi. Keep a tire gauge in your
glove compartment, and check your
pressure periodically while on the road.
Very wide temperature fluctuations can
also affect your tire pressure (e.g. driv-

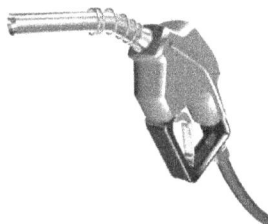

ing from a very warm climate to a very
cold one), so check your pressure again
after driving into a different climate
area.

In most cases, regular
unleaded gasoline is
just fine.

**7. In warmer weather, when using the air condition-
ing, set the control to "MAX" or "RECIRC" to recirculate
air already inside the vehicle and save energy.** When the
weather isn't as warm, but you still want a little ventilation in the
car, turn on the vent instead of the air conditioner. You'll save gas
by keeping the compressor off.

8. Skip the premium gas. Regular unleaded is fine for
most cars and is just as good for gas mileage as more expensive
grades. In my personal experience, premium gasoline may eliminate spark knock, but does little to nothing for gas mileage. In fact,
the few times I've tried it on a trip, my gas mileage actually went

down! Regular grade gas is just fine unless your vehicle's manual specifies otherwise.

9. Slow down. Keeping your speed to 55 really does save gas. If you don't believe it, try keeping your speed to 55 miles per hour for an entire tank, and monitor your gas mileage. Look at the tachometer on the instrument panel; the engine works hardest at speeds above 55. Since interstate traffic moves much faster than that, consider taking two-lane roads instead. Nearly all two-lane highways east of the Mississippi cap speeds at 55, and those west of the Mississippi usually keep speeds to 65 or below. Even if slowing down doesn't improve your gas mileage, driving the speed limit *will* save money in the long run. Speeding tickets are expensive!

10. Consider driving fewer miles each day. If your destination is negotiable, seriously think about driving significantly fewer miles per day. When gas is $4.00 a gallon, each hour of interstate driving costs about $9.00 (assuming fuel economy of 25 mpg). So, planning for shorter days puts money back in your pocket. Try stopping for the evening two hours earlier each day. Not only will you save about $15.00 a day, you'll also leave more time to explore the local area. Now, if you have a specific destination in mind, this suggestion won't work too well, but for road trips where you're 'wandering', it works just fine.

Ways to Save on Lodging

11. Take advantage of free Wi-Fi. In the last chapter, I discussed free wireless internet as one of the amenities offered at nearly every roadside chain hotel. But what does it have to do with saving money on your hotel room? Well, some of the best hotel deals are found online. (More about that later.) And if you can't get online, you won't have access to those prices. So if you have a laptop computer, search for a Wi-Fi signal.

One of the best places to get online is in your hotel room itself. Get in the habit of looking for hotel deals at tomorrow's destination *today*. You'll save yourself the hassle of having to get online to make a reservation late in the afternoon, when you're already getting tired. Other spots offer a free wireless signal, too. Many restaurants attract customers with free Wi-Fi. For example, most Burger King and McDonald's have free wireless internet, along with several other smaller businesses.

Several public places offer free Wi-Fi as a municipal service and don't mind if you borrow access for a few minutes. Many libraries, hospitals, schools, interstate rest areas, and even churches now have open Wi-Fi signals. Although it's not a service that's likely advertised on billboards like it is at motels, many facilities, especially libraries, welcome motorists who need to use the internet.

12. Use Priceline.com to save money on hotels. Every hotel has days when its occupancy is low. Many hotels, from extended-stay properties to high-end hotels, auction off their unoccupied rooms at Priceline.com. If you're somewhat flexible with your plans – and most of us are – Priceline is a great way to save up to 50% on even the lowest advertised rate available. Of course, to use this website, you'll need a computer with web access and a major credit card.

To bid on a hotel room, input the dates you want to check in and check out. Enter a city or town, and the number of rooms you need. Look for the "Name Your Own Price" option. After you click "Enter" or "Bid Now", you'll see a list of neighborhoods and star levels. Click on the neighborhood where you want to stay.

"Star levels" refer to the level of amenities available to guests. They don't necessarily refer to the quality of guest rooms. In other words, a room at a 4-star hotel may not be significantly nicer than a room at a 2-star hotel. What's the least you need to know about Priceline's star levels? High-end hotels are generally found in the 5, 4, 3 ½, and 3 star levels. Most roadside chains fall into the 2 ½ and 2 star levels. Extended stay properties are normally 2 stars, but they're occasionally rated as 1 star. Although independent motels are usually not available on Priceline, when they are, they'll probably be rated as 1 star, along with the cheapest of the roadside chains.

After you've decided where you want to stay and the star level you want, decide on a fair price to pay. How much should you offer? This is the tricky part of the bidding process. Offer too much and you'll overpay; offer too little – your offer will be denied and you'll have to wait 24 hours before trying the same offer combination again. If you don't want to wait, you'll need to change dates, neighborhoods, or star levels. Under some circumstances, though, you can immediately get a chance to rebid without waiting 24 hours – something called a 'free rebid' – and it involves recognizing that certain Priceline neighborhoods don't contain hotels at the star levels on which you're bidding.

Be warned, though! Priceline is not for the extremely picky or for anyone who *has* to stay at a certain hotel; you won't know which hotel you'll be staying at until your bid is accepted. And once your bid is accepted and you learn the name of the hotel, your credit card is charged immediately, and there's no turning back – no refunds or changes.

Sound complicated? It can be, if you've never tried it before. Priceline is almost like playing a game, and you need to know the rules before you play. Fortunately, Priceline's website interface is quite intuitive, and there are at least two discussion forums dedicated to helping people get the best prices for hotels on Priceline – betterbidding.com and biddingfortravel.yuku.com. Both forums are quite large and should help anyone who wants to learn to use Priceline most effectively.

Bidding on Priceline involves taking a risk, namely, trusting that your $70 bid on a 4-star hotel is really going to land you at a 4-star hotel. Usually it does; but that 4-star hotel might have a few crummy rooms. Some hotels assign their worst rooms to Priceline guests, but most hotels treat winning bidders just like anyone else. I use Priceline to book as many as 80% of my hotel stays. If you travel often, it could easily save you thousands of dollars a year. Over the years, I've stayed at some very nice hotels for very little money.

The savings are real: How about Nashville's Sheraton Music City for $31 a night? I've stayed at the Venetian Las Vegas for $99. The Hyatt Regency Chicago O'Hare was only $45 a night. My stay at the Sheraton Suites Houston Galleria? $40. The Hyatt Suites Atlanta? $40. My lowest price of all time? Just $22 a night at a Quality Inn in Dallas. Although you might not get these same low prices, they're a sample of the amazing savings you can rack up on Priceline.

In each of these cases above, the hotels were worth every bit what I paid – much more, in fact. The rooms were clean, and I was never discriminated against because I got a low rate. Personally, using Priceline is my top way to save money on lodging while on the road. It not only offers flexibility and savings, but it also works well for last-minute lodging decisions.

If you like to decide where to spend the night at the last minute, use your computer or phone's data plan or WiFi signal to connect to the internet. Once online, you're ready to 'Priceline' a hotel. Since you're bidding, quite literally, at the last minute, you won't be able to wait 24 hours to bid again if your offer is unsuccessful. And you may need to make use of the 'free rebid' strategy in order to win a hotel. To make the most of your bidding opportunities, try consulting one of the discussion boards mentioned earlier

Priceline Same-Day Bidding

Priceline.com allows you to bid for hotels up to 11:00 p.m. Eastern time the day of your intended stay. In other words, it's possible to bid for a hotel while online in the parking lot of a hotel, have your bid accepted at that very hotel, then go inside five minutes later to check in. If it sounds like a seamless process, be careful – there are a few potential snags that could happen.

Don't make a same-day bid much later than 6:00 p.m. local time. Priceline may claim the hotel has rooms available, but when you arrive, they may already be sold out – it's happened to me. If you must make a same-day bid late in the evening, stick to 2½-star properties or higher. Many hotels below this level are extended-stay properties which don't even have 24-hour front desk service. Your bid might be accepted, and your credit card *will* be charged, but no one may be at the hotel to retrieve your reservation and check you in. It's a lesson I learned the hard way.

to see what the 'going price' is for certain zones and star levels in a particular city.

Make no mistake, though: bidding for hotel rooms on Priceline at the last minute is risky. If you use all your free rebids without getting an offer accepted, you're out of luck. You'll have to book conventionally or walk up to a hotel and ask for their best rate. Be aware, also, that many hotels at Priceline's 2- and 1-star levels are extended-stay properties, which typically provide only one bed per room. These hotels just don't work well for groups of three or more.

If you use Priceline to reserve a room at the very last minute, try to book before 6:00 p.m. It takes a few minutes for a hotel to receive your reservation. More importantly, some hotels put their front desks on 'autopilot' at night and aren't ready to handle new reservations, although Priceline has already charged you for the room. If you're assigned to an extended-stay property, for example, the front desk may close completely after 8:00 p.m. Even when Priceline faxes your information to the front desk, there may be no one there to get it. Once again, you're just out of luck.

13. Use Hotwire to save on hotels. The savings at Hotwire.com on hotel rooms are not usually as great as on Priceline, but they're nothing to sneeze at, either. Some travelers feel more comfortable with Hotwire because you're given a list of amenities and a fixed price; you either take it or leave it. Hotwire is often a better choice on the road, because you don't have to make several bids before winning a room, or worse, having all your bids denied. With Hotwire, you take their offer, and after it's accepted, you find out the name of your hotel.

Since there's less guesswork with Hotwire, the prices are a few bucks higher, but often it's worth the money to know the amenities you're getting in advance. One area where Hotwire really shines, though, is when traveling with a group of three or more. Priceline guarantees only that your room will hold two people, but with Hotwire, you can specify a room for up to four adults. That's an important feature, because with Hotwire, a group of four people won't be assigned to an extended-stay property designed for two.

So, what's the verdict? Priceline and Hotwire are both great ways to save money on hotels, but if you're traveling alone or with just one other person, Priceline will net the better deal most of the time. If you don't have the time to worry with bidding, or if your group has more than two people, the nod goes to Hotwire.

14. Book with Expedia, Orbitz, Travelocity, or another site. With these online booking engines, your savings won't normally be as great as with Priceline or Hotwire. However, you'll know exactly which hotel you're getting before making the purchase. Occasionally, these websites will offer coupons to save up to $40 off a stay of three days or more, or a 15% discount on any purchase. If you stick with roadside chains, that savings may come close to beating the lowest rate available on Priceline or Hotwire. Keep your eyes open for these coupons, sometimes they're advertised on the front page of the websites under "Deals", and they're usually sent to customers via a weekly e-mail.

15. Stay in independent motels. If you're willing to stay at locally owned, non-chain motels, it's possible to save up to $20 off even the best Priceline or Hotwire rates for roadside chains. Although the amenities may be fewer, you won't have to worry about making a bid or scrolling through lists of hotels when you're already tired and would rather be *in* your hotel room. If you don't have internet access, this is probably the cheapest way to sleep, not counting hotel/motel alternatives.

16. Use coupons or other discounts available to you. In the last chapter, I mentioned the coupon booklets available for free at larger gas stations and rest areas. Roadside chain hotels provide most of these discounts, so the hotel names will likely be familiar. If you travel around the holidays or another high-occupancy period, remember that most coupon discounts won't be valid. In that case, you'll have to rely on some other discount method, such as a AAA or AARP membership card. If you're not a member, ask the desk clerk for a discount anyway. Usually, he or she has the final say as to the rate you'll pay.

17. Join frequent-stay programs. If you have a favorite hotel chain, join their frequent-stay program. It may eventually net you discounts or other perks, such as free breakfasts or room upgrades. Stay often enough, and you'll earn free hotel nights and even better perks. It's usually free to join these programs, and rewards usually start flowing after just a few stays.

18. Think about traveling off-season. January and February are the slowest months for hotels in most of the country. It's no coincidence that those months have the best deals. Most hotels have lower rates in the autumn, too, so consider traveling in September or October. The weather is still agreeable in most of the country, and prices usually are, too. Likewise, midweek prices are normally lower for roadside chains than on the weekend.

19. When visiting the city, stay in suburban areas. Downtown hotels often cost twice as much as suburban hotels. Staying in the suburbs not only saves money on the hotel rate itself, but it also keeps you from paying for parking in most cases. Even if you drive a few miles into the city for sightseeing, the money saved by staying out of town outweighs what you'll pay to park for a few hours. Suburban hotels usually offer more dining and shopping options in the evenings and on weekends; most downtown areas go dormant after 5 p.m.

20. Look for cheaper cities. Some cities are just more inexpensive for lodging than others. Kansas City, Dallas, Orlando, and Atlanta are a few cities known for lower hotel rates, especially if you're willing to stay in the suburbs.

If you're searching for a low rate alongside the interstate, look for small towns located about halfway between larger cities. These towns often have lots of rooms for little money. About halfway between Albuquerque and Amarillo, for example, you'll find the little town of Tucumcari, New Mexico – home to over 1000 motel rooms, most of them very inexpensive. Halfway between Nashville and Chattanooga is the town of Manchester, Tennessee; rooms start at $30. Texarkana is on the Arkansas/Texas state line about halfway between Little Rock and Dallas; rooms are advertised starting at $34.99 a night.

21. Try camping. Campsites cost less than hotel rooms, and you'll get to connect with nature and enjoy your road trip that much more. Of course, camping isn't much of an option in the wintertime, and many campgrounds close for the season after October.

22. Sleep in the car. When all else fails, you can always sleep in your car. You probably won't sleep too soundly, but it's free. This is really a last resort, though, and should only be attempted in safe places. See the previous chapter for details.

Ways to Save on Food and Drink

23. Make lunch your big meal of the day. Instead of pigging out in the evening, eat a big lunch and a lighter dinner. Especially if you plan to be in the car for a while, you won't be able to burn as many calories from a heavy dinner, so it's actually healthier to eat a bigger lunch when traveling. Since prices are generally cheaper at lunchtime, you'll save money. Some restaurants have their biggest crowds around noon, so visit between 1 and 2 p.m. to avoid the masses.

24. Stay at hotels with free breakfast. If breakfast is the most important meal of the day, then it's even more important when you travel. A hearty breakfast is the perfect way to start your travel day, and it's even better when you don't have to pay extra. Four people eating breakfast in a restaurant could easily pay $30, even in an inexpensive diner; save that money and take advantage of your hotel's free breakfast. Never skip the free breakfast offered at a hotel; you've already paid for it with your room rate. Even if you're not hungry or a big breakfast eater, take a piece of fruit for when you *do* get hungry.

25. Visit super-markets and buy your own food. Supermarket deli sandwiches cost less than most restaurant lunches. Drinks and snacks, like candy bars and chips, will be much cheaper at a supermarket or even a convenience store. To save some time, do your grocery shopping on or before the

Free breakfast at your hotel can save several dollars per person

first day of your road trip at a market near home. By shopping close to home, you'll know where to find your favorite snacks without wasting time or money.

26. Fill your own water bottles. Bottled water is one of the most overpriced products on the market today. If it tastes any different, it's because the bottled water has been filtered or boiled – two steps you can do at home for much less money. Install a filter on your kitchen faucet at home and purify your own water. Another option: instead of paying close to $1.00 a bottle, fill your own empty bottles with water from a drinking fountain. If you *must* buy bottled water, buy it by the gallon at the supermarket and fill your own smaller bottles as needed. One gallon of water from a grocery store costs less than a 16-ounce bottle at a convenience store.

Restaurant coupons can
save you money when
traveling

27. Carry restaurant coupons. Most chain restaurants offer nationwide coupons through their websites. Take a few minutes before your trip to look for coupons you might use, and print as many as you can. Each chain has coupons featured quite prominently on its website. You may already receive some in the mail or in your Sunday newspaper.

If you're thinking of finer dining on the road, check out the options at **www.restaurant.com**. Their site features discounted gift certificates for finer independent restaurants across the country. Menus are available for most of the restaurants, and you can even make a reservation online. And what about the discounts? For most restaurants, $25 gift certificates are usually available for $10 or less. Other coupon codes are often available that slash another 50% off that already heavily-discounted price.

28. Visit local diners. At locally owned restaurants, the meals are probably a little cheaper. You're also more likely to sample regional specialties. The desserts are often homemade, too.

29. At fast food places, check out the value menu. Most fast food restaurants offer a 'value menu' or 'dollar menu' for budget-minded customers. Often, the value menu can net you a burger, small salad, and small drink for as little as $3 to $4. Or substitute the small drink for another dollar item and drink water instead. The price is perfect for those on a budget.

30. Order a big meal and split it. Many sit-down restaurants serve big portions – sometimes too much for one person who'll be sitting in the car for the next several hours. Instead, try ordering one big meal and asking for a second plate. You're likely to eat just as well – better, in fact – as you would having eaten the big meal by yourself. It's cheaper, too. One big meal costs less than two big meals, and in most cases, it's even less than two small meals. Just don't try this at a buffet!

31. If you're *really* hungry, look for a buffet. Buffets offer wide variety and exceptionally good value. Everyone in a group can get what he or she wants. At lunch, when prices are cheaper, it's possible to enjoy a full meal, with dessert included, for well under $10. Just be careful, though, because it's easy to overeat. For this reason, when on the road, I recommend buffets primarily for lunch, because you'll have more time to burn those extra calories.

32. Order water. Aside from the obvious health benefits of avoiding sugary soft drinks, ice water is usually free at restaurants. If you have a favorite soft drink, you're probably carrying it in your car anyway, so wait to enjoy it *after* your meal. Have you noticed that most sit-down chain restaurants don't even include soft drink prices on their menus? They've learned that if customers knew ahead of time what drinks cost, they'd order water instead. Drinks are one of their major profit centers, and it's not uncommon to be $2.00 or more for what amounts to a few cents worth of syrup. Save yourself the empty calories and the money and just ask for water instead.

33. If you *must* buy fountain drinks, get them at convenience stores. Many convenience stores advertise low prices on fountain soft drinks to get customers in the door. Whereas the smallest soft drink at a fast food restaurant will cost at least $1.00, convenience stores usually offer drinks that are twice as big for the same price. So, if you've run out of cans in your cooler and need a fountain drink, find one of these stores.

AAA, AARP, and union membership cards may get you discounts on admission

Saving Money at Your Destination

34. Visit free museums and historic sites. Some cities have more free museums than others. The best museums in Washington, DC are free, as are most of the major museums in St. Louis. Even if the museums you visit charge admission, they're likely more economical than going to a theme park or even a trip to the mall. Historic sites, such as those found in most state capitals, are fun, educational, and almost always free. Other sites worth mentioning include battlefields, ghost towns, national forests, and beaches.

35. Ask for a discount. Many museums and theme parks offer discounts to senior citizens, children, and AAA members. Likewise, if you're in the military, a full-time student, teacher, in-state resident, or AARP member, you're likely to get a discount, too. Ask before you pay admission; the discount could range anywhere from 10% all the way to free admission.

Budget Cities

Some cities tend to be cheaper for road travelers. Here are a few cities where you're likely to spend less on your visit:

St. Louis – Lodging is abundant and inexpensive, especially in the suburbs. The zoo, science center, and art museum all offer free admission.

Washington – Lodging in the suburbs is less expensive than in the city. Forget parking in Washington; leave your car in the suburbs and take the Metro into town. All the Smithsonian museums and most other major sites are free to visitors.

Dallas – Plenty of cheap lodging options at all levels. Most attractions here do charge admission, but consider taking the DART light rail, which is inexpensive and convenient to downtown.

Las Vegas – Some of the most inexpensive lodging in the nation, that is, if you're willing to stay off the Strip or at smaller properties. Dining options range from the dirt cheap to the utterly expensive. For the best deals, be willing to dine at odd hours. If you have a car, think about staying in Laughlin, instead, an hour to the south, where hotels start at $19 a night.

Atlanta – Hotels here, especially in the northern suburbs, are quite inexpensive. You'll find plenty to see and do in the downtown area, too.

Orlando – If you're going to visit the theme parks here, try visiting during the fall. October, early December, and mid-January have the best deals in this popular tourist city.

36. Go downtown on the weekend. Most cities don't charge to park on downtown streets during the weekend. You'll likely find downtown less crowded then, and cheaper, too. Beware, though: although choices for visitors are abundant in most downtown areas, a few cities empty out on the weekends, especially in the evening. You may find fewer dining and shopping choices, too.

37. Look for discounts online. Many museums, theme parks, and other attractions that charge admission offer discounts if you buy your tickets online. It's convenient, because you print your own tickets at home and save time, avoiding lines at admission. Even if the online price isn't discounted, it's a good idea to print your tickets ahead of time to allow more time for sightseeing and less time waiting in line.

38. Take pictures. Instead of buying expensive souvenirs you're likely to lose or never use, take lots of pictures. With digital cameras and memory very inexpensive, anyone can take dozens, even hundreds of pictures with ease. Remember to take plenty of batteries. Take snapshots of anything you'd like to be reminded of when you get back home. Taking pictures and reminiscing about the excitement of a road trip is almost as thrilling as being there. Your pictures will bring back memories and help you remember things you'll want to tell friends back home.

39. Avoid the crowds. Steering clear of typical tourist trap crowds can lower your stress level. You'll save money, too, because high prices tend to follow crowds. Most major tourist attractions are surrounded with high-priced food, overpriced drinks, gouged parking fees, and expensive souvenirs. Instead, opt for a park, a hiking trail, or one of the less-frequented museums in town. It will be less stressful, less crowded, and likely cheaper.

One Last Idea to Save Money

40. Stick to a budget. Hopefully you've already planned how much money is available for your trip and budgeted it accordingly. A very wise person once said, "Take half as many clothes and twice as much money." And in many respects, that statement is true. Any vacation can easily go overbudget, especially if hotels end up being more costly than planned, or if gas prices spike.

Even with unexpected expenses, you can still save plenty of money, especially by sticking to lower-end hotels, getting deals online, and watching dining expenses. But don't try to be so frugal that you stop enjoying your road trip. Sure, eating peanut butter sandwiches and sleeping in the car will save money, but after two days of that, will you *really* be having a good time?

Remember, you can still splurge on occasion without breaking the bank. Keep an eye on the budget, and if you're cutting it close, keep a written log with *all* expenses listed. Total your expenses every day, and if you're going over your daily allotment, cut back a little. But most of all, have a good time! If you follow the tips in this chapter, you can save money and have a great time, too!

13

Roadtripping Solo

Many travelers end up driving alone by circumstance; others do so by choice. In either case, nothing is stopping you from having a wonderful time on a road trip by yourself. Still, it takes a special person to decide purposely to embark on a multi-day road trip alone. Most of us would rather have company on such an adventure, but solo road trips are actually one of my favorite type.

Think about this: When traveling alone, you get to make all the choices. You get to decide when to begin driving in the morning and when to stop in the evening. You'll choose where and when you eat and the stops you'll make along the way.

Taking a road trip by yourself is a perfect time to reflect on life, but beware: some solo travelers also tend to isolate themselves. That's why it's especially important to make an effort to talk to people while you're on this type of road trip.

Whether you attend a religious service or talk to tourism guides at interstate welcome centers, try to start conversations and make friends on the road. If you're in a local eatery on a solo road trip, ask the server a question about the area. Tourist guides at interstate welcome centers or local chambers of commerce are usually quite friendly and are glad to share information and tips about a particular area.

When traveling alone, avoid becoming your own worst enemy. Without friends or family along the route to tell you when to take a break, a solo driver can get fatigued much more easily. From experience, I've found that I tend to push myself to drive more than I should when alone.

It's easy to feel overconfident, especially in the early evening, just before sunset. Several times, I thought I had enough energy to drive through the night, only to get very drowsy around 1 to 2 a.m. By then, it's really too late to check into a hotel. Avoid this mistake by recognizing your limitations. Driving through the night when alone is not only dangerous, it also seriously reduces your ability to enjoy the following day's drive. Make plans to get a full eight hours of sleep each night, especially when driving alone.

Before you leave home, decide how long you'll drive before taking a break. If you've never taken an 'independent road trip' before, a good rule of thumb is to stop *at least* every two hours. Set a countdown timer if you must, but force yourself to stop, walk around, and eat at regular times.

Do You Really Like to Drive?

That question is key to knowing how far you'll be able to drive when traveling alone. Traveling solo means you can't switch drivers when tired. So if you don't really like to drive, and if you haven't done a long trip by yourself before, you'll want to keep your driving day short: 8 hours maximum or about 450 miles. If you drive longer than that, try to take more frequent breaks – possibly every hour or so.

On the other hand, you may really like to drive. If you've taken a solo road trip before, you may be able to advance farther in a day. For a one-day trip, you could advance as much as 800 miles, which is about 14 hours worth of driving. If you're planning a multi-day trip, 600 miles a day is more reasonable, which averages to a little over 10 hours a day. Even these amounts may be a bit ambitious for some; the main thing is to drive only as far as you feel comfortable. When you get tired, stop and rest; take a nap in your car at a rest area if you have to.

Special Challenges of Driving Alone

Boredom. When traveling with friends or family, you have the chance to fill the hours with interesting conversation. When that gets old, you can always turn on the radio or listen to CD's. When driving alone, there won't be any conversation, but you can still stay entertained with the radio.

Even though you won't have the benefit of conversation, you can still listen to talk radio. If you enjoy radio, I recommend sub-scribing to satellite radio. You'll have access to dozens of music channels, several of which you're sure to like. There are talk radio stations to fit nearly any interest or political persuasion. With satel-lite radio, I can personally say that I've never been bored on a solo road trip.

If you don't want to commit to satellite radio, consider down-loading some podcasts of your favorite programs. Hundreds of free and interesting podcasts are available on iTunes and BlogTalkRadio (including my own Road Trip Radio show!), and you're sure to find something to your liking, no matter what your taste. Thousands of audiobooks can be downloaded from audible.com. Books on CD are also available at any bookstore, at truck stops and travel centers, and even some restaurants. The Cracker Barrel restaurant chain even allows travelers to rent audiobooks with the ability to return them at any other Cracker Barrel restaurant in the country.

With so many options to keep your mind occupied on the road and so many interesting things to listen to, you don't have to be bored on the road, even when driving solo! Of course, if all else fails, just turn off the radio for a while and enjoy the scenery as it passes by.

Loneliness. If your drive lasts just a day or two, you likely won't have time to get lonely. But if you're planning a multiday trip, or especially a solo road trip of several weeks, being away from friends and family might start to wear on your nerves. Of course you'll want to stay in touch with those back home, whether by phone, e-mail, or Skype. But what if that's not enough?

Even when travelling alone, you'll enjoy yourself more when you reach out to the people around you. Talk to people. Ask for directions. Ask people about places to eat. Interacting with others will help keep you from feeling as lonely.

Exercise also improves a person's state of mind. Try to get out of the car at least twice a day to take a walk – once in the morning and once in the evening. Although a rest area will do, try to find a park or a neighborhood that will put you in the company of local residents. Some of the greatest scenic treasures in the country are found right in someone else's backyard, so make time to enjoy community parks and neighborhoods when you get a chance. It will help keep you from feeling lonely on the road.

Sharing the Ride

If you're taking a solo road trip, especially during busy travel periods, it's likely that someone else in your area may be headed to the same destination. It might be possible to divide expenses by carpooling. Check out websites like www.rideshare-directory.com for nationwide opportunities to carpool or share the ride. Not only will you save money, you'll make new friends. Many online rideshare bulletin boards offer secure posting methods, so you can safely screen potential carpool buddies.

Eating. A lot of solo roadtrippers feel self-conscious about eating by themselves. Most people dine out in a group. As a result, some single travelers feel strange eating out somewhere other than a fast-food restaurant. My best advice is not to worry about it. Some restaurants will ask if you want to sit at the bar; only do that if you want to. You're entitled to a table or booth as much as anyone else. Take a book or magazine with you while you eat. When I eat alone in a restaurant, I take my Kindle or tablet to catch up on some reading.

Solo travelers tend to eat in fast-food restaurants, which honestly are the worst choices for dining on the road. Even eating in slightly nicer sit-down restaurants can be a bit better, but not by much. At least once a day, try to eat fresh food. Visit a supermarket or farmers market to find fresh produce. Eating better will help you feel better, especially if you're traveling alone.

Lodging. One of the biggest disadvantages of making a solo road trip is that you don't have anyone to share expenses with. Although a hotel room for one costs less than a room for four, *your* cost is higher, since solo travelers pay the complete price themselves. Because of that, it's even more important to find the best rate for your room. Use the strategies in the rest of this book to get the best price possible. Use coupons, discount rates, and opaque booking sites like Hotwire or Priceline to pay as little as you have to for a hotel room.

When driving alone, no one will be there to tell you it's time to stop for the day. And since there won't be anyone helping you drive, you'll probably get tired earlier than you would otherwise. Aim to stop early, before dark if you can. You don't want to find yourself getting drowsy, only to realize that there are no decent hotels nearby.

By being kind to your body, you'll be able to relax and enjoy your time on the road. If you plan to be on the road several days, plan to alternate long driving days with short ones. If you make every day a long one, you'll tire very quickly and stop enjoying your trip within a couple of days.

Since you won't have anyone to help drive, you may have to cover less distance each day of your solo trip. On the other hand, you likely won't need to stop as often as a family traveling with kids, so you may cover more distance. Again, the key is to plan for your own limitations. Bring along your favorite CD's or audiobooks. Satellite radio will keep your mind occupied, especially if you're a talk radio fan.

Consider documenting your trip to share it with others later. Taking pictures of roadside scenery or attractions, recording videos, or writing a journal will help you remember not only what you see, but also the feeling of freedom that goes along with being an independent traveler. If you feel awkward writing on your trip, take along an audio recorder – the cheap digital kind that costs $20 will do – and record your impressions as you drive or at stops along the way. Later, you can make a road trip album as a memento to your solo road trip.

Taking a road trip by yourself can be an exhilarating experience. It can give you a feeling of freedom that's a little bit different from other types of journeys. Over the years I've come to enjoy solo drives as much as other trips. I get to catch up on some talk radio and a couple of audiobooks along the way. Although they have their own challenges, making a long-distance drive by yourself can still be an adventure to remember.

14

Unconventional Road Travel

O ver the past several years, a new trend has emerged among a few serious roadtrippers. RV travel has a faithful following and has morphed into its own lifestyle, with RV clubs and parks operating all over the country. However, record-high fuel prices have forced many RV'ers to reconsider. With most rigs getting no better than 10 to 12 miles per gallon, traveling the highways costs about 30 cents per mile at current prices. Hundreds, if not thousands of almost-new RV's have gone up for sale across the country!

Many travelers would like the freedom associated with RV travel, without the monetary commitment, especially for a vehicle they may use only a few weeks a year. A few of them have bought vans and converted them into simple RV's at a much lower expense than buying a full-sized rig.

Other travelers who wouldn't really be that interested in RV travel have done this because it gives them greater freedom and helps them save money. Several have told me they travel this way because it allows them to spend more time on the road and be where they want to be.

Camper-Van Design

The best vehicle for a mini-camper conversion is a full-size van. The favorite seems to be a full-size cargo van or work van. Other travelers have had success converting a minivan, box van, or even a school bus, but a simple white work van offers an excellent balance between fuel economy and living space. These vans are easy to find on Craigslist or at a local dealership and tend to be easy to sell when you're ready to get rid of one. If you prefer, these vans come already converted from the factory and can be purchased as a *Class B motorhome.*

Work vans tend to have an interior width of about six feet, which is just barely enough to install a full-size mattress. A common design is to build a box over the wheelwells in the back of the van and elevate the bed over the box. With a double layer of sturdy plywood as support, you won't need box springs. Although a high-quality pillow-top mattress can be installed, many opt for memory foam, since it can be cut to fit your available space, especially if your van is a tad too narrow to fit a full-sized mattress.

Elevating the bed in the back of the van has another advantage – additional storage space. You can use the space in the box underneath the bed for storing emergency supplies, clothing, or even food.

The mid-section of the van can be designed however you like. Stackable plastic drawers can be added for storing supplies and clothing. Add a cooler for food storage. Most van campers have at least a couple of comfortable foldable camping chairs stored for relaxing in the evening at a park. Some even have a small work table next to the bed, such as a small laptop cart, that can double as a nightstand.

The design of camper vans is as flexible as you want to make it. Some travelers opt for simple designs that can be undone in just a few minutes, while others go all out and even install paneling and carpet in their vans. Others install entertainment monitors on the wall. Many install an electrical system to run small appliances or electronics while inside. Dozens of interesting designs can be found online; check out Chapter 23 for places to find them.

Advantages of Camper Van Travel

Cost-Savings. By camping in a van, you can reduce or even eliminate hotel expenses from your budget. When hotels cost upwards of $70 a night, you'll save hundreds of dollars on road trips, even if your van gets lower fuel economy than a smaller car.

Comfort. Many people have trouble sleeping in a hotel room or on unfamiliar beds. By camping in your van, you'll be guaranteed to sleep in your own bed every night. It will be as comfortable as you choose to make it.

Storage. Vans are simply bigger than cars, and they'll have more room to store your gear. You'll be able to store things underneath the bed and in the mid-section interior. The camper van setup is perfect for one or two people, with plenty of room for luggage.

See More on the Road. If you're limited more by money than by time, you'll be able to spend more time on the road van-camping than by staying in hotels. If hotels run $70 a night, you'll save $70 every night you sleep in your camper-van. That's $70 you can use for traveling farther, getting into museums or shows, dining, or other attractions that interest you.

Frees Up Your Schedule. By camping in a van or a similar Class B motorhome, you won't have to make reservations at hotels days ahead of time. If you find a national park or area you like, just stay there a few more days! This type of travel embodies freedom; you won't be tied down to any schedule.

Enjoy the Outdoors More. In a camper van, you probably won't spend that much time in the van itself – just for driving and sleeping. It's more likely that you'll spend more time living *around* the van instead of *in* it, enjoying your surroundings, visiting parks, barbecuing or having a picnic outside.

Easy Parking and Driving. Camper vans handle much more easily on the road than a full-size Class A motorhome. You can park in nearly any parking spot, too, something that can't be said for a larger rig. Some toll roads also charge more for heavier vehicles, while vans get through on the same toll as a passenger car.

Challenges of Camper-Van Traveling

If you decide to buy a Class B camper van or your own van to renovate, don't think that it's the key to an easy life on the road. The van travel style has challenges of its own, but some good planning will make your life on the road in a camper van much easier.

Showering and Staying Clean. Some of the more ambitious van conversions include an installed shower. Still, all but the largest vans are simply too small to make this a comfortable fit. Some van campers decide to opt for some kind of discreet sponge bath inside the van itself.

However, the best shower option is probably to visit a truck stop and shower there. Professional drivers use these showers, because their trucks don't have facilities either. These showers aren't restricted to professional drivers, though; anybody can shower there for a fee of about $10. They're cleaned after each use, and they're scattered all over the country, so there's probably one located near you. Many public campgrounds also offer showers for a fee. With these options, staying clean on the road isn't really much of an obstacle, even if you decide to camp in your van.

Overnight parking. Finding a place to park your van overnight can be a challenge, especially if you happen to be staying in a large city. One favorite for RV'ers is the ever-present Wal-Mart parking lot, since most of these stores are open 24 hours a day and normally considered quite safe. A van can park there much less conspicuously than a big RV.

Two other favorites are National Forests and Bureau of Land Management (BLM) areas. The latter are more common in the mountain West and desert Southwest; the former can be found all over the country. Some travelers just stop at the nearest Interstate rest area and sleep there; check signs to see if this is allowed. In some places, parking overnight at rest areas may not be safe or legal, so use your best judgment.

One obvious choice would be to visit an official campground and reserve a space, just like an RV. Some state parks, lakes, and even beaches make great parking spots for camper-vans, but check local regulations, since some of these places close at sunset and don't allow camping.

Some vandwellers have made the art of *stealth parking* into a science. Stealth parking means choosing a parking spot to blend in with the surrounding neighborhood, so that no one knows you're sleeping inside. Often, this means parking in plain sight, such as at hospitals, near 24-hour restaurants or gyms, casinos, or even on a residential street between two houses. Stealth parking can be risky, as it often involves making use of private property. Obey parking signs and other regulations before you decide to stealth-park, and give preference to public property to avoid trespassing. When in doubt about parking on private property, such as at a hospital or grocery store, asking permission first is the best policy. There's no need to make a big issue of the situation; just say you need a place to park and get some sleep for a few hours before moving on in the morning.

Another option is a paid parking lot. Long-term parking at airports can be a cheap, no-frills way to park overnight. These lots are well-patrolled and usually very safe. Beware: restroom facilities may be non-existent, so plan ahead. Some park-and-ride facilities located on the edge of many cities have cars parked 24 hours a day, and a van wouldn't arouse any suspicions. Once again, get a feel for the area, and have a back-up plan in case your first parking choice doesn't work out.

Fuel Economy. One reason to camp in a van is to save money, but if it gets poor gas mileage, you won't be saving much. Cargo vans or older vehicles tend to get low mileage, sometimes as low as 10 to 12 mpg. Newer vans and smaller work vans often get as high as 25 mpg, which will stretch your travel budget a lot further.

If you're concerned about fuel economy, avoid towing trailers or other vehicles with your van. Travel as light as possible, too, since a completely loaded vehicle will burn more fuel than one with less gear.

Long-Term Van Camping

Over the last decade, a new class of van camping has gained in popularity – the permanent vandweller. Some folks have taken to living in their camper vans and Class B rigs for months – or even years – at a time. Some of them have been able to retire early or live on a much lower income than would have been possible had they maintained a more conventional home. By cutting out most housing expenses, they've learned to live well on much less than $1000 a month. This lifestyle certainly isn't for most of us, but it *can* be done. Plus, the thought of being on a never-ending road trip is interesting enough to make for some interesting reading. Several books about living permanently in RV's and vans are available for sale.

Part Three

Places to Go
and
Road Trip Ideas

15

Route 66

Route 66 is without a doubt the most written-about highway in history. Since its inception in the 1920's, Route 66 was the highway taken by millions of motorists heading west to California, either on vacation or looking for a new life out West. It was the highway taken in John Steinbeck's novel *The Grapes of Wrath*, in which the Joad family leaves the Dust Bowl of Oklahoma in search of a better life in California. In fact, you could say that *The Grapes of Wrath* was the first great American road trip novel.

Don't look for Route 66 on your road atlas, though, because you probably won't find it there. The highway started being signed as "U.S. Highway 66" around 1928, shortly before the beginning of the Great Depression. It was the route taken when traveling from much of the Midwest to southern California. During the Dust Bowl period, a combination of poor economic conditions, antiquated farming methods, and severe drought led many farmers and their families to abandon their homes in Oklahoma, Kansas, and other rural states in favor of the booming economy of California.

As the economy improved after World War II, Americans became increasingly mobile and the modern road trip was born. They took to the highway like never before, and Route 66 was *their* road, too. Vacationers headed to California, the Grand Canyon, St. Louis, and everywhere in between. The highway was immortalized in the song most famously sung by Nat King Cole, "Get Your Kicks on Route 66." And it was Route 66 that took them where they wanted to go. Traffic was so congested on the highway, in fact, that the road was eventually expanded, and much of it became a four-lane highway.

Route 66 was the road to a better life for many

Many nostalgic travelers feel that Route 66 lost much of its charm when it became a four-lane road, yet progress was inevitable. Four-lane roads became the standard, especially at the end of the 1950's when the Interstate Highway System started to replace many of the older two-lane routes. Sure, the new highways were faster, but they also bypassed many of the small towns that gave the older roads their personality and charm. Many of those small towns relied heavily on traffic from Route 66 to make ends meet. As the traffic from 66 dried up, so did many of the towns. Eventually, in 1985, the federal government decided the highway was unnecessary and removed the designation from the register of U.S. highways.

The Old Road's Revival

Over the past few decades, highway nostalgia has revived Route 66, attracting roadtrippers from around the world. Many bikers flock to the "Mother Road" on motorcycle, others make the drive in their cars to experience what it must have felt like to travel west decades ago. Most states along the route have made it easy to follow old Route 66, especially as it meanders through smaller towns along the way. Even where the interstate has completely superseded the old road, you'll find signs for "Historic Route 66" that guide motorists along the classic route.

As the song says, Route 66 "winds from Chicago to L.A." And yes, it is "more than 2000 miles all the way." If you're really interested in traveling "Main Street of America," as it's often called, visit the travel section of your local bookstore or library; you're likely to find several volumes documenting the trip. I won't even try to cover everything that's found along the route, as other books completely devoted to Route 66 do a much better job. In the pages that follow, I'll give a short summary that may whet your appetite for an exciting trip across the heart of America.

Following the Route

Thanks to several Route 66 historic societies around the country, it's pretty easy to follow the old highway. In fact, nearly 80% of the original route is still driveable, and a few sections still have the original pavement dating back to the 1930's. Traveling from Chicago, most of old 66 parallels Interstate 55 through Illinois. In the city of St. Louis, much of 66 follows surface streets until joining up with Interstate 44 through most of Missouri.

Near Joplin, Missouri, 66 diverts from I-44 for a few miles to take a brief jaunt through Kansas before rejoining the interstate in

Oklahoma. The Mother Road parallels I-44 all the way to Oklahoma City. From there all the way west to Barstow, California, Route 66 usually runs alongside or concurrent with Interstate 40. Beyond Barstow, follow Interstates 15 and 10 for most of the remainder of the route.

For more specific details on following the old road, look for a Route 66 guidebook at your local bookstore or library. Many of them include mile-by-mile maps documenting every town along the route and interesting sights to see along the way. Several documentaries have also been made about 66; you'll want to watch one or two before planning your trip.

Highlights of Route 66

Traveling south along I-55 between Chicago and St. Louis, you'll notice a narrow two-lane road paralleling the freeway most of the way; that's old Route 66. One small city along the road worth a visit is Springfield, Illinois. This is the site of the only home Abraham Lincoln ever owned. The house still stands, and tours are given several times daily. Lincoln's entire neighborhood is a pedestrian mall showcasing life in the mid-19th century.

The Abraham Lincoln Presidential Library and Museum is also here in Springfield. If you're into Civil War era history, this museum is a must-see. Also of interest is the Illinois state capitol, located downtown. Route 66 passes almost directly in front of the capitol, not to mention other historic sites in town.

Crossing into Missouri

About 100 miles south of Springfield is the bigger city of St. Louis. An interesting attraction on the north side of the city is the Chain of Rocks Bridge. Originally used as one of the alignments for

Route 66 around the city, today the bridge is closed to vehicle traffic and is used as a pedestrian and bicycle path.

About 45 minutes west of St. Louis, near the town of Eureka, Missouri, is Route 66 State Park. The park has a small visitor center and provides access to the nearby Meramec River. Probably the most interesting thing about the park, though, is that it's built on the site of the deserted town of Times Beach.

The Gateway Arch is
St. Louis' main landmark.

Considered a major environmental disaster, throughout the 1970's the streets of the little town were accidentally sprayed with oil contaminated with dioxin, a lethal chemical.

No one suspected much until dozens of area horses started dying. Shortly thereafter, it was discovered that practically the entire town had been contaminated with the chemical. When the Meramec River flooded in late 1982, dioxin contamination allegedly spread from the streets to the soil and homes of town residents.

In 1983, the federal government decided to buy out the entire town of Times Beach and evacuate the residents. By 1985, the town was shut down and completely sealed off. Only after contaminated soil was removed and incinerated did the state of Missouri decide to open the former town as a state park. Visitors say the abandoned streets in the ghost town are still visible.

Destination: St. Louis

Often called the "Gateway to the West", St. Louis, Missouri, has plenty to see and do. Well before crossing the Mississippi River into the city, the most familiar landmark is the 630-foot-high Gateway Arch. A visit to the Arch is the perfect way to begin your trip to St. Louis. Even if you don't take the five-minute elevator journey to the top, check out the museum underneath the monument commemorating America's westward expansion and the Lewis and Clark expedition, which began near here. Admission is free to the museum, and it costs about $10 to go to the top.

After visiting the Arch, head toward Forest Park – larger than New York's Central Park – where many of St. Louis' finest museums are found. The St. Louis Art Museum, Science Center, and Missouri History Museum are all located here. Each of these attractions require at least two hours to see well, and special exhibitions will require more. Best of all, admission is free to all three museums. The St. Louis Zoo, also located in the park, is normally considered one of the top twenty zoos in the country. Admission is also free.

About a mile southeast of Forest Park is the Missouri Botanical Garden. Admission is about $8 for adults and makes for a leisurely afternoon. The Garden was founded in 1859, making it the oldest continuously-operated botanical garden in the nation.

Sports fans won't be disappointed here, either. All the major stadiums are downtown. The baseball Cardinals play in Busch Stadium, the NFL's Rams play in the Edward Jones Dome, and the NHL's Blues play in the Scottrade Center – all located within a few blocks of each other.

Also located in the downtown area is St. Louis' historic Union Station. Although the old train station may no longer serve passengers, the property has been restored as a downtown shopping and dining center.

About an hour to the west of town along Interstate 44 is Meramec Caverns, thought to be Jesse James' hideout. Whether you're interested in roadside attractions, big-league sports, or fine museums, St. Louis has a little of everything.

Kansas and Oklahoma

Route 66 continues west paralleling Interstate 44 through most of Missouri. Near Joplin, State Route 66 takes over where the interstate leaves off. From here through Baxter Springs, Kansas, it's easy to follow the original highway, as signs marking "Historic Route 66" mark the old route quite well. Even though 66 passes through only about a dozen miles of Kansas, the Kansas section is one of the best-maintained and easiest to follow.

The state of Oklahoma has made a great effort of promoting the old road. Nearly every town along the route boasts "Historic 66" signs to make it easy to follow. Many of the original Route 66 travelers were from Oklahoma – like the Joad family in Steinbeck's novel – invoking the pejorative 'Okies' to refer to Midwestern migrants.

The Texas Panhandle: Cattle Country

Although Texas is the biggest state in the lower 48, Route 66 crosses its Panhandle for a mere 177 miles. Through most of Texas, the old road runs as a parallel frontage road to Interstate 40. Although the route through the state is relatively short, it's full of interesting sights, many of which are visible or easily accessible from the interstate. All the way through

Route 66 passes through the Texas panhandle

Texas, Route 66 is pancake flat; only a few rolling hills dot the landscape.

About an hour west of the Oklahoma state line, near the town of Groom, Texas, you'll see two roadside attractions that make many travelers break out their cameras: a giant cross on one side of the highway and a leaning water tower on the other. The cross welcomes visitors, but the water tower, labeled "Britten USA", lured travelers to a truck stop which shut down years ago.

Almost halfway through Texas is the city of Amarillo. Amarillo really is a cow town, and it's proud of that designation. The area around the city is one of the largest beef-producing regions in the United States, if not the entire world. You'll see cattle ranches all over this area.

One of the most popular places to sample some of the local beef is the Big Texan Steak Ranch, located right off Exit 74 in Amarillo. You've probably heard of this restaurant, famous for its free 72-ounce steak. If you can finish the steak dinner in one hour, it really is free. Of course, they offer smaller steaks for more normal appetites, but you have to pay for those.

Also in the Amarillo area is a famous site called the Cadillac ranch. Between Exits 60 and 62 along I-40 lie ten old Cadillacs, mostly dating from the 1950's, buried halfway, face down. It's supposed to be art, a testament to the golden age of the road and Route 66. The cars are covered in graffiti, and visitors are welcome to add more of their own. Although it's a somewhat offbeat place to visit, thousands of people flock to the 'ranch' every year to see it and add their own message.

An hour west of Amarillo, right on the Texas/New Mexico state line, lies one of the casualties of the interstate highway system – the town of Glenrio. Although Glenrio was founded when the railroad passed through well over a hundred years ago, it was Route 66 that made it prosper. Few people actually lived in the little town, but it was a convenient stopping point for travelers along the old highway.

Located exactly on the state line, Glenrio had restaurants, a filling station, and a motel. But with the construction of Interstate 40 a few hundred yards to the north, Glenrio didn't have enough pizzazz to lure motorists off the expressway. Today it's a ghost town; the buildings still stand, but most of them are abandoned. You'll be hard-pressed to find a single person in town. Glenrio is easy to find; take Exit 0 just over the Texas state line. After looking around at what's left of the town, you may agree that the exit number is eerily appropriate.

New Mexico: The Heart of the Southwest

Through much of New Mexico, Route 66 has been buried underneath the endless ribbons of interstate asphalt, as a testament to the millions of travelers from decades past who discovered the America of yesteryear along this same highway. Although the old road is gone, many of the

The Blue Swallow is one of many classic motels in Tucumcari

towns and sights are still there and worth a visit.

The town of Tucumcari, New Mexico, is located about halfway between Albuquerque and Amarillo. Although fewer than 10,000 people live here, the little town boasts well over 1000 motel rooms, most of which are locally owned. In fact, you could call Tucumcari the independent motel capital of America!

Some of these motels are the same ones that operated when Route 66 was in its heyday back in the 50's. Tucumcari's motels were most famous for their classic neon signs. At one time, the neon lights of Tucumcari welcomed well over 1,000 visitors every night as travelers stayed here on their way to places all over the nation. Even today, many businesses in town have survived. Of course, it helps that it's the only sizable town in a 60-mile radius. Thousands still spend the night in Tucumcari in the independent motels that dot Old Route 66 through town. In fact, for decades billboards advertising "Tucumcari Tonite!" have invited travelers to spend the night here.

Once you get past Tucumcari and near Albuquerque, you'll notice the terrain changing noticeably. Although the last thousand miles of road have been flat plains, with the exception of a few spots in Missouri, things change considerably about an hour east of New Mexico's largest city. The level land you saw from Illinois all the way through Texas now changes to rolling hills. And the rolling hills suddenly give way to rugged mountains, before descending into the valley where Albuquerque lies.

Not to worry, though, the grade is much easier than most other mountain highways in the country, and even the least powerful of cars will easily handle the mountains along Route 66 / Interstate 40 – one of the reasons the route was so popular back in the day.

Desert Country

After passing Albuquerque, the path through western New Mexico becomes rocky, dry, and relatively flat, except for a few hills. This is the terrain you'll see from here all the way to Flagstaff, as you enter the arid Colorado Plateau, where the high plains and mountains give way to desert. Along that same plateau, about a half hour before arriving at Flagstaff, you'll find an interesting formation at Exit 233. Simply called Meteor Crater, it's the place where a meteor – or technically, a meteorite – crashed into the earth's surface 50,000 years ago, leaving a hole nearly 600 feet deep and a mile across.

Meteor Crater, or the Barringer Crater as it's sometimes called, is located in the middle of an otherwise flat desert. Plan to spend two hours. During good weather, tour guides will lead visitors on a walk around the rim of the crater, narrating the history of the crater's discovery and exploration. If you look closely, you'll see where the crater was used for mining in the early part of the 20th century. In fact, the ruins of mining structures are still visible around the rim of the crater. Look for the wreckage of a plane that crashed in the crater back in 1964. And don't forget to ask about the astronaut training that NASA conducted in the crater, due to the similarity of the crater's base to the lunar surface.

About halfway through Arizona is the city of Flagstaff. The highest major town in the state, it's an interesting place to visit, if only for the unusual terrain. Flagstaff is located at over 7000 feet above sea level, and as a result, the city boasts alpine forest, is surrounded by mountains, and has a cooler climate different than most of Arizona. The unusually high elevation keeps winters cold and summers refreshingly cool, and as a result, Flagstaff is a popular summer resort destination.

Further west is the town of Williams, Arizona, often called the "Gateway to the Grand Canyon." Although Williams itself has only 3000 residents, it's a popular stopping point for passing motorists, even those not headed to the Grand Canyon, as it's the last town on the interstate for the next 100 miles.

One of Williams' main attractions is the steam locomotive found in town, and it's also the end of the line of the Grand Canyon Railway. Williams also claims to be the last town along Route 66 bypassed by the interstate. Due to fierce local opposition, Interstate 40 around town wasn't opened until 1984.

Heading west out of Williams, you find yourself in the vast unforgiving desert. Towns, restaurants, gas stations, and other services are few and far between until the small city of Kingman, more than 100 miles down the road. So savor the desert scenery, and take old Route 66 at Exit 139. It's more scenic than the interstate, and you'll pass a few more towns that the interstate left behind, like Seligman, Peach Springs, and Valentine. All used to be important stops along the dusty old road; when you pass through today, you can still visualize the thousands of motorists who passed through every day back in the heyday of Route 66.

At Kingman, much of the traffic turns north, heading to Las Vegas. Others head straight west, making the long, steep descent into Bullhead City and Laughlin, Nevada. Those following the old road head toward Oatman and over Sitgreaves Pass, traditionally considered one of the most treacherous parts of Route 66, with hairpin curves that gave this section the name 'Bloody 66.' Interstate 40 makes a sharp turn to the south, as it heads toward Needles, California, and eventually Barstow, where I-40 ends.

Route 66 near Oatman was called 'Bloody 66' for curves like these

From Barstow, continue on Interstate 15, heading south, to experience some of the scenic vistas for which southern California is famous. You'll pass Victorville and San Bernardino, then head west on Interstate 10. Eventually, you'll end up in Santa Monica, where the old road ended. Although the Interstate superseded 66 in most places, you'll still see signs pointing out the old alignment.

This brief description is really just a cursory glimpse at the endless sights along the Mother Road. True, Route 66 may not be the most scenic way to cross the country, but it is one of the most historic. And it's one of the best for catching a glimpse of past small-town glory, while enjoying a leisurely drive in the present.

After driving the route, you may want to come back and do it again. Plenty of Route 66 roadtrippers are repeat visitors, and when you make *your* visit to the old road, you'll see why it's called Main Street of America!

16

Road Trip Ideas for the Eastern U.S.A.

World class cities, rugged mountains, beautiful beaches, and the nation's best fall colors beckon road travelers to the Eastern United States every year. Although it's the most geographically compact part of the country, it's also the most diverse. Unsuspecting tourists are likely to be surprised at the vast treasures to be unearthed within 100 miles of the nation's most crowded cities. So explore these roads that offer some of the best of the East.

Vermont's Main Street – Brattleboro to Plymouth VT
65 miles – about 1 ½ hours

This route traverses some of the most spectacular fall foliage in the nation, passing through attractive small towns and villages along the way.

Start in Brattleboro, home to the New England Center for Circus Arts, where lessons are offered in performing circus tricks. They offer group workshops and private lessons.

In June, visit the quirky Strolling of the Heifers festival. A spoof on the Running of the Bulls in Pamplona, Spain, the festival celebrates local farms and livestock. And of course, there's a big parade where all the livestock stroll through the center of town. If you've brought your bike, they even have a Tour de Heifer cycling race.

Head north along Highway 30 to wind around the mountains and hills that make Vermont famous. Near the community of Townshend, check out the Scott Covered Bridge, the longest wooden bridge in Vermont. Built in 1870, at 277 feet long, it makes for a great photo spot.

The trails passing through Green Mountain National Forest offer some of the best views of fall foliage around. Here you'll find famous Mt. Snow, probably the most accessible ski area to most major cities in the northeast. By the way, Mt. Snow isn't actually named for snow; it's named for Reuben Snow, the man who owned the land around here years ago. Whether you prefer to golf or spend time taking the scenic 2 ½ mile chairlift ride to enjoy the fall colors, the scenery here is splendid.

Jamaica State Park, near the little town of Jamaica, boasts miles of hiking & biking trails, playgrounds, and camping facilities. Here you'll find raging white waters and winding rivers perfect for all types of outdoor recreation. The entrance fee is $3 per person.

From here, head north on State Route 100, often called Vermont's Main Street.   It's a near non-stop blend of exceptional fall colors, well-kept communities, dairy farms, white-steepled churches, with history and unforgettable scenery sprinkled throughout.

Near Plymouth is President Calvin Coolidge State Historic Site. This is the spot of Silent Cal's birthplace and boyhood home, as well as his gravesite.   Interestingly enough, this is also the place where Coolidge was sworn in as president upon the death of his predecessor Warren Harding. This park is pretty much preserved as it was back in the 1930s, and you can enjoy plenty of stunning views from different spots in the park.   Plan a visit to the Frog City Cheese factory, one of several spots here in the park where you can get a taste of rural life in Vermont.

Adirondack Northway – Albany NY to Plattsburgh NY
160 miles – about 3 hours

This route roughly follows Interstate 87 in upstate New York as it crosses cities, villages, mountains, and wilderness and cuts its way north to the Canadian border.

Start in Albany, a pleasant small city of about 100,000 residents. Visit the ornate New York state capitol building. Resembling a castle built in the classical and Romanesque styles, it took over 30 years to build, costing $25 million dollars by the time it was completed in 1899 (equivalent to half a billion dollars in today's money). Tours are offered of this magnificent building; there's even

New York's State Capitol is built in the Romanesque style

a special Hauntings Tour, for those interested in hearing the mysterious legends of the capitol.

The New York State Museum hosts everything from gems and fossils to fine art, historical displays, and film festivals. Ongoing exhibitions include displays of Adirondack wildlife, local archeological findings, and Metropolis Hall where the story of New York City's history is told. Look for the free carousel dating back over 100 years that kids of all ages can enjoy. Admission is free to the main exhibits, and the facility is open from 9:30 to 5:00 every day except Mondays and major holidays.

History buffs will want to visit the tomb of President Chester Arthur. Generally considered one of the better late 19th century presidents, he was raised here and worked as a teacher and school principal. After a successful term as president, he returned home to Albany where he died in 1886. He's buried in Albany Rural Cemetery, next to an American flag and a small staircase.

From Albany, head north on I-87, the Adirondack Northway, connecting New York's more populated south with the upstate forests and mountains in the Northeast quadrant of the state.

In the little town of Ballston Spa, the National Bottle Museum tells the story of the economy over a period of 150 years – with glass bottles. The museum is open most days from 10 to 4 with a collection of over 2000 bottles of all types, some of which date back to the 1830s.

The town of Saratoga Springs is the site of historic Canfield Casino, opened by local resident John Morrissey back in 1870. Saratoga Springs was a gambling center– the American Monte Carlo – long before places like Atlantic City or Las Vegas even became viable cities. Increasing anti-gambling sentiment caused the closure of the casino shortly after the turn of the century.

The little town of Wilton holds the cottage where President Ulysses Grant died. The former Union general and commander-in-chief had been diagnosed with throat cancer and arrived here in June of 1885. He spent his last five weeks resting and completing his memoirs, and today the cottage is much as it was when Grant was here over a century ago. The Grant Cottage is open during the summer months – Memorial Day through Columbus Day – and admission costs $5 for adults, $4 for children.

Heading north on I-87, especially past Glens Falls, the free-way leaves the confines of small town upstate New York and forges into the scenic wilderness that is Adirondack Park. At nearly 9400 square miles, Adirondack Park is the largest park in the lower 48 states. Located on the historic territory of the Mohawk First Nation of Native Americans, it's neither a national park nor a national forest, but rather a state park. It's larger than the entire state of New Hampshire, and larger than Yellowstone, Grand Canyon, Rocky Mountain, and Great Smoky National Parks combined. The Park occupies a full fifth of the land area in New York state.

Admission to the park is free. There are no gates to cross the park's boundary, often referred to as the 'blue line'. Here are found the ancient Adirondack Mountains, along with the less famous Alder Brook Mountains. The park has 3000 lakes and 30,000 miles of streams and rivers, not to mention 2000 miles of hiking trails. Look for diverse wildlife like moose, osprey, and the Canadian lynx.

North of the park is the small city of Plattsburgh, on the shores of Lake Champlain. This region has been inhabited continuously since the 17th century, when fur traders headed to Montreal took advantage of the area's geography and proximity to beautiful Lake Champlain.

Coastal Maine – Ellsworth to West Quoddy Head ME
120 miles – about 3 hours

The historic DownEast region of coastal Maine abounds with rich colonial culture. The French settled here as early as 1613, and the British followed soon thereafter. A series of wars were fought between the French & the British over a series of nearly 100 years, all for control of this valuable coastal land.

Start in the small town of Ellsworth, an excellent base for exploring the entire DownEast region. The first schooner was built here in 1773, called the Susan & Abigail. The city had some rough times, being ravaged by a flood in 1923, then by fire 10 years later, but they rebuilt bigger and better than ever.

Head south to the Bar Harbor area and Desert (prounounced: duh-ZURT) Island, home to Acadia National Park, the oldest National Park east of the Mississippi. It's the second largest island on the eastern seaboard of the US, with numerous summer colonies attracting visitors with natural beauty, seclusion, peace, and quiet.

Bar Harbor, population 5000, is the largest town on Desert Island. Many visitors arrive on cruise ships, visible in the harbor throughout the summer. Bar Harbor is also famous for long-distance cyclists, with hundreds each year participating in cross-country events that begin or end here, like the Atlantic Coast Bicycle Route, which runs from here to Key West, Florida – over 2,500 miles.

Once in Acadia Park, experience the dozens of miles of carriage roads – unpaved roads designed for the horse and carriage – many of which were bankrolled by John Rockefeller & Edsel Ford. About 55 miles of these primitive roads are open to pedestrians, hikers, cyclists, and other non-motorized traffic – the best way to enjoy the park.

Acadia Park's Bar Island at low tide

Back in town, tours take visitors to see lobster, whales, seals, puffins, lighthouses, and seabirds. Bar Island is close by, and at low tide the sand is exposed just enough so that you can walk from town to the island to enjoy some shelling. Others just walk across the sandbar for the experience of seeing what lies underneath the water.

The main highway circles all the way around Desert Island and heads back to the mainland, where you can rejoin U.S. 1 and keep heading east. The highway is never more than a few miles from the coast. You'll cross several scenic rivers and pass countless quaint little towns.

When you can't drive any farther east, you've arrived at West Quoddy Head, the easternmost point in the United States. Here, at the cusp of Canada's Atlantic Provinces, just barely in America, you'll hear the ocean crashing against rocks in the distance. The most famous landmark here is the West Quoddy Head Lighthouse, a beacon for ships from afar, and a historic reminder of times past. Here, you're actually closer to Ireland than to Los Angeles. If you're looking for salt-filled coastal air, unique natural beauty, and maybe even some solitude, coastal Maine makes for an excellent choice.

Civil War History – Harpers Ferry WV to Frederick MD
50 miles – about 1 ¼ hours

This short drive highlights the Maryland, West Virginia, and Virginia tri-state area and the Civil War history in the area.

Begin in the little town of Harpers Ferry, West Virginia, within easy access of Interstates 70, 81, and U.S. Highway 340. This community of about 300 residents is the easternmost settlement in West Virginia, where the Shenandoah and Potomac rivers converge. This attractive village is wedged between mountains and rivers, giving it a strategic location during the Civil War era. A military arsenal was located here, and on October 16th, 1859, radical anti-slavery activist John Brown and his 21 men staged a raid. After a three-day standoff, most of his men were killed, and Brown was captured. He was soon tried for treason against the state of Virginia, convicted, and publicly hanged.

During the Civil War, control of Harpers Ferry changed hands eight times. The biggest battle held here took place from the 13th to the 15th of September, 1862, when the South captured the town and held it for almost two years.

From here, follow Highway 230 north to Shepherdstown, where yet another key battle was fought, the bloodiest ever fought on West Virginia soil. Many today view it as a turning point in the Civil War. Just two days after Shepherdstown, President Abraham Lincoln issued the Emancipation Proclamation. Visit the well-preserved battlefield and relive the history at the small but interesting Shepherdstown Museum.

From here, cross the Potomac River driving east into Maryland, continuing onto State Route 34. Just a few miles past the river, the town of Sharpsburg is where the bloodiest battle of the Civil War occurred. Just days after Harpers Ferry and a few days before Shepherdstown, the Battle of Antietam on September 17th,

1862, marked the most tragic single day of fighting, with nearly 23,000 total dead, missing, or wounded.

You can experience the battlefield via an 8.5-mile driving tour with 11 stops. Experience Antietam National Cemetery, a field hospital museum, the visitor center, and stone-arched Burnside's Bridge which allowed troops to cross Antietam Creek during battle. It's a somber, yet interesting place to visit, and a third of a million visitors stop here every year.

Down the road at Crystal Grottoes Caverns, you'll find more geologic formations per square foot than any other cave in the country. The cave is maintained in the most natural state possible, so you can experience the stalactites, stalagmites, helectites, flowstones, and bacon rinds (as they're called) as they were meant to be seen. Admission costs $20 for adults, and you can expect a fascinating 40-minute tour of the cave featuring the various creatively-named rooms, such as Fairyland (with light blue formations), the Blanket Room, and the Golden Lake. The cave is open from 11 – 4 weekends only during the winter months, and from 10 – 5 every day April through November.

At Boonsboro, turn right onto U.S. 40 Alternate – also known as the Historic National Road. One historic monument follows another until we reach Frederick. Just 50 miles from Washington, the National Museum of Civil War Medicine chronicles how wounded soldiers were treated and cared for in such difficult circumstances – as well as the medical advances that helped many of them survive.

From here, you're within an easy drive of our nation's capital Washington DC, as well as Baltimore or any number of cities on the east coast.

Overseas Highway – Florida City FL to Key West FL
130 miles – about 4 hours

One of America's favorite road trips is U.S. Route 1 through the Florida Keys. This route starts south of Miami in Florida City and winds its way across the Keys over bridges and causeways that, in themselves, are feats of engineering. Along the way, you'll spot interesting wildlife, parks, restaurants, quaint shops, places to party, and plenty of water.

About 12 miles outside of Florida City, as you skirt the edge of the Everglades, you also leave the U.S. mainland and enter the Florida Keys. Although the road is quite modern, it was actually placed on the bed of the former Overseas Railroad. After the railroad was destroyed during a hurricane in 1935, the right-of-way was sold to the state for $640,000. Since then, millions of tourists have travelled this way for vacationing, sightseeing, and some in search of the laid-back island lifestyle.

Although most people traveling this road are headed to Key West, two other important towns along the way are Key Largo and Islamorada. The more scenic part of the route starts at Marathon, though. At the south edge of Marathon, you'll come upon Seven Mile Bridge, one of the most photographed bridges in the world. Pull into the parking lot before you drive onto the bridge and walk around a bit. You might see iguanas in the parking lot, sharks in the water, and maybe even a giant ray.

Key West is a mere 90 miles from Cuba

Farther down the highway, near Big Pine Key, you'll enter the National Key Deer Refuge, where you'll have a good chance of seeing the tiny Key Deer. They average 2 1/2 feet tall, and they're found in abundance throughout the refuge.

When you finally get to Key West, you'll be closer to Havana than to Miami. In fact, on a clear night, you can see the lights of Cuba from the waterfront. The Overseas Highway is a slow-going highway, and although the speed limit on most of it is 45 mph, expect to go much slower when there's traffic. Motorhomes and lots of leisure travellers clog the highway at times, so it's no use getting in a hurry. Allow at least four hours to savor the ocean breeze, natural beauty, and wildlife along the way. And don't forget to bring your camera on this trip – one of the most unique drives in America!

The Grand Strand – Myrtle Beach SC to Murrells Inlet SC
25 miles – about 1 hour

For beach enthusiasts, take a journey down to the famous Grand Strand of coastal South Carolina, most famous for the beach resort town of Myrtle Beach.

To get there, head down U.S. Highway 17; Myrtle Beach and the surrounding coastal communities are located just south of the North Carolina state line. The drive along U.S. 17 is much more laid back and scenic than busy Interstate 95, roughly 50 miles to the west. This route is never more than a couple miles from the ocean; much of the time, you're within direct view of the beach.

Myrtle Beach is a tourist town, and aside from hotels, restaurants, and beachside businesses, there's a huge golf industry here, too. This is also the miniature golf capital of the East Coast; one local favorite is Captain Hook's Adventure Golf, a Peter Pan themed course offering an afternoon of fun for about $10 a person.

Check out the award-winning Carolina Opry, a two-hour show featuring country music, comedy, and dancing. If you're not into country music, they have other shows too, including a revue of popular music from the 60s and 70s. Adult prices start at about $33 each.

Don't miss out on the Oceanfront Boardwalk. Completed in 2010, the 1 ¼ mile long promenade runs from 14th Avenue down to 2nd Avenue, offering a picture-perfect view of the beach, with dozens of restaurants and shops for every taste. During the summer, the boardwalk plays host to countless events and festivals, plus live music acts. National Geographic has rated it the third best boardwalk in the nation.

Nearby is the Skywheel, a 200-foot ferris wheel right on the oceanfront. Completed in 2011, the Skywheel offers a unique view of the Atlantic Ocean. Tickets cost $13 for adults and $9 for kids. Each ride gives you three revolutions around the wheel, which may not sound like much – but this is one big ferris wheel – you'll be in motion for 12 minutes.

Kids will enjoy Family Kingdom Amusement Park. Admission to the park is free – patrons pay as they ride. With over 30 rides, including roller coasters, bumper cars, go carts, and the ever-popular Log Flume, you'll also want to enjoy the free entertainment while you're there, like stilt walkers, jugglers, clowns, and magicians.

Off the beaten path, Myrtle Beach State Park (Admission $5 for adults, $3 for kids) will wisk you away to a more tranquil part of the beach. Fish from the pier, walk along the beach, or sit on the oceanfront and savor the

The resort area at Myrtle Beach

waves as they crash upon the shore in front of you.

About 10 miles to the south of Myrtle Beach lies the little fishing village of Murrells Inlet. This town of 9000 is most famous for its fresh-caught seafood. Known as the "Seafood Capital of South Carolina," Murrels Inlet offers fishing cruises from the marina that will give you the chance to catch your own. Or, if you prefer, you can wade into the water and find clams, crabs, or oysters on your own. Of course, you can just enjoy one of the dozens of seafood restaurants that beckon with mouth-watering lunches fresh from the ocean.

Florida's Hwy A1A – St. Augustine to Daytona Beach
84 miles – about 2 hours

Travel rustic two-lane highway A1A as it meanders down Florida's Atlantic coast. The breathtaking 84 miles between St. Augustine and Canaveral National Seashore, to the south of Daytona Beach offers some of the most stunning ocean views per mile along Florida's Atlantic coast.

Begin in historic St. Augustine, 40 miles south of Jacksonville. St. Augustine, capital of the Florida Territory until 1824, claims to be the oldest town established by Europeans in America, founded by a Spanish admiral back in 1565. Ponce de León explored the area

that is now St. Augustine as early as 1513 as he allegedly searched for the fabled Fountain of Youth.

Visit Fountain of Youth park in St. Augustine, where Ponce landed in the early 16th

The view of the coast from Florida's
Highway A1A

century. Drink out of the supposed Fountain of Youth. Enjoy cannon demonstrations, a planetarium, discovery globe, and knowledgeable guides that help keep the legend alive. Admission is $12.00.

Awe-inspiring Castillo de San Marcos, also in town, is operated by the National Park Service. This giant fort was built during the 1670's by Spanish conquistadors. Today the Castillo is the oldest masonry fort in the United States, located about 2 miles from the mouth of the Matanzas River.

While in St. Augustine, don't miss the kitschy roadworthy attractions like the Oldest Wooden Schoolhouse, Ripley's Believe It or Not museum, and St. Augustine Alligator Farm.

Halfway between St. Augustine and Daytona, you'll spot the ocean from the highway for the first time, and about 2 miles after that, you'll arrive at Marineland Dolphin Adventure. Here you'll see dolphins in their 'oceanarium'. General admission is affordable at $10 for adults, $6 for kids, but if you'd like to swim with the dolphins, pet them, feed them, or even train them for a day, those options are available as add-ons.

South of Palm Coast, Highway A1A becomes one of the most picturesque beach roads in the country, paralleling the Atlantic Ocean with an unobstructed view of the shore for nearly 18 miles. At any time, you're no more than a couple hundred yards from the water, with dozens of access points to pull off the road and enjoy a day on the beach.

Farther south, Daytona Beach has built itself as a beach city and world-renowned Spring Break destination. Highway A1A runs beachside as Atlantic Avenue, and its 'Strip' boasts hotels, restaurants, and bars as far as the eye can see.

For a more subdued beach scene, try Canaveral National Seashore. Sharing its name with Cape Canaveral, which incidentally, is located just a few miles to the south, this pristine shoreline offers

quiet walks on the beach, majestic sunrises, and an isolated environment that's largely unchanged from the way the Florida coast
was when the conquistadors landed here over 500 years ago.

17

Road Trip Ideas for the Midwest

Don't call it the Rust Belt. The American Midwest keeps inventing itself, with some of the most iconic road trip stops just a short journey away. The land here may be flat, but it's rarely boring if you're willing to seek out the hidden treasures here. Here you'll find robust cities, the tranquil beauty of farmers' fields, majestic waters, and tales of generations past that settled here – or left these lands – in search of a better life. The Midwest has a little of everything.

The Great River Road – St. Louis MO to Tiptonville TN
220 miles – about 5 hours

The Great River Road winds its way over 2000 miles through ten states near the shores of the Mississippi River. Starting its

Chester, Illinois is the original
home of Popeye

journey in northern Minnesota and ending at the Gulf of Mexico nearly 100 miles south of New Orleans, Louisiana, the 'Big Muddy' evokes images of riverboats, wooded forest, and even Huck Finn. This route focuses on the small towns that dot the riverfront between St. Louis and Memphis.

Heading south from St. Louis on the Illinois side of the river, follow State Highway 3. Stop in Chester, 60 miles south of St. Louis. This is the home of Popeye. Elzie Segar, born in Chester, created the original Popeye cartoon and the comic strip *Thimble Theatre.* The community park houses a 6-foot statue of Popeye, and other Popeye characters have been getting their own statues around town. True Popeye fans should head to Chester during September for the annual Popeye Picnic on the river.

South of Chester on Route 3, the highway winds past panoramic views of the river before turning east. Your last stop in Illinois is the hauntingly interesting town of Cairo. Named after the city in Egypt but pronounced KAY-ro, it was once one of the largest towns in Illinois, and arguably one of its most important. Located at the confluence of the Mississippi and Ohio Rivers, Cairo was an important strategic point during the Civil War. Giant 19th century homes and historic architecture abound here. One of the highlights is Magnolia Manor, a Victorian-era historic home and museum showing off the history of the town. Another noteworthy stop is Customs House Museum, a fine example of period architecture. Fort Defiance Park is located where the two rivers converge, and it's a nice spot to watch barges pass by as they head to the Gulf of Mexico. Sadly, most of Cairo is run-down and in a sorry state of disrepair. Apart from the worthy Shemwell's Barbecue, you'll find few tourist services or restaurants.

Cross the Ohio River and stay just to the east of the Mississippi. The Kentucky side of the river holds Wickliffe Mounds, a reminder of ancient peoples that once called this vast area home. At Bardwell, turn right onto Highway 123 and check out Columbus-Belmont State Park. An attractive park with camping, picnic areas, and even a museum, check out the historic earthworks made during the Civil War, where soldiers tunneled out large pathways as a protection from opposing enemy fire from across the river.

Just past the Tennessee state line lies another body of water with quite a story. Reelfoot Lake – most of which is actually a shallow swamp – was formed by the powerful earthquakes that shook this region over 200 years ago. Eyewitnesses at the time said that the Mississippi flowed backwards for nearly an entire day, filling the low-lying bottoms with enough water to change the landforms of the entire area. Reelfoot is the biggest natural lake in Tennessee, and it's famous for fishing.

The Lake Huron Circle – Port Huron MI to Port Austin MI
90 miles – about 2 hours

This drive follows Michigan's scenic Lake Huron Circle Tour, following state highway 25 in search of relaxation, great food, and breathtaking scenery.

This drive begins near the U.S./Canadian border at Port Huron. The Blue Water Bridge was built in 1938 and is one of the busiest crossings between the United States and Canada. Over a mile long, it's easily one of the most photographed bridges in Michigan, and likely one of the most scenic, especially at night.

Ten miles north of Port Huron is Lakeport State Park, with camping right on the shores of Lake Huron, spectacular scenery right along the rocky beach, all surrounded by rustic woods. Lakeport is known for its sandbars and the ease with which you can take a walk along the shore. You'll want to have your camera ready to snap a picture of the beautiful blue-green water.

Farther up the road, the small town of Lexington comes to life during summer tourist season. Wine connoisseurs will want to visit Old Town Hall Winery and Lexington Brewing Company; both are located along historic Main Street. Friday nights during summer, enjoy the free live outdoor music.

Heading north along the lakefront, stop in Harbor Beach, located in the world's largest man-made freshwater harbor and home to historic Harbor Beach Lighthouse. Built in 1885, it warned – and welcomed – approaching freighters as they neared the rocky shore. Today, the lighthouse has been restored to its old-style grandeur, and for $20, you'll get to take a one-mile boat ride out to the light, a tour inside the structure itself, plus you'll gain admission to the Grice Museum, a small museum dedicated to local history.

For a glimpse of 19th century Michigan life, don't miss Huron City Museums, a small community of restored buildings from the 1880s. Stop in and peruse the village, which includes the Victorian-style House of Seven Gables, church, restored general store, community inn, as well as a log cabin built in 1837.

Up the highway in Port Austin, sample some local cuisine at *The Bank 1884*, located in – what else? – a restored bank building from 1884. Another option is *The Farm Restaurant*, known for comfort food with a local touch.

Just past town is picturesque Port Crescent State Park, offering beautiful private beaches, hiking paths, a playground for the kids, and camping. The park is famous for its breathtaking sunsets. Few other places in the Eastern United States have as beautiful a sunset.

Midland Trail – Charleston to White Sulphur Springs WV
115 miles – about 2 ½ hours

This unique mountain road trip takes a detour from the bustling interstate and heads east on scenic U.S. Highway 60 through West Virginia's Midland Trail.

Although U.S. 60 is a lot more curvy and mountainous than the freeway – not to mention slower – the trip is much more satisfying than taking the interstate. The Midland Trail swings past more roadside attractions, natural wonders, plus the highway itself is more authentic WV, wild, rugged, and mountainous.

This highway was founded in 1790 when then-President George Washington first ordered the Midland Trail cleared. Stagecoaches & overland travelers made use of the Trail on into the 19th century, and it was a major route through the Civil War era.

Start your tour in Charleston, West Virginia's capital. Check out the vibrant downtown; most top attractions are centered right near the Capitol building.

Head over to the handsome state capitol building and the West Virginia State Museum. Admission is free, and it's one of the nation's best museums dedicated to the history, life, and culture of Appalachia, decade by decade.

The gold-covered dome across the lawn is the state capitol building. At just over 290 ft, it's the tallest building in West Virginia. Check out the nearby

West Virginia's state capitol is the tallest building in the state

Clay Center for the Arts & Sciences or just take a stroll along the Kanahwa River.

Heading east on U.S. 60, the humble hills quickly become more rugged mountains, and the road gets curvier – and hillier. About 30 miles from Charleston, you'll find yourself at Kanawha Falls, a picturesque cascading waterfall with easy access to the trail.

A few miles to the east, the Mystery Hole is a spot where they claim the Laws of Gravity are suspended – up is down and balls roll uphill. If you like optical illusions, stop in and see for yourself. Guided tours last about 20 minutes and cost $6.50 for adults.

At the village of Hico turn about 5 miles south, to the New River Gorge Bridge – a steel arch bridge that hovers 876 ft above the breathtaking New River. It's the 5th highest bridge in the world, and one of the most scenic. The bridge was opened in 1977, and today the bridge has become one of the most photographed sites in the state, and even made its way onto the back of the West Virginia state quarter. Cross the bridge around sunrise, and you may very well find yourself driving *over* the cloud line, a sight you won't soon forget.

The New River Gorge Bridge hovers nearly 900 feet above the river below

Back on the Midland Trail, you'll continue motoring over mountains and around countless curves, a seemingly endless hilly road, until you get to the town of Lewisburg. This little town of 4000 hosts the West Virginia State Fair every summer. Lewisburg may be best known for its cave formations. Lost World Caverns is the most famous and offers 45-minute guided tours

- $12 for adults, $6 for kids. If you're a well-heeled spelunker and want something a little more intense, try the 4-hour Wild Cave Tour for $70, where you'll see places in the cave few others get to experience. You do have to make reservations ahead of time, and you *will* get mud-soaked. But the granddaddy of cave tours will let you experience unusual formations such as the Drain, the Squeeze Box, and the Birth Canal.

Farther east is the town of White Sulphur Springs, home of the famous Greenbrier Resort. Surrounded by the Allegheny Mountains, the 700-room resort was founded in 1778, boasting the world's only five-star mineral spa, whitewater rafting, a casino, over 3 dozen retail shops, and a golf course.

Much of the mystique at the Greenbrier involves the formerly top-secret government bunker located here. Designed to withstand a nuclear blast, the underground compound was designed as a post-apocalyptic national capital in the event Washington DC were destroyed by nuclear attack. The bunker's existence was declassified in the 1990's, and today you can tour the formerly-secret compound for $30.

From the weird to the wild and wonderful, this motor route is a little bit different, a bit off the beaten path, but well worth every mile.

Great Northern – Bemidji MN to Grand Rapids MN
70 miles – 1 ½ hours

For your next summer road trip, consider a trip up north to Minnesota, where average high temperatures usually hover a little bit below 80°, even in the hottest months. Summer nights almost always drop into the 50s, making it one of the most comfortable summer road trip destinations.

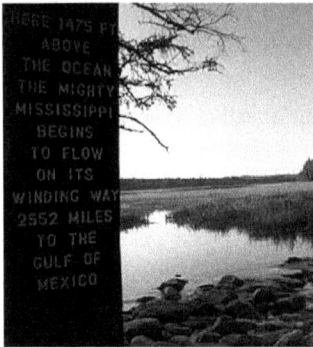

The headwaters of the mighty Mississippi River

Start in Bemidji, a pleasant community and the biggest town within a 50-mile radius. Don't miss the larger-than-life size statues of Paul Bunyan and Babe the Blue Ox. Both date back to 1937 and have greeted visitors every summer at tourist season.

Also here is Paul Bunyan's Animal Land, a petting zoo with 100 animals representing every continent, including lions, tigers, bears, deer, porcupines, and several exotic birds. Admission is $7 for teenagers and adults, $6 for kids 3-12. They're open from 10-6 every day during the summer tourist season.

A detour about 40 minutes to the south takes you to Itasca State Park and the headwaters of the mighty Mississippi River. From the visitor center, you can talk an easy walk to the location where the Big Muddy begins its 2,500-mile journey to the Gulf of Mexico. And if you're in the mood, you can kick off your shoes and walk across the river. You'll be able to tell your friends back home that you walked across the Mississippi River – and lived to tell the story!

Back on U.S. 2, picturesque Chippewa National Forest covers two-thirds of a million acres with plentiful camping, fishing, bird-watching, and hiking opportunities. Plenty of bald eagles call this forest home; here you'll find one of the highest density of the National Bird in the country.

Logging has always been a huge industry in Minnesota, but due to a mapping error back in the 1880s, a 140-acre swath of forest was never cleared here. These "Lost Forty" hold some of the oldest trees in Minnesota, some nearly 400 years old. A walk through the Lost Forty is a treat year round, but especially comfortable in the late summer and early fall.

The town of Grand Rapids holds the Forest History Center, a re-creation of a logging town from the turn of the century. See how blacksmiths, cooks, and other residents functioned back then.

Most tourist activities around here are only open during the summer, but one year-round family attraction is the Children's Discovery Museum in Grand Rapids. Complete with a dinosaur exhibit, maze, model train village, antique dolls, and even a talking tree, it's a treat for the whole family. Admission is $7.

Grand Rapids is also the birthplace of Judy Garland. You can tour her childhood home, as well as peruse the gift shop filled with enough Wizard of Oz memorabilia to satisfy even the biggest fan. Admission is $7.

The next time you're headed north, or driving across the country, consider taking U.S. 2, the "Cooler Route" as they used to call it in the days before car air-conditioning, a route with countless treasures.

Badlands and Black Hills – Philip SD to Keystone SD
85 miles – 1 ½ hours

This year, over 3 million people will head for Mount Rushmore, that granite mountain in South Dakota with the images of four American presidents carved into its side. Although Mount Rushmore is quite a sight unto itself, you won't be disappointed at the scenic beauty and attractions nearby.

This route begins as we drive from the east on I-90. By the time you get to Exit 110 you've likely driven across this state for over 300 miles and are ready for a break. Here in Wall, South Dakota, you'll find the famous Wall Drug.

Wall Drug opened in the early 1930's as a little store offering free ice water to weary travelers. Although that tradition hasn't changed, the store is now a huge 76,000-square-foot emporium with restaurants, souvenirs, and even a small amusement park for the kids. You'll see a replica of an old West town, a Tyrannosaurus Rex, and more than a few stuffed renditions of the mythical Jackalope – half jackrabbit, half antelope. They still sell cups of coffee for a nickel, and their cinnamon rolls are famous.

Wall is also the western gateway to Badlands National Park. Don't miss the 35-mile Loop Road that takes you through the best of this geologic wonder. Often ranked as one of the world's best drives, you'll see the eroded spires, buttes, and ravines that give an otherworldly ambience to this park. With plenty of pull-offs and scenic vistas, this is one of the most satisfying park roads out there. Look for the wildlife too; you're likely to find bighorn sheep, deer, bison, and prairie dogs as you drive the loop. For a special treat, visit the road early in the morning, right around sunrise, as the morning dawn against the rock formations form a rich palette of colors that make for an unforgettable view.

The otherworldly formations at Badlands National Park

For a much different type of tourist attraction, take Exit 131 and tour Minuteman Missile National Historic Site. For nearly the entire Cold War, the nuclear missiles held here had the power to destroy civilization as we know it. Now, free tours are available every day except Tuesday, and they serve as a thought-provoking reminder of that era in history.

West of Wall and the Badlands is Rapid City. This small city of 70,000 is the gateway to Mount Rushmore. If you're traveling with kids, don't miss Reptile Gardens, where there are more species of poisonous reptiles than any other park in the world. This is the place to see snake handlers and lizards from around the world. An educational experience for visitors of all ages, admission costs $16 for adults, and $11 for kids.

In Rapid City's historic downtown, statues of different presidents are found at just about every corner. Check out the quaint shops, restaurants, and outlets featuring Native American art and jewelry. Rapid City is also home to the South Dakota Air and Space Museum. Admission is free, and you'll find over 30 different aircraft on display, including various fighter planes. You can even travel down into a Cold War-era missile silo.

Rapid City is the gateway to Black Hills National Forest. Covering over 1 ¼ million acres, the name is derived from the extremely dark color of the ponderosa pine forests here. Spearfish Canyon Scenic Byway forms a breathtaking 20-mile loop through the bottom of Spearfish Canyon, where you'll be greeted by waterfalls, mountain vistas, trout-filled streams, limestone cliffs, and countless wildlife.

Another driving tour worth taking is the Peter Norbeck National Scenic Byway. This 68-mile byway begins near Keystone. With more twists and curves than the Spearfish Canyon trail and plenty of tunnels bored through the hills, it was the same route Lewis & Clark passed on their monumental voyage west over 200 years ago. This byway also offers a spectacular view of Harney Peak, which at 7242 ft, is the highest mountain in America east of the Rockies – impressive enough that the Lakota Native Americans believed it was the center of the world. Along the way, don't miss Peter Norbeck Turnout, where you can enjoy a breathtaking view of Mt. Rushmore.

Admission to Mt. Rushmore is free, but parking costs $11 per car. The best views of the sculpted monument are had in the evening, as the sun sets over the massive granite sculpture. During the summer months, stay for the nightly lighting ceremony which starts at 9 p.m. and lasts for 30 minutes.

Ohio's Lincoln Hwy – E. Liverpool OH to Mansfield OH
115 miles – about 2 ½ hours

The Lincoln Highway was first proposed in 1912 by the inventor of the automobile headlight, Carl Fisher. In time, this historic auto trail would stretch over 3000 miles from Times Square in New York to Lincoln Park in San Francisco, passing through 14 states at one time or another. This road trip highlights the 115-mile stretch of the highway extending across Eastern Ohio.

Over the years, the Ohio section of the Lincoln Highway evolved from a dirt road to a gravel, macadam, and even brick highway in later years. Eventually, progress and concrete won out, and much of the original Lincoln Highway through the Buckeye State has been covered by four-lane U.S. Highway 30. Although the route looks much different than it did 50 or 100 years ago, most of it is easy to follow and well-signed, passing through dozens of little towns and villages.

The Lincoln Hwy enters Ohio from the east at East Liverpool, the Pottery Capital of the USA. Visit the Museum of Ceramics, located downtown in the old Post Office, showcasing thousands of pieces produced near here over the past 150 years.

Farther west in Hanoverton, check out historic Plymouth Street, where most buildings date back to the mid-1800s, like the Spread Eagle Tavern and Inn, where guests dine surrounded by antiques in a building dating back to 1837.

The original brick-paved Lincoln Highway near Robertsville, Ohio

West of Hanoverton, the highway strays away from the Appalachian foothills and into more level terrain. In the little town of Minerva, you'll find its restored filling station that dates back to around 1910, which actually predates the Lincoln Hwy by a couple of years.

In Robertsville, look for original Lincoln Highway alignments that were paved with brick. The best section is Baywood Street, just outside of town, with 2.4 continuous miles of original brick paving that dates back to 1919. A definite must-see, if only to experience what it was like to drive the original Lincoln Highway as it was a century ago.

Canton is a bustling town most famous as the birthplace of professional football. The Pro Football Hall of Fame is located here; tickets are $22 for adults and $16 for kids 12 and under. Canton is also the home of former President William McKinley and the McKinley Presidential Library and Museum. Canton's Classic Car Museum, located downtown in a building that used to be a Ford-Lincoln dealership, holds dozens of cars that date back to the golden age of the Lincoln Highway, some as early as 1901. Admission to the car museum is $7.50 for adults and $5 for kids under 18.

The 30-mile stretch between Wooster and Mansfield offers some of the most sweeping scenic vistas in all of Ohio. You'll revel in mile after mile of rolling hills and beautiful views. In Mansfield, check out Richland Carrousel Park; it opened in 1991 with the first new, hand-carved carousel built in the United States in over 60 years. Rides for the kids cost about a dollar, and it offers plenty of fun and memories for kids of all ages.

If you've seen the movie Shawshank Redemption, based on the Stephen King novel, you might want to take a drive down the Shawshank Trail, highlighting 14 of the sites in the Mansfield area where filming of the movie took place.

The Lincoln Highway offers miles of historic sites, activities, and scenic vistas everyone can enjoy. After this drive, you'll agree that some of the most satisfying miles of the Lincoln Highway are in Eastern Ohio.

Kansas High Plains – Oakley to Liberal Kansas
150 miles – about 2 ½ hours

If you ever thought Kansas is boring, then get off the interstate and explore the state's beautiful two-lane roads. This north-south route follows U.S. 83 between Oakley and the Oklahoma border, a trip of about 150 miles.

There are no cities along this highway – only small towns. And many of the roadside stops are quirky, bizarre, and sometimes just downright weird. Others will seem completely alien in these flat Great Plains, but that just makes the trip that much more worthwhile.

Driving south from Interstate 70, our first stop is the little town of Oakley, home of the Fick Fossil & History Museum. A small family operation, the Fick Museum showcases over 10,000 shark teeth as well as hundreds of other fossils and historical artifacts highlighting the rich heritage of the High Plains. Admission is free.

Leaving Oakley, you'll find yourself on the arrow-straight and pancake-flat highway 83. Take some time to savor the open spaces and wide expanses that surround you – one of the joys of this route is the lack of traffic. After about 20 miles, you'll see a sign for Monument Rocks. Take this little detour down a dozen miles on gravel roads.

At the end you'll see one of the most unusual sights in Kansas – chalk pyramids, over 70 feet tall, carved naturally from limestone bedrock over thousands and thousands of years. A surreal sight amid the flat land surrounding, it's a formation that might look more at home in Utah or Nevada. Due to its isolation, there are no services, and you may very well be the only human visitors when you stop.

Monument Rocks, the 'Stonehenge of Kansas'

Back on the relatively comfortable confines of Route 83, keep going south. About 10 miles north of Scott City, turn off to the west, over to the El Quartelejo ruins. This site holds the remains of the northernmost Indian pueblo, likely dating back to the 1690's when some of the Pueblo from New Mexico fled to the north, trying to escape Spanish domination. Several fled as far north as Kansas, and the ruins of their community are on display in Lake Scott State

Park. If you decide to spend the night here, there's a campground open during the summer months, and a small beach for swimming.

On down Route 83, Garden City is the largest town along our route. Stop at Lee Richardson Zoo, the largest zoo in western Kansas; it highlights both native animals as well as animals from around the world, such as elephants, kangaroos, flamingos, and lions.

The most refreshing place in town, though, is the municipal pool. Hand-dug back in the 1920's, and later enlarged during the Great Depression, Garden City's public pool was then advertised as the World's Largest Free, Outdoor, Municipal Concrete Swimming Pool. Today, the 'Big Pool' is larger than a football field and has 50-meter Olympic swimming lanes, and well as 3 water slides and a children's pool. It can easily accommodate over 2000 guests. Admission to the pool is $1.

Farther south, near the Oklahoma state line, lies the town of Liberal. As the story goes, one of the town's founders had a policy of offering free water to tired travelers back in the 1870s. Supposedly, several of the recipients of that hospitality responded by saying "That's mighty liberal of you." And so the name stuck.

Liberal is the home of Dorothy from *The Wizard of Oz*. Pay a visit to "Land of Oz" park, also called "Dorothy's House", where you can peruse memorabilia and props from the original movie set. Tour the 'Yellow Brick Road' and have your picture taken next to life-size statues of characters from the movie.

Liberal is also home to the Mid-America Air Museum. This is one of the largest flight museums in the central United States; over 100 aircraft are on display.

From Liberal, you're only 2 miles from Oklahoma, 40 miles from Texas, 70 miles from Colorado, and 130 miles from NM. Although the drive from Oakley to Liberal can be driven easily in 3 hours, there are enough unique places to enjoy for days here in the High Plains of Kansas.

Nebraska Treasures – Omaha to Kearney NE
180 miles – about 3 hours

This route highlights the interesting and unusual things to see as you drive along I-80 through the plains of Nebraska.

Starting in Omaha, known for one of the nation's best zoos and for its steaks, downtown you'll see the modern urban art sculpture often called "Geese Flying into a Building." The real name is "Spirit of Nebraska's Wilderness," and it's a huge city sculpture taking up 6 city blocks composed of 100 pieces. The giant artwork features the American bison, a pioneer wagon train, and makes for some great picture taking while you're in downtown Omaha.

The Chef Boyardee statue calls Omaha home

Over on South 10th Street just south of Interstate 480, in ConAgra Plaza is a life-sized statue of Chef Boyardee. One Omaha native that made it big was Gerald Ford, the 38th President of the United States. His birthplace is commemorated with a gazebo and small museum at the corner of Woolworth Avenue and South 32nd Street. The gazebo and nearby park make for a nice stop while you're visiting Omaha.

West of here in Nebraska's capital, Lincoln, you can admire architecture and chambers of the only unicameral state legislature in the nation. Also check out the National Museum of Rollerskating, housing one of the nation's largest collections of skates and skating memorabilia. Among the collection are some skates that date back to 1819, as well as some gasoline-powered skates. Admission is free.

You may not have known that Lincoln was the birthplace of the dial tone. The Frank Woods Telephone Museum hosts a wide array of telephones and operator equipment representing the entire history of the telephone, much of which is centered right here in Lincoln. This was the original home of LT&T – Lincoln Telephone & Telegraph – and this city takes pride in its phone service; Lincoln was one of the first cities in the country to boast dial service on its telephones. The museum is open Sunday afternoons from 1 to 4.

Nebraska's unusual log archway spans I-80 near Kearney

Driving west from Lincoln, the expansive plains of Nebraska seem to go on forever, but at 75 miles per hour, you can drive the 130 miles from Lincoln to the small city of Kearney in just under 2 hours. Just east of Kearney, though, is a giant log archway stretching over the interstate. Usually called The Archway, this structure commemorates the early 'road trips' made by countless settlers and pioneers who passed through here over the past 200 years. The bridge was actually assembled offsite, then wheeled into place during the night. They shut down the interstate for an 8-hour period back in 1999, and by morning a bridge was there.

Parking isn't allowed on the shoulder of the interstate, but take the exit and visit the worthwhile museum, where actors in period attire will guide you through time on a tour of the western frontier, much as it was 150 years ago. You'll get a glimpse of what those westward travelers experienced on their travels. Admission to the museum is $12; plan at least an hour or two to enjoy the museum and archway to the full.

18

Road Trip Ideas for the South

Today's southern United States is a tapestry of contrasts. While the traditions of the past are proudly celebrated, her modern cities are a beacon of progress. Here you'll find towering pine forests, fog-laced swamps, pristine beaches, and farmland as far as the eye can see. For a land of contrasts, head south and follow one of these routes.

Blue Ridge Parkway – Waynesboro VA to Cherokee NC
469 miles – about 12 hours

The Blue Ridge Parkway is a delightful 469-mile tour through the Appalachian Mountains, where scenic wonders and delightful cultural sites are around nearly every bend.

The Blue Ridge Parkway is often called "America's Favorite Drive" because it's the most visited unit of the National Park Service, attracting over 15 million visitors a year. It's a living history museum, chronicling the passage of time and progress that early settlers made on their journeys west across the forbidding Appalachian Mountains.

The Parkway was built during the Great Depression as a recreational motor road, linking the Shenandoah Mountains of Virginia with the Great Smoky Mountains in North Carolina. Along its nearly 500-mile trek, it traces a path along the spine of the Blue Ridge Mountains, sometimes reaching right up into the clouds, at times within a stone's throw of the region's highest mountain peaks.

The parkway's top speed is 45 miles per hour and is enforced rigorously. In many places, the limit drops to 35. It was designed to be a slow-paced drive that gives access to some of the most stunning and diverse scenery in the country. The mileposts are numbered from 0 on the northeast corner down to 462 on the southeast end.

Around milepost 6, near the beginning of the parkway, is historic Humpback Rock. One of the most unusual mountains along the parkway, it sticks out like a sore thumb due to its craggy, rocky peak, unlike most

Lots of natural beauty on the Blue Ridge Parkway

other peaks here that are covered with vegetation. A hike to the top of Humpback Rock is difficult, yet one of the most accessible peaks along the Parkway. The trail to the top is just a mile long, but it ascends 740 feet in the process. When you finally stand on the rocky precipice, you'll be treated to a spectacular panoramic view of the surrounding terrain.

Near milepost 61 is the crossing of the James River. This historic river served as the Colonyof Virginia's first highway. Ships would deliver goods from Europe as far inland as Richmond, and later smaller vessels could head even as far as the Blue Ridge Mountains. Check out the James River Visitors Center near Milepost 64.

At the 120 mile mark, the parkway skirts the edges of Roanoke, Virginia, and the Mill Mountain Star, an 88-foot neon star that lights up the countryside and claims to be the world's largest star. The view of Roanoke from here is excellent, especially at sunset. It was here where a 24-year-old George Washington spent the night as he was headed west inspecting Appalachian forts.

On the Virginia/North Carolina border at milepost 213 is the Blue Ridge Music Center. During the spring and summer months, natives and visitors alike spend weekend evenings in the refreshing outdoor theater enjoying bluegrass, country, and folk music. The Roots of American Music museum are also on the grounds.

After crossing into North Carolina, the views will continue to take your breath away as you swing around mountains on state-of-the-art bridges and flyovers. One such marvel is the Linn Cove Viaduct. This elevated roadway slinks around Grandfather Mountain at mile marker 304. It took 9 years to build and was the last part of the Blue Ridge Parkway to be completed, at a cost of over $8000 per foot. Ten miles down the road is Linville Falls, one of the most serene – yet majestic – waterfalls in the Blue Ridge Mountains. Legend has it that the falls were used by Native American tribes to execute prisoners; a plunge down the final cascade was considered unsurvivable.

Near mile marker 364, you'll find Craggy Gardens. Throughout the spring and summer, a visually-stimulating palette of colors tantalizes the eye as the mountains come alive with wildflower blooms of all sorts. Whether it's the purple of rhododendron in June or the orange of Turkscap lily later in the summer, the mountain vegetation, mixed with an often foggy background, make for a surreal landscape as you walk the paths laid out before you.

Not far from here is the Folk Art Center and the vibrant city of Asheville, North Carolina, home to the Biltmore Estate, the largest privately-owned house in the United States.

Motoring on down the Parkway, near milepost 407, is Mt. Pisgah. The 1.6 trail of moderate difficulty leads you up to the peak of the mountain, which at over 5700 feet, will offer a magnificent view of the valleys below.

The final 40 miles of the parkway are increasingly elevated, mountainous, and curvy. Expect to go slow for much of the final hour. You'll have some excellent mountain scenery to enjoy at the stops through here, though, with one of the best being Waterrock Knob at mile marker 451. Plan for at least two, maybe three days to enjoy this classic road to its fullest.

Louisiana Bayous – Grand Isle to Baton Rouge LA
145 miles – about 3 hours

Louisiana Highway 1 follows the banks of Bayou LaFourche until the waterway literally empties into the Gulf of Mexico. You'll see shrimpers at their docks, drawbridges connecting the little communities on either side of the waterway, floating homes, and stands selling fresh-caught seafood. Keep on going, and Hwy 1 turns to the east and you'll be riding just a couple feet above the waters of the Gulf as you head toward Grand Isle. This is about as far south as you can go in LA, and by the time you get to Grand Isle, most of the homes are on stilts because of frequent floodwaters and hurricanes.

If you're driving along I-12, stop in Abita Springs, site of the famous Abita brewery. The town has a quaint historic downtown with shaded streets, art galleries, and restaurants that make a perfect stop along your road trip. Stop at the Abita Mystery House, an interesting museum full of area folk art, unusual machines, miniatures, and odd pieces such as the 'bassigator', some sort of animal that seems to be half bass & half alligator. Down the road, Angola Prison is best known for its rodeo, where the public comes to watch the inmates compete in barrel racing, bull riding, and racing.

The 'bassigator' at Abita Mystery House

If you're looking for interesting yet quirky places along the road, you'll find them scattered throughout southern Louisiana. Along I-12 sits the town of Covington, home of world's largest Ronald Reagan statue. Crowley, along I-10, boasts a giant accordion and guitar. A little to the east, in Lafayette, you'll find a giant saw, as well as a giant, rotating loaf of bread tucked inside a billboard for Evangeline Maid bread. Lafayette also serves as the center of Cajun country. Stop at Acadian Village for a taste of 19th century life around here – plenty of exhibits and homes showcase the rich history & culture of the area. About 10 minutes away is Breaux Bridge, the crawfish capital of the world, a perfect place to sample some of the world's best crawfish & gumbo.

Louisiana is known for its heat & humidity, especially in summertime. But if you're up for something a little hotter, head south from Lafayette to the town of Avery Island, the world capital of Tabasco sauce. The famous hot chile sauce isn't the only attraction in town, though; you'll also find a bird sanctuary and well-kept gardens.

A little bit further down US 90 headed toward New Orleans is Morgan City, home of the Rig Museum. The Gulf of Mexico is home to hundreds of operational offshore oil rigs, and here you can take a tour of a real oil rig (nicknamed Mr. Charlie) that was in use in the Gulf for over 30 yrs.

History buffs will want to visit Baton Rouge, capital of Louisiana and its 2nd largest city. At the state capitol building, you'll be reminded that Huey Long was a famous populist senator assassinated right here, in 1935, at the prime of his political career. Look for the plaque that shows where he was shot, an X marks the spot where Huey Long fell, and the bulletholes are still present in the wall from the assassination.

Kentucky Horse Country – Lexington to Louisville KY
80 miles – about 2 hours

To experience the best of Kentucky horse country, start in Lexington, the Horse Capital of the World. Although the more famous Kentucky Derby is held in Louisville, Lexington has a rich horse breeding and racing tradition that's unrivaled anywhere else. Don't miss Kentucky Horse Park, a working horse farm and educational theme park on the north edge of town.

You'll see thoroughbreds from around the world, plus enjoy shows and tours of the farms. You can go horseback riding, and children under 12 can take a pony ride if they'd like.

One of North America's favorite racetracks is just across town at Keeneland Race Course. Known for being a classic race course that suggests a rich historical ambience, Keeneland takes pride in its tradition. It's the last racetrack in the country to broadcast race calls via loudspeaker. You may recognize the course as the filming site for most of the race scenes in the popular movie *Seabiscuit*.

Head west on U.S. 60, avoiding faster-paced I-64. As you head out of town, look for an unusual castle on the north side of the highway.

The next town in our westward tour is Frankfort. For a state capital city, Frankfort is small – the 5th smallest in the nation. But it's been here a long time, having served as capital continuously since 1792. It also qualifies as one of the country's most unusual capital cities. One time I had to go to the state capitol for a meeting, one cold February morning. I followed the road signs, and so I followed the sign to the Capitol building. When I made my left turn, I found myself on a narrow country road with overgrown trees forming a canopy over the road. I thought to myself, "Surely this isn't the way." Well, sure enough, after a few twists and turns along the Kentucky River, this country road rounded a bend, and the stately Capitol building emerged in front of me.

The world's largest bat stands in front of the Louisville Slugger museum

Tours are available, and the grounds are especially well-kept. It makes for a nice walk any time of year, but especially in the spring.

Our last stop is Louisville, the largest city in Kentucky, and home to one of horse racing's most iconic courses, Churchill Downs. Downtown you'll find the home of the Louisville Slugger factory and museum, where baseball bats have been made for decades.

Everybody who takes a tour gets a free mini-bat as a souvenir!

Downtown Louisville is also where you'll find the Muhammed Ali Center, a museum and interpretive center dedicated to the story of the one-of-a-kind boxer. It's also the perfect place to enjoy the historic riverfront, where if you visit at just the right time you might hear the whistle of a classic riverboat 'singing' folk songs.

Texas Tropical Trail – Kingsville to S. Padre Island TX
130 miles – about 2 ½ hours

This road trip follows the 130-mile Texas Tropical Trail, a unique adventure through desert, cowboy country, a major urban center, and to the warm Texas Gulf coast.

Start in Kingsville, four hours south of Houston. On U.S. Highway 77 about half-an-hour southwest of Corpus Christi, Kingsville is in the heart of cowboy country. The main attraction here is the King Ranch, a 825,000 acre ranch founded by New Yorker Richard King. Although the ranch is over 160 years old, today it's a conglomeration of modern industry and traditional ranching and farming. A tour will give you a glimpse of the immense cattle production that goes on here, not to mention breeding of quarterhorses and thoroughbreds, some of which have gone on to win racing's Triple Crown.

Also in Kingsville is the Old Railroad Depot and Museum. It's over a century old and gives visitors a glimpse of early 20th century cowboy days. Every November, Kingsville hosts its annual Ranch Hand Festival, complete with a cowboy dress-up contest, showings of old-time cowboy movies, and even a tequila tasting.

Heading south, make sure you fill up the gas tank; it's 60 miles from Kingsville to the next gas station.

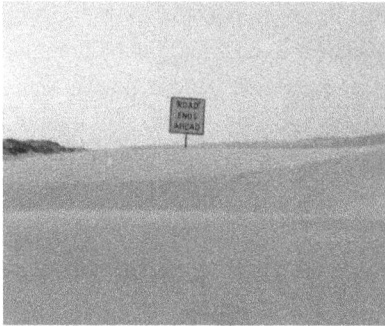

Just five miles from South Padre Island, sand dunes completely cover the road

At Raymondville, take a detour east until you reach the little town of Port Mansfield, one of the top 10 fishing spots in the nation. Located right on the coast of the Laguna Madre, the 113-mile long Padre Island is just offshore. Although the island separates Port Mansfield from the Gulf, a channel was cut right through the island in 1962, giving the village easy boat access to some of the best deep sea fishing in the country. Try your hand fishing for marlin, sailfish, snapper, grouper, and amberjack.

Back on U.S. 77, we keep motoring south until we reach Harlingen, the first city in the Rio Grande Valley. The valley metro area has a population of over 1.1 million, but it's more or less a loose chain of smaller communities. This area is hugely popular with snowbirds - Winter Texans as they're called here - between November and March. Harlingen has a couple of major shopping centers, warm weather year round, and the lowest cost-of-living in the United States.

Farther south, though, you'll find the beach resort town of South Padre Island. Highway 100 crosses over the Laguna Madre at the festive town of Port Isabel. Here you'll see billboards and shops advertising beachwear, souvenirs, and fresh tropical fruit. The causeway over the laguna is over 2 miles long - the longest bridge in TX. Watch for pelicans as you cross.

For most of the year, South Padre Island is a laid-back resort town, complete with inexpensive motels, seafood restaurants and souvenir shops dotting the main drag through town. Things get wild in March, though, as tens of thousands of college students converge on the island for Spring Break. The rest of the year, though, it's a perfect place to relax and enjoy the sand, sun, and calming waves of the Gulf. For a fun beach walk, drive north along the island until the road stops, then get out and enjoy a quiet stroll along the shore, looking for shells and exotic birds.

Padre Island is one of the nation's best spots for birding, being one of the only places in the US to see certain species of tropical birds. So grab your binoculars and join one of the many birding tours on the island. Families will enjoy Sea Turtle, Inc, the best spot in town for spotting sea turtles. Check out the Dolphin Research & Sea Life Center, an economical way for your family to learn about dolphins, in their natural habitat.

Natchez Trace – Nashville TN to Natchez MS
444 miles – about 10 hours

The Natchez Trace is one of the country's most historic byways. Starting outside Nashville and winding its way through southern Tennessee, northwest Alabama, and into the heart of Mississippi, its 444-mile-long course passes through forest, farmland, rivers, and plenty of small towns. It's one of the greatest road trips in the South, and the summer or autumn are perfect times to savor the surreal scenery of this trail.

Settlers used the old Natchez Trace as a way west, and as the decades wore on, the soft soil was pressed down by so many travelers and their wagons that the trail actually became sunken. Several sections of the Old Trail are like this, pressed down a few feet below the surrounding land.

Throughout the late 18th and early 19th centuries, the Trace was a well-used route, but it was also a magnet for highwaymen, bandits, and gangs that robbed travelers – or worse. Still, the Old Natchez Trace was one of the first roads with a well-organized pattern of 'stands' – the network of inns and stops along the road.

Today's Natchez Trace Parkway runs parallel with the old route, running for two lanes all the way, and takes you within eyeshot of nearly all the history and scenery along the way. Our trek starts just west of Nashville, and the mileposts count down the distance to the end of the road in Natchez, Mississippi.

Make sure to stop at Birdsong Hollow, near milepost 438, just a few miles from the parkway's northern terminus. Here you'll enjoy panoramic views of the hollow and the hills in the distance. The Trace crosses the hollow via a 155-foot-high, double arched bridge. Its own beauty and design excellence makes this one of the most photographed bridges in Tennessee.

Down at milepost 405, you'll find signs leading you to Jackson Falls, one of the most popular short hikes along this road. The paved trail here will lead you down a steep 900 foot drop in elevation into the gorge leading to famous Jackson Falls.

Near milepost 401, stop at Old Trace Drive. This two-mile section of the Old Road is probably the easiest place where you can actually drive your car down the same path that travelers & settlers used centuries earlier. This little jaunt gives you some breathtaking views of the surrounding forest, but it's a one-way path, going from south to north only; no RVs or heavy trucks allowed.

The road briefly meanders into Alabama, crossing the Tennessee River near milepost 327. Today a modern bridge crosses the expansive river, but 200 years ago, this was the location of a travelers' 'stand' and ferry operated by Mr. George Colbert, a leader in the Chickasaw Native American Army. The river is a perfect place to stop for a picnic or to enjoy some fishing or boating.

Once you cross into Mississippi, where the majority of the Parkway resides, you'll meander through Tishomingo State Park, near a dozen scenic overlooks, and – at milepost 269 – to a small cemetery where 13 unknown Confederate soldiers are buried. Located right on the Old Trace, this spot remains a mystery to historians and visitors alike.

Outside of Tupelo, at milepost 266, peruse the Natchez Trace Visitor Center to get acquainted with the historic and cultural sites along the parkway. Check out the exhibits, orientation film, and bookstore to learn more about the history of this unique road.

The original Natchez Trace was sunken from decades of wagon and foot traffic

About 30 minutes outside Jackson is one of the most surreal places along the Parkway – Cypress Swamp. Located at milepost 122, a half-mile trail through the swamp takes visitors along an elevated boardwalk. The atmosphere is eerie as you walk surrounded by the bald cypress and water tupelo trees. If you look closely, you may even see an alligator or two in the swamp below.

Check out the ghost town of Rocky Springs at milepost 55; the town was already in decline by the time of the Civil War. A yellow fever epidemic devastated what was left, and today, all that remains are a building or two, the cemetery, and some trails where the streets might have been. A popular spot for primitive camping, you're likely to be the only resident here if you spend the night!

Built in 1780, the Mt. Locust Inn, around milepost 15, is the only remaining 'stand' on the Parkway, where weary travelers could find food and lodging for the night.

The Natchez Trace Parkway showcases some of the best scenery the South has to offer. Whether you're looking for history, culture, natural beauty, or all of the above, you won't want to miss this byway or any of its countless treasures.

Talimena Byway – Pine Ridge AR to Talihina OK
73 miles – about 2 hours

This road trip starts about an hour west of Hot Springs, Arkansas, in the little town of Pine Ridge. From here, you'll enjoy a breathtaking scenic drive through western Arkansas and eastern Oklahoma through the Ouachita Mountains. With some of November's best fall foliage, an abundance of cultural offerings, and friendly people, it's a favorite destination for a late fall road trip.

Pine Ridge is where a couple of local boys by the names of Chet Lauck and Norris "Tuffy" Goff got their start in the radio business. One night back in 1931 they tried out a comedy routine, playing the role of two country storekeepers. Before long, they had their own radio show. Chet and Norris became the stars of the Lum & Abner show that ran for decades.

Here you'll find the Lum & Abner Jot em Down Store & Museum, which pays tribute to the story and talent of these two local residents. They sell plenty of old Lum & Abner comedy routine recordings, which make for some great listening while you're on the road.

About 15 miles west of here is the town of Mena. A charming community in the hills of Western Arkansas, you'll find the scenery attractive, the people friendly, with plenty of interesting places to see. Look for the restored Esso filling station, originally built in

1928. Now refurbished to its former glory, it houses a museum of classic cars from the golden age of automobiles.

Janssen Park, in the middle of town, houses a log cabin that was built in 1851. Local legend has it that Jesse James used the cabin as a hideout. Later it was used as a community hospital, city hall, and post office, even surviving a near-direct hit from a tornado in 1993.

Four-wheeler and ATV enthusiasts won't want to miss Wolf Pen Gap Trail, just a few miles from here. The trail has dozens of miles of ATV trails for both beginners and experts. You're likely to see owls, deer, and even bears along the way, and you'll want to make a special trip to enjoy Little Missouri Falls.

Driving west from Mena, follow Arkansas State Highway 88, designated as the Talimena National Scenic Byway. It's a 50-mile scenic road that curves through the rustic beauty of the Ouachita Mountains. It's an especially fascinating drive in early to mid-November, when fall colors are at their peak.

The Ouachitas are one of the only mountain ranges in the nation that run East to West, making for a diverse range of wildlife and plant life as you drive through here.

The byway, although rural and remote with few services, has plenty of scenic vistas offering a birdseye view of the mountain valleys below. One must-see spot is Queen Wilhelmina State Park, located right on the byway. The crown jewel of the park sits atop Rich Mountain, 2600 feet up. The historic Queen Wilhelmina Lodge dates back to 1898, and it's often called the "Castle in the Clouds."

As the Talimena Byway crosses into Oklahoma and through the Winding Stair National Recreation Area, you'll be treated to a part of Oklahoma that most people never see -- winding mountain roads and scenic vistas. On a clear night, stargazers will get a special treat. This 50-mile driving trail ends near the little town of

Talihina. Plan on 3-4 hours to take this historic, scenic drive from Pine Ridge to Mena to Talihina along the Talimena Scenic Byway.

Great Smoky Mountains – Knoxville TN to Deals Gap NC
55 miles – about 1 ½ hours

This drive starts in Knoxville, the largest city in Eastern Tennessee. Check out the East Tennessee History Center and Museum in downtown Knoxville. You'll find exhibits highlighting the area's rich history, including the Cherokee that once called this area home, the pivotal Civil War battles fought not far from here, and the history of country music. The museum is open every day except holidays.

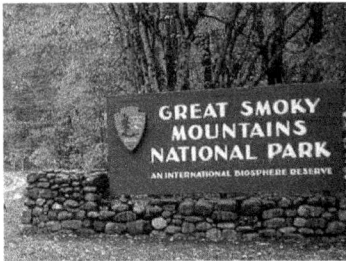

One of the most visited national parks in the Eastern United States

Knoxville was the birthplace of both the touchscreen and Cherry Coke. Both of these innovations made their dubut at Knoxville's 1982 World's Fair. The most conspicuous reminder of the fair, the 266-foot-tall Sunsphere, is located downtown. It sports a 75-foot gold-colored glass sphere at the top. Back in 1982, visitors to the World's Fair had to pay $2 for a ride to the top, but now you can go up for free. The 4th level has an observation deck, and the 5th level boasts a restaurant with a panoramic view of the city.

A few miles south of Knoxville, in Maryville, is the Parkway Drive-In. Right on the main drag, this old-fashioned drive-in movie theater takes visitors back to the golden age of cinema. Although it's only open on the weekends, it's a great family destination.

From here, our journey down 129 quickly becomes much more rural, not to mention mountainous. If you're looking for a more scenic route, take U.S. 321 east out of Maryville and then go south on the beautiful Foothills Parkway. This byway takes you right through the gorgeous Appalachian foothills with breathtaking vistas at just about every turn.

After rejoining U.S. 129, heading southeast, you're going to want to hang on to your hat – or your steering wheel, armrest, or whatever else you hang on to – because you're now on a famous stretch of road known as The Dragon – the curviest highway in America – 318 curves in 11 miles. That's an average of 29 curves every mile, if you're counting. Motorcycle riders from all over the world come here to try out their skill. With the Smoky Mountains on one side of the road and a lake on the other, there are no drive-ways, side roads or pullouts on this twisty byway. Some of the curves are famous, with names of their own, such as the Gravity Cavity, Copperhead Corner, and Hog Pen Bend. Near here are some great resorts where you can regain your breath and enjoy the scen-ery of the Smoky Mountains. The most famous is the Deals Gap Motorcycle Resort, just over the state line in North Carolina, cater-ing specifically to motorcyclists taking on The Dragon's challenge.

Skyline Drive – Front Royal VA to Waynesboro VA
105 miles – about 3 hours

Back in 1931, the WPA started the long and difficult process of building a road right along the spine of the Blue Ridge Mountains in Virginia. It was a dangerous job, but 8 years later, the 105-mile Skyline Drive was opened to the public. Although it took a few years to catch on, this three-hour, two lane road cruise has become one of the easiest ways to enjoy the best of the Blue Ridge Moun-tains.

About 70 miles west of Washington, D.C., near Front Royal, Virginia, visitors pay the $15 entrance fee to Shenandoah National

Park, which is good for an entire carload – multiple entries – for an entire week. During the winter, the fee drops to $10. Although this is a twisting mountain road, it's perfectly safe as long as you watch your speed and look out for wildlife that may cross in front of you.

The Drive has plenty to delight even the most avid roadtrippers, whether you're here to experience the blazing palette of colors in the autumn, or the wide variety of birds and wildlife – such as deer and bears – that populate the park in the summer. The wildflowers, trillium, and azaleas of spring, and even the peaceful snows of winter make this road a pleasure any time of the year. The park has the highest density of black bears of anywhere in the country. So pack your binoculars, and be prepared to take advantage of the 75 scenic overlooks that dot the Drive.

Be warned: the speed limit is a strictly enforced 35 mph the entire length; you won't want to take those switchback curves and steep grades too fast. Most services in the park, such as the lodge, restaurant, and some of the best camping are found right at the center of the Drive, around milepost 51, at Big Meadows. This is also the only place in the park where you can buy fuel, so plan accordingly. Although you're likely to see wildlife – especially wild turkeys, deer, and black bears along the drive – you'll want to appreciate them at a distance. Park regulations prohibit feeding the animals.

Right around milepost 32, you'll approach Mary's Rock, which at 3500 feet, is one of the highest peaks in the park. One of the engineering feats of the road is Mary's Rock Tunnel, which is a 610-foot-long tunnel blasted right through the mountain. Check your height, as the clearance through the tunnel is 12'8"; tall loads are prohibited.

Near milepost 42, you'll find the Skyland resort area. This is the highest point on the drive, at an elevation of nearly 3700 ft. Back in the 1850s, copper was discovered at Skyland, and the Virginia Cliff Copper Company offered to buy this whole parcel of land for a million dollars. Well, they soon found that copper mining wouldn't be profitable in these mountains, which were rather inaccessible at the time. Around the turn of the century, a travel promoter named George Pollock bought the land on credit, developing it into a resort venue for middle-class businessmen and their families trying to escape the hustle and bustle of the nearly cities.

Pollock built restaurants, recreation halls, and cabins, which became quite popular in the region. But he also put on costume parties, jousting tournaments, formal balls, pageants, and other unique entertainment, which kept his resort popular. Today, about a dozen of the original Skyland structures still stand, and you can stop here and see what life was like back in this unusual resort community back at the turn of the century, not to mention enjoying a satisfying dinner up at Skyland Lodge.

Now earlier, I mentioned Big Meadows, the main visitor center in the park, located at mile 51. If you like a little hiking, and you like waterfalls, then don't want to miss Dark Hollow Falls. From the parking area, follow the trail about ¾ of a mile down to the picturesque falls 440 feet below.

Serious hikers know that most of Skyline Drive parallels the world-famous 2200-mile-long Appalachian Trail. The scenery along this section is some of the trail's finest; so enjoy it and take your time driving down the road. Skyline Drive is one of the most satisfying two-lane mountain roads out there, well worth a detour or even a special trip.

Sweet Home Alabama – Mt. Carmel to Huntsville AL
80 miles – about 2 hours

This drive begins a few miles from the point where Alabama, Georgia, and Tennessee come together. If you're driving near here through I-24 on the Tennessee side, you'll notice one fireworks superstore after another; take Exit 152 and head to the southwest on U.S. 72. The hilly terrain continues as you quickly cross the Alabama state line.

Just south of the state line, near the tiny town of Mount Carmel, you'll find a historic, geologic, and scenic wonder – Russell Cave National Monument. There's evidence from flint arrowheads and charcoal remains that Russell Cave has been inhabited for thousands of years. Researchers believe that several prehistoric families spent the winters here, due to the constant water available inside and the animal skeletons that they've found, including remains of the now-extinct passenger pigeon.

This is one of the longest caves in Alabama, with over seven miles of mapped caverns and an internal natural spring that eventually flows to the Tennessee River. Plenty of unusual animal species call the cave home, including a species of scorpion that's been found nowhere else in the world. You can enjoy one of the picturesque nature trails or take a tour of the cave itself. Russell Cave is operated by the National Park Service and is open daily from 8 to 4:30; admission is free.

The Saturn V rocket at Huntsville's Space and Rocket Center

From here, head west on U.S. 72, roughly paralleling the Tennessee River. Throughout the 1930's and 40's, the TVA built several dams along the river, creating expansive lakes that fill much of the river's length through

Alabama. As a result, thousands of fishermen, boaters, and hunters flock here every year.

About 30 miles from Russell Cave sits the pleasant town of Scottsboro. The most famous attraction here is the Unclaimed Baggage Center. Here, unclaimed baggage from buses, planes, and trains is put on display to be purchased at low cost. It's like a giant thrift store, so if you like rummaging through used merchandise looking for treasures, then don't miss stopping here.

Payne's Soda Shop, an old-fashioned soda fountain, has been doing business on the square next to the Scottsboro courthouse since 1869 and will make you think you've gone back in time.

From here, U.S. 72 veers away from the river and heads through more mountainous terrain on its way to Huntsville. The largest city and cultural center in Northern Alabama, Huntsville is home to NASA's Marshall Space and Flight Center, where rockets are designed and astronauts are trained. The main space-related attraction in town is the U.S. Space and Rocket Center, right on Interstate 565 just west of town. Here you'll experience the story of space exploration from its humble beginnings down to the current day. The museum contains one of the most comprehensive rocket collections in the world. The center is open daily from 9 to 5; admission is $25 for adults and $20 for kids ages 6-12 and includes your choice of an IMAX or 3D movie.

19

Road Trip Ideas
The West

The American West is known for wide open spaces, vast emp-ty deserts, adventure-loving cowboys, picturesque mountains, and some of the most beautiful sunsets in the world. Most any roadtripper will find a worthwhile adventure by heading west. Try one of these unforgettable journeys.

Pacific Coast Hwy – San Francisco CA to Mendocino CA
170 miles – about 5 hours

One of the most picturesque road trips in the world is the Pa-cific Coast Highway in northern California.

Start on the north edge of San Francisco. While you're in the 'city on the bay', enjoy some five-star shopping at Union Square, ride one of the famous cable cars, and don't miss the spooky former prison on Alcatraz Island. By the time we drive north out of San Francisco's hustle and bustle, we're at one of the world's most recognizable landmarks – the Golden Gate Bridge.

The Golden Gate Bridge from below

No matter when you visit this iconic bridge, you're sure to be amazed at the architecture, the water nearby, not to mention the fantastic view of the city. Tours of the bridge are offered through the spring and summer – until early October – and begin at the Round House on the southeast end of the bridge.

Even without a scheduled tour, you can still enjoy the 'bridge experience.' Although the Golden Gate is a toll bridge, tolls are only collected on vehicles driving south into the city, so driving north is free! Just north of the bridge, the rest area offers free parking and a breathtaking view of the bridge and the city of San Francisco. If you're up to a walk, consider walking across the bridge; pedestrian access is free. But be forewarned, the bridge is over 1 ½ miles long, so pace yourself, and don't forget your camera!

North of the Golden Gate Bridge are the beautiful, rugged Marin Headlands. This former military base has been reclaimed for recreational use, where you'll find Native American history, hiking trails, historic Point Bonita Lighthouse, and breathtaking views of the coast. Check out Rodeo Beach, an otherworldly beach complete with rocky vistas and unusual red and green pebbles dotting the sands.

Driving north, follow the signs for California Highway 1. This coastal road gives sweeping vistas around nearly every bend. At the northern edge of Marin County, keep an eye out for Point Reyes National Seashore, where you'll find unusual flora and fauna, and everything from hiking to camping to cycling to beaches to history.

Hikers will enjoy Bear Valley Trail, which starts out from the visitor center and follows a picturesque stream right into a canyon, eventually delivering the most spectacular ocean view in the park. The 140-year-old Point Reyes Lighthouse is a popular spot for whale-watchers. The migration of Gray Whales can be seen here in both January and March. Tule Elk can also be spotted throughout the northern part of the park.

Continuing along Highway 1, the road curves away from the coast for a few miles, but then heads right back, passing through the sleepy towns of Bodega Bay and Jenner, where the highway crosses the Russian River. North of here, much of the coast is undeveloped, with the next hundred miles dotted with abundant state parks and state beaches.

Well up the coast is the town of Mendocino. This little town of 1000 residents is within view of the ocean and has become a haven for writers and artists, not to mention vacationers escaping the daily grind. Try one of the locally-owned restaurants and cafes that will give you a taste of the good life while passing through.

Farther north up the coast is the iconic Avenue of the Giants, where redwood trees tower over you, with one of the most memorable roads in the world offering plenty to see and do.

Extraterrestrial Highway – Ash Springs NV to Rachel NV
45 miles – about 1 hour

For decades, conspiracy theorists and alien researchers alike have paid special attention to the elusive Area 51, located in the desolate expanse of the Nevada desert. The closest you can legally get to Area 51 –likely a testing area for experimental military aircraft – is to head north out of Las Vegas on U.S. 93 for about 100 miles.

Once you've arrived at Alamo – population 1000 – you've crossed a mountain range and have gained significant elevation, and you'll find that the weather up here is crisper and the nights cooler than down in the Las Vegas Valley. Plus you'll have some of the clearest views of the night sky in the country, perfect for catching a glimpse of aircraft – or something a little more 'out of this world' – as you motor up the highway. Alamo may be small, but it's the largest town you'll see for several hours. Make sure you gas up here, because there are no fuel services along the Extraterrestrial Highway.

Just past Ash Springs, you'll come to a junction – Nevada Highway 375. Turn left here and you'll be on the E.T. Highway. Near here, under a big tree, you'll see the famed 'Crystal Springs Park and Ride', where several Area 51 employees catch a mysterious white bus that shuttles them to work each day.

If you decide to drive down Highway 375 and down to the Area 51 border, remember: this is open range, so cattle and other critters roam freely across the road. Don't drive this road at night, since cattle can't be seen until it's too late. Very few vehicles drive this highway – about 200 a day on average – and you won't want to get stranded. Cell phone service is spotty to nonexistent, so if you break down, put your hood up and turn your flashers on; locals will usually help a stranded motorist. This is the desert, so have enough water for the day, and a blanket for the night.

From here, it's a deserted 14 miles to an unmarked dirt road that heads to the main entrance of Area 51. If you're feeling brave, take the unmarked dirt road going southwest around mile marker 34.6. Head about 13 miles down this dirt road until you see some warning signs. Whatever you do, do not pass those signs! At this point, you are officially at the border of Area 51.

Get out of your car if you want to, but watch your step! There are some orange plastic posts every few hundred feet; those posts line the border of this top secret military installation. Look over to your left on top of that big hill – see that SUV parked up there?

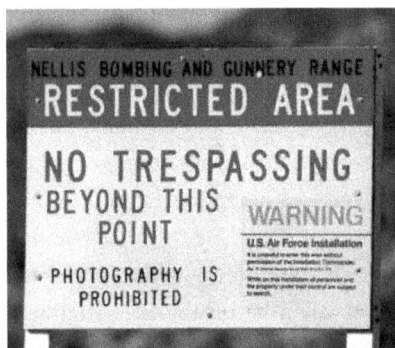

A not-so-warm welcome to Area 51

They're watching YOU. Sensors placed along this dirt road let them know that a curious roadtripper was in the area, and they've made a special trip just to make sure you don't cross that line of orange posts.

And if you do cross that line, they're authorized to use deadly force.

Once you're back on Hwy 375, head another five miles west toward an unusual landmark – the 'Black Mailbox'. As it turns out, the Black Mailbox is a white mailbox. But years ago, U.F.O. enthusiasts thought this mailbox belonged to Area 51 itself, and they had the bad habit of ruffling through its contents to see if any top secret, classified letters might just be randomly left out in the open box. Well, the mailbox actually belonged to a local rancher, and he quickly grew tired of having his mail stolen. He put up the steel reinforced, locked white mailbox that you see today. At night, especially during the summer, those who believe in UFOs gather here and claim to see spooky lights in the sky, off to the south over the military installation. There's even a place to pull off the road and camp for the night.

But our path takes us about 20 miles up the highway to the little town of Rachel. And this tiny spot on the map has a full-time population of 54, according to the last census. There's only one business in town, and that's the Little A'le'inn, a small restaurant, bar, souvenir shop, and motel. They've been open for over 20 years, and they've adopted the whole alien theme, even in their menu. Try the Alien Burger, it's a variation on a hamburger with special sauce and served on a homemade roll. And don't forget the souvenirs! Anything you could possibly want with a green alien head on it can be found here. It's an 'out of this world' experience!

A drive along the Extraterrestrial Highway can be an otherworldly experience, even eerie at times. Every now and then, you'll hear the sonic boom of experimental air force planes sweep past you, reminding you of your nearness to the most top secret facility in the world.

Glacier National Park – Shelby MT to West Glacier MT
130 miles – 2 ½ hours

This journey starts in Shelby, Montana, 30 miles south of the Canadian border, where U.S. 2 intersects the Interstate 15 freeway. If you're driving from the east, you've already crossed 1000 miles of flat plains and ranchland, wondering if you'll ever make it to the mountains. Although Shelby is small – with a population of less than 4000 – the world heavyweight boxing title between Jack Dempsey and Tommy Gibbons was held here (of all places) back in 1923. Oil had just been discovered here, and prospectors thought

Shelby could be the Chicago or New York City of the West. They built a 40,000-seat arena, but only 7000 bought tickets to see the fight. Over 13,000 people were let in for free to keep the arena from looking too empty. It was one of the biggest flops in the history of boxing, and four banks went belly-up because of it.

About 20 miles west is the town of Cut Bank, where you'll find a 27-foot talking penguin claiming that this is the coldest spot in the nation.

Heading west out of Cut Bank, you quickly enter the Blackfoot Nation, which covers much of northern Montana and southern Alberta in Canada. The Blackfoot were once the most powerful Native American tribe on the northern plains; they had innovative and ingeneous ways of hunting buffalo and an advanced civilization. The tribe is headquartered in nearly Browning, where you'll find the Museum of the Plains Indian. Here you'll experience the richness & diversity of the tribes' historic arts. During the summer, explore the Native American tipi exhibit, where you'll get a glimpse of how traditional Plains Indians lived.

Going-to-the-Sun Road, the crown jewel of Glacier National Park

Once you've arrived at Glacier National Park, head north on famous Going-to-the-Sun Road, a 50-mile-long engineering marvel that some say is the most scenic road *in the world*. Although the section of the road along Lake McDonald is open 365 days a year, the most awe-inspiring parts generally open by mid to late June.

The area receives an unthinkable amount of snow each year, so the snow plows work overtime all spring and into early summer to get the road ready for visitors. Most years, the complete road is open to passenger vehicles by the third week in June.

Without stopping, the road takes about 2 hrs to drive, but most visitors take an entire day to savor the road. Make sure to stop around Logan Pass, where at 6700 ft in elevation, you'll see a spectacular palette of colors as the wildflowers put on a natural show in early summer. Save some time and energy for hiking, as some of the most satisfying trails take you to scenic overlooks at Hidden Lake and the famous High Line Trail. More experienced hikers opt for more rugged Hidden Lake, while High Line Trail is flatter, less strenuous, and accessible to just about anyone. The park is one of the few places in the world where you can see a real glacier, such as Grinnell Glacier. Some of the rooms in Many Glacier Lodge actually offer views of Grinnell.

There are several fine places to stay in the park, but a favorite among visitors is Lake McDonald Lodge. Here you'll enjoy a welcoming lobby with bearskin and buffalo rugs. Rooms in the lodge run about $180 a night, although there are some motel-style rooms near the lodge for a bit less. Just outside the park, you'll find lots of excellent accommodations too, such as the Great Bear Inn, in the parkside town of West Glacier.

Without a doubt, Glacier National Park and its surroundings will treat your senses to some of the best scenery on the planet.

The Arizona Strip – Mesquite NV to Marble Canyon AZ
185 miles – 3 ½ hours

One of America's most unusual – yet remote – places is the Arizona Strip, the ribbon of land in Arizona that lies to the north of the Grand Canyon. Since the canyon is up to 18 miles wide, no bridges cross the canyon. As a result, the Arizona Strip is culturally and geographically isolated from the rest of the state and most of the country. Although it's larger than Massachusetts, it has a population of just 8000, and 5000 of them live in the insular town of Colorado City, right on the Utah border.

Most visitors to the Arizona Strip pass through its northwest corner traveling on I-15 between Las Vegas and Salt Lake City. The main attraction on this short stretch of interstate is the Virgin River Gorge, a 2000-foot-deep canyon that's as little as 20 feet wide, carved out by the Virgin River. When I-15 was built in the 1970's, it reportedly cost over $100 an inch to excavate and build the highway through the gorge. As you whiz through the canyon at 55 miles per hour, you'll see limestone crags towering more than 500 feet straight above your head.

If you're feeling brave, take the Cedar Pockets exit to explore the gorge at a slower pace. In addition to being a scenic drive, it's also popular with hikers & campers.

Once you're through the canyon, Interstate 15 sneaks into Utah near St. George. From here, take Exit 16. Make sure your gas tank is full, because fuel services through the eastern half of the Arizona Strip will be few and far between. At the little town of Hurricane, Utah, follow highway 59 up the steep mountain and then through the hamlet of Apple Valley on your way back into northern Arizona.

The highway re-enters the Grand Canyon State at the town of Colorado City. With 5000 residents, you'd think there would be a few gas stations, maybe a few restaurants catering to the weary traveler. Well, you'd be wrong. There is absolutely nothing here that invites the passing traveler, not a McDonald's, not a motel, not a campground – nothing.

That's because Colorado City is one of – if not the most – insular town in the United States. It's a town that's run by polygamists; members of the Fundamentalist Latter Day Saints have set up shop here and essentially own the town. Large unfinished houses are found all over the dusty town, inhabited by the adherents of plural marriage. If you drive into the town, there's a good chance you'll be followed around by men in pickup trucks with darkened windows – not exactly the most welcoming place to visit. As a result, there's not really much here to welcome travelers other than a passing curiosity for what it holds locked inside.

Continuing down Highway 389, the high desert road curves around to the town of Fredonia. Originally inhabited by the cliff-dwelling Anasazi centuries ago, today Fredonia is the gateway to the Grand Canyon's North Rim, as well as a popular junction for visitors on their way to Zion and Bryce Canyon National Parks in Utah, just a few miles away.

At Fredonia, we turn right onto Highway 89A, which quickly lifts visitors to some of the most beautiful scenery in the Arizona Strip. While the last 30 miles traversed high desert terrain, the road becomes even more elevated as it enters beautiful Kaibab National Forest. From Fredonia at an elevation of 4,600 feet, US Highway 89A eventually reaches a peak of nearly 9,000 feet, as the scenery changes from dusty desert to majestic Ponderosa pines on both sides of the highway. And in the wintertime, snow coats the hills and slopes surrounding the highway, giving it a refreshing alpine feel.

Kaibab National Forest in December looks nothing like the desert surrounding it

If you're traveling in the

summer, it will be here, near the highest point along the highway, where you'll turn to head toward the North Rim of the Canyon. During wintertime, the North Rim is closed. Over the course of the next 10 miles, the highway twists and turns around one switchback after another on its way back down into the desert.

Once the road returns to the desert floor, you'll spot some bright red rock formations to the east. These are the Vermilion Cliffs National Monument, nearly 300,000 acres of geologic wonders unspoiled by civilization to excite the senses. Be warned, though, that this is one of the most remote spots managed by the federal government, with no creature comforts. Poisonous reptiles, flash floods, extreme heat, and rugged terrain are just a few of the hazards you may encounter if you decide to hike these cliffs.

A view of Marble Canyon from the Old Navajo Bridge

When you finally arrive at Marble Canyon, which is basically a smaller upstream version of the Grand Canyon, you'll cross the Colorado River on its only bridge between here and Hoover Dam, 250 miles away. Here, you can walk across the old Navajo Bridge, which was completed in 1929. You can walk across Marble Canyon and look straight down, 470 feet to the Colorado River, the powerful river that carved through millions of tons of rock over countless generations to form this canyon, as well as the Grand Canyon, just a few miles away.

From Navajo Bridge, it's an easy, relatively flat 217 miles to Four Corners Monument, or a slightly more elevated 123 miles to Flagstaff. Either way, you're sure to encounter plenty of treasures that few people ever see, right here in the most remote stretch of the Arizona Strip.

The Loneliest Road – Fernley NV to Ely NV
286 miles – about 5 hours

U.S. Highway 50 through Nevada has been a road for a long time. It was part of the original Lincoln Highway – the first coast-to-coast auto trail across the continent, and dates back 100 years. Before that, it was a stagecoach trail during the late 19th century, taken by the fabled Pony Express as dozens of riders traversed the dusty trails of Nevada as far back as 1860.

The success of this trail was hitched to the dreams of silver miners from the 1800s. When the mines boomed, so did the towns along the old trail. And when those mines went bust, the fortunes of these old towns went bankrupt too. And the road between them got very lonely.

Through most of the 20th century, hardly any traffic passed through here. And when the interstate was built about 80 miles to the north, even fewer motorists had a reason to take the old road. Although it takes the better part of 6 hours to make the trek from Ely to Fernley without stopping, you can count the towns you pass on one hand.

In the summer of 1986, *Life* magazine published an article warning travelers about U.S. 50 through here. They called this 286-mile ribbon of pavement the "Loneliest Road in America" and quoted a AAA agent as saying, "It's totally empty. There are no attractions and no points of interest. We warn all motorists not to drive there unless they're confident of their survival skills."

Big skies and endless views stretch before you on Nevada's Loneliest Road

The state of Nevada decided to turn the backhanded insult into something positive. They embraced the "Loneliest Road" moniker, jumped at the chance to attract visitors, and made the label official. Today, you can pick up a special Loneliest Road passport and get it stamped in the five different towns along the road, and they'll send you a special signed certificate dubbing you an official Highway 50 Survivor.

From the west, you'll start your journey in Fernley, just a few miles outside of Reno. This pleasant city of 20,000 has a wide array of creature comforts, so fill your gas tank, because the loneliest part of the Loneliest Road lies ahead.

About 28 miles east of here lies the town of Fallon, literally your last chance to fill up and prepare yourself for crossing the high desert and nine mountain ranges ahead. This area is home to vast sand flats that may make you think you're half a world away. At the same time, this pleasant town of 8,000 is called the Oasis of Nevada, because of its widespread irrigation. This is an agricultural center, and if you stop at the right time of the summer, you might just arrive in time to sample the local Heart O'Gold cantaloupes. It's surprisingly green through here; you'll see alfalfa fields in the spring and summer.

But "Last Chance" is no joke; driving east, you're 111 miles from the next town and the next gas station.

About 20 miles east of Fallon is the Sand Mountain Recreation Area. This 600-foot-high sand dune is two miles long, and it sings when the wind hits it just right. Anyone interested in exploring this unique dune can buy a one-week permit for $40 per vehicle; Tuesdays and Wednesdays are free for everyone.

About 30 miles past Sand Mountain are the ruins of Cold Springs. Back in 1860 a Pony Express station was built here, as they did at regular ten mile intervals. The horses and riders would run a giant relay from one station to another, linking St. Joseph, Missouri to Sacramento, California. Here in Cold Springs lies the rubble of one of these stations, and you can see it from the road if you look for it. The 110' by 50' stone and mud structure housed horses and kept riders sheltered from the elements while they waited to ride to the next station. Today, the abandoned site stands as a silent reminder of a past that's been all but forgotten.

The next town is Austin, a living ghost town. In its heyday, over 10,000 lived here; less than 200 reside here today. Located at nearly the exact geographical center of the state, it's one of the best places to explore where silver miners prospected 150 years ago.

One of the most interesting and relaxing things to do here is about 20 miles east of town – Spencer Hot Springs. A natural hot tub, hot water flows from holes in the ground, and you can bathe in them, completely free of charge. You're likely to be the only visitors, as Spencer is located hours from the nearest resort. The springs are a little hard to get to, but worth the experience. Just south of U.S. 50 on Highway 376, there's a turn-off near mile marker 99. Follow the dirt road for about 10 miles; the springs are on your left. But be careful! At times the springs may be too hot for comfort; always check the temperature before taking a dip.

One of the most awe-inspiring things about the Loneliest Road is the way it extends before your eyes as you drive, straight as an arrow in many spots. The road disappears into the horizon over what might be 10, 20, even 30 miles in front of you, twirling up and over the next mountain range. Out here, distances can be deceiving, and the mountains that seem so close may be 40 miles away.

Back on the Loneliest Road, 70 miles – and two mountain ranges – separate Austin from Eureka. Although Eureka County is as big as Connecticut, less than 2000 people live here, making this the loneliest county on the Loneliest Road in America. Although Eureka was originally settled by silver prospectors, lead mining became the town's bread-and-butter through the latter 19th century. Money poured in, and builders erected impressive structures that seem out of place. The beautiful crimson and white Jackson House Hotel was built in 1877 and still stands today. The Eureka Opera House was built in 1880, and its Old West architecture, horseshoe-shaped balcony, and rugged façade hold secrets of decades long past.

Another hour and a couple of mountain ranges down the road is the town of Ely. With over 4000 inhabitants, it seems like a major city after the loneliness of the past 300 miles. Copper was discovered here in 1906 and has kept this town on the map ever since. Right in the center of town stands the Hotel Nevada. At six stories, it was the tallest building in Nevada until the 1940s. The Nevada Northern Railway Museum does a fine job telling the story of how the railroads shaped the history and fortunes of this area. Ely is a tourist town more than anything, though, and with several state and national parks near here, there's always something to do. Great Basin National Park and Cave Lake State Park are favorites around here.

From here, you can head north to Wendover and the Bonneville Salt Flats, or continue east toward the next town – Baker, Nevada (population 68) and on into Utah. If you've made it this far, then you've survived the Loneliest Road in America! If you know where to look, it's filled with surprises , serene beauty, and plenty to see.

Southern California Desert – San Diego to Felicity CA
160 miles – about 2 ½ hours

Although most road trip purists shy away from the interstate system, a few of these expressways provide an endless variety of scenery. California's Interstate 8 is one such interstate, running between San Diego and Yuma, Arizona.

Interstate 8 begins its journey a mile from the Pacific Ocean, near the best beaches in San Diego. For a fun diversion off the beaten tourist path, head over to La Jolla Cove for a chance to view sea lions in the wild.

Driving east on Interstate 8, passing the sprawl of San Diego, the highway quickly ascends into Cleveland National Forest. The freeway then turns south to avoid the majestic Vallecito mountains that you'll see rising to an elevation of over 5000 feet, just to your north.

A great spot to enjoy the view is Exit 77, In-Ko-Pah Park Road, at the historic Desert View Tower. Built here back in the 1920's, the tower is 70 feet high and affords visitors a fantastic view of the surrounding desert terrain. For the price of admission ($2), you get to climb to the top of the tower, explore the three-story museum, which holds several historic photos of the area over the past 150 years, as well as numerous historical artifacts. And the kids – as well as the young at heart – get to explore Boulder Park, the rock formations that have been worn down into cave-like structures and narrow sheltered walkways, not to mention some that have been sculpted to look like animals. In the 1890's, the 170-mile trip between Yuma and the Pacific Ocean took a month, from surviving the desert crossing, to navigating the mountain passes, and scaling the countless hills and mountains through here.

Today, though, our journey is much easier, and we keep motoring east, now making the 3000-foot descent into In-Ko-Pah gorge in just over 10 miles. Located right on the eastern edge of San Diego county, the gorge brings travelers from the high desert to the fertile plains of Imperial County, and by the time you get to the bottom, you'll be very close to sea level, if not a little below. The road twists so much that the eastbound lanes are over a mile and a half away from the westbound lanes.

Eventually, you arrive at El Centro. Its name implies a location smack dab in the center of California, but it's actually one of the southernmost towns in the state, and one of the lowest in the country, situated over 50 feet *below* sea level. Winter vegetables and farming are big business here.

The next stop is the Imperial Sand Dunes. Here, at Exit 156 – Grays Well Road – travelers marvel at the sand dunes that have been shifting through here for thousands of years. The dunes attract fans of off-road vehicles from all over the world. Between October and May, while the rest of the country languishes in cold wintry weather, the weather here is comfortable, usually in the 60s or 70s during the day.

Keep going east for a few miles on I-8 before taking Exit 164, Sidewinder Road, for our last stop before crossing into Arizona. The little town of Felicity, population 2, is the home of Jacque-Andre Istel, a marine from the

Granite pyramid at the "Official Center of the World"

Korean War. Decades ago, he bought thousands of acres of desert in this area and wrote a children's book proclaiming Felicity "The Center of the World".

Istel built a 21-foot-tall pink granite pyramid and put a little metal dot on the floor, which marks the official center of the world (at least according to the sign). By planting your foot here, you're told to make a wish and are then presented with a certificate proclaiming that you've been to the official center of the world.

Colorado Peaks – Colorado Springs to Pikes Peak CO
30 miles – about 1 ½ hours

Colorado Springs was founded by Civil War general William Jackson Palmer back in 1871, his intention was to build a railroad from Denver through the city and eventually all the way to Mexico City. When he founded the city, he was struck by the natural beauty of the area and wanted to build a major resort city here, with tourists stopping off via the railroad to visit. Within just a couple of years, thousands of tourists indeed were visiting Co Springs. In fact, the town quickly gained the nickname "Little London", because of all the English tourists that visited, many of whom decided to settle in the area for good.

Much of this part of Colorado is gold country. Around 1860, gold was first discovered here, beginning the famous Pike's Peak Gold Rush. Over the next several decades, gold ore was processed and shipped along the very railroads founded by Palmer.

The most visible attraction here is Pike's Peak, sometimes called 'America's Mountain' because of its accessibility. If you spend much time in Colorado, you'll eventually hear the word 'fourteener', referring to the 54 mountains in the state with a peak elevation over 14,000 feet. Pike's Peak rises to 14,115 feet, and it's the easternmost fourteener in America. It's arguably the easiest to climb, thanks to the accessible paved road that leads all the way to the top. The Pike's Peak access road starts just ten miles west of downtown on Highway 24.

Incidentally, the first road trip to the top of Pike's Peak took place back in 1913, when William Brown drove his car up to the peak, a trip of 20 miles. It took him 5 ½ hours to make it to the top, but today, you can reach the peak in less than an hour. Plan about three hours for the round-trip journey – an hour to go up, an hour to head back down, with about an hour at the top.

The gateway to the mountain is at an elevation of 7400 feet, but you'll rise quickly, passing an alpine wonderland filled with scenic beauty, mountain lakes, rising above the timberline, driving literally into the clouds. Along the way to the top you'll pass the North Slope Recreation Area, the Historic Glen Cove Inn Hotel, the Crystal Reservoir Gift Shop, with plenty of opportunities for fishing, hiking, and picnicking, not to mention the breathtaking view once you get to the top.

Unusual rock formations at Garden of the Gods Park in Colorado Springs

If you prefer to stay closer to the ground, you'll enjoy Garden of the Gods park, founded in 1909 and donated to the city by founder Charles Perkins. Admission is free and is one of the area's most popular attractions. You'll find miles of trails that pass along the unusual and steep rock formations in the park. It's known for rock climbing, and of course for its wonderful natural beauty. The park's unusual name came from two surveyors passing through the area, when they stumbled upon the sandstone rock formations and were amazed by the view here. One of them said that it would be a "capital place for a beer garden." The other surveyor, Rufus Cable, replied, "Beer Garden! Why, it is a fit place for the gods to assemble. We will call it the Garden of the Gods." They never put a beer garden here, but the name Garden of the Gods was quickly adopted.

While in town, visit the Colorado Springs Pioneers Museum, the premier history museum in the area. Highlighting the rich cultural framework around here, the Pioneers Museum boasts numerous exhibits covering everything from Native American clothing to historic photographs of the early history of Colorado Springs.

Land of Enchantment – Roswell NM to Magdalena NM
290 miles – about 5 hours

This route follows two-lane byways across New Mexico – the Land of Enchantment – in search of interesting and quirky things to see.

We start our voyage in Roswell, in the southeast corner of the state. Famous for the mysterious object that crashed on a ranch here in 1947, people flock here to investigate for themselves. Although the local newspaper called the object a 'flying saucer', the government insists that it was nothing more than a weather balloon. Others say that the object was a high-altitude, experimental aircraft that went awry. Skeptics gather at the Roswell International UFO Museum and Research Center, where you can look at mockups of the supposed alien autopsy, watch conspiracy videos, and read newspaper articles and exhibits about the 1947 Roswell incident. Tinfoil hats not included.

Roswell is a fun place, and the locals have embraced the whole alien theme; even the lampposts are shaped like flying saucers. The local fast food places get in on the action, too, with alien-themed decorations. It's a fun place to visit, even if you don't buy into the whole alien idea.

From Roswell, head south to Artesia, then west on U.S. 82 to the town of Alamogordo. Here you'll find White Sands National Monument, a huge place where visitors find smooth gypsum sand dunes covering the land for as far as the eye can see – 275 square miles of it – the world's largest gypsum sand field. The most popular activity here is sand sledding. You can buy a special plastic disc for about $12 and slide down the sand, a lot like sledding or skiing down a snow-capped mountain. For the best views, stay until sunset, when the sun's rays dance across the sands, making for a spectacular show. Moonrise over the sands also gives visitors quite a visual treat.

While you're in the area, check out the New Mexico Museum of Space History, where you'll find exhibits dedicated to rockets, space travel, and the U.S. space program.

A few miles north of Alamogordo is the little town of Three Rivers. Turn east from here and head over to the Three Rivers Petroglyph Site. Here, there's a one mile trail that winds through some of the most prolific and most accessible prehistoric stone petroglyphs in the world. Over 21,000 glyphs have been discovered here, and many of them can be spotted by tourists on the trail. It's said that they were created by the indigenous peoples that lived here nearly 1000 years ago. For a charge of $5 per carload, you can wander all over the hills and cliffs and enjoy the entire site.

A couple hours west of here on U.S. 60 is an unusual site that science buffs won't want to miss. About 50 miles west of Socorro, you'll see huge radiotelescope dishes towering over 100 feet into the air. This is the National Radio Astronomy Laboratory, sometimes called the Very Large Array, or *V.L.A.* Each dish measures 82 feet in diameter, and there are 27 of them scattered across the bowl-like expanse. If you saw the 1997 science-fiction movie *Contact*, you'll be familiar with the site. Here, you can take a self-guided walking tour

Giant radiotelescope dishes in the New Mexico desert

through a small museum and get an up-close look at one of the dishes. Admission is free, and you'll see a special exhibit about the filming of the movie *Contact*, which did in fact take place onsite.

Bonneville Salt Flats – Salt Lake City UT to Wendover UT 125 miles – about 2 hours

This route follows a segment of the Lincoln Highway that was one of the most feared and certainly one of the most desolate. Expanded today as Interstate 80, this route between Salt Lake City and the Nevada state line is one of the straightest and flattest roads in America.

This road trip starts in Salt Lake City, the capital and biggest city in Utah. Usually considered one of the prettiest capital cities in the nation, you're within easy access of hiking, skiing, plenty of outdoor recreation, and sweeping mountain vistas in just about every direction.

Salt Lake may be considered small and sleepy by some people's standards, but it's the only serious urban area within a 400-

mile radius. You won't find any other city even close to this size until Denver, Las Vegas, Reno, and Boise.

As you probably already knew, many of the attractions in town are of interest to members of the Church of Jesus Christ of Latter Day Saints, also known as the Mormons, such as Temple Square. However, there's plenty to do here for everybody. If you're interested in researching family genealogy and history, multiple genealogy libraries, such as the Family Search Center and the Family History Library, make researching your roots an educational and fun adventure.

A must-see while in town is the Natural History Museum of Utah. An excellent science museum housed in a beautiful new building, its interior is built in the shape of a spiral. You can explore astronomy, dinosaur bones, Navajo tapestry, and more during your visit.

What looks like snow is actually salt on the eerie Bonneville Salt Flats

Outdoor recreation and hiking enthusiasts won't want to miss Big Cottonwood Canyon. Beautiful no matter the season, there's plenty here to do, such as skiing, snowboarding, and snowshoeing in the winter, plus hiking, fishing, and rock climbing in the summer. At the top of the canyon, you may spot some interesting wildlife, such as moose, up at Silver Lake, which provides some absolutely breathtaking views.

Leaving Salt Lake City, headed west on I-80, you'll quickly find yourself squeezed between the mountains to your south and the famous Great Salt Lake to your north. If you look carefully to your north, you'll catch a glimpse of the beautiful Antelope Island, a popular park located on an island in the lake. Since the lake has no outlet, it's even saltier than seawater. It hosts millions of birds, shrimp, and other wildlife, so it's by no means a "Dead Sea." This lake is big enough and its surface warm enough that winter evaporation causes huge lake-effect snows on the surrounding land. In fact, the lake seems to cause much of the 42 feet of snow that falls on the Wasatch mountain range each year – something the locals call the "Greatest Snow on Earth."

After passing this unusual inland sea, the highway winds around a couple more peaks before angling down to become the flattest and straightest road in the country. You've arrived at the famous Great Salt Flats, the most famous of which is the Bonneville Salt Flats near the Nevada state line.

This stretch of road is often called one of the most boring stretches of highway in America. And it's true that, at 35 miles long, it's the longest stretch of completely straight interstate in the country. It's also the longest stretch of interstate without an exit. Still, there are a few interesting things to look for through here. If you're headed west, around mile marker 26, to the north of the highway is an unusual sculpture that looks somewhat like a fruit tree. It was built in the mid-1980s by Swedish artist Karl Momen. He called it "Metaphor: The Tree of Utah." It's nearly 90 feet tall, and is said to represent the variety of natural treasures found in the state. It's an interesting sight when you're surrounded by the white salt flats in every direction. Unfortunately, if you want to take a picture of the sculpture, you'd better do it fast, because parking on the shoulder isn't allowed.

The only place to stop on I-80 here is a rest area. Here, travelers can take a closer look at the curious salt covering, which is up to 5 feet deep. At the rest area, there's a view station where you can get a bird's eye view of the salt, which looks a lot like snow, but is composed of over 90% sodium chloride.

If you're visiting in mid-August or early October, you're likely here for some of the land speed races hosted at world-famous Bonneville Speedway. This part of the flats has been used for land-speed racing for over a century, where rocket-powered and jet-powered cars climb to speeds over 620 mph. You can have your own speed race at other times of the year, but remember to take plenty of water, snacks, and a GPS so you don't get lost, since there are no landmarks out on the flats. The Flats are one of the most unusual places on earth; it's a sight you won't soon forget.

The closest town is Wendover, right on the Nevada state line. And as you'll find with most places on the Nevada border, there's a thriving resort town right across the line, in West Wendover, Nevada. Look for the cowboy statue, Wendover Will, welcoming you to town and encouraging you to stop and stay a while.

Without a doubt, this 120-mile stretch of the Lincoln Highway has intrigued drivers for decades. Although it's sometimes considered an arrow-straight shot across the western Utah desert, there are surprises and wonders just waiting to be found.

20

Coast to Coast:
A Cross-Continent Adventure

Countless travelers dream of taking a weeklong – or even a monthlong – trek across the continent. It was this dream that inspired the Lincoln Highway, America's first named coast-to-coast road. When that highway first starting taking shape over a century ago, it was little more than a string of rustic wagon trails linked together – barely a road at all. The route in this chapter is a hybrid of several classic highways – the Lincoln, U.S. 50, I-70 over mountain passes, and more. It's one that winds from the Atlantic to the Pacific, passing some of America's best scenery along the way.

This route begins in Ocean City, Maryland, at the shores of the Atlantic Ocean. This is also the eastern terminus of U.S. Highway 50, which we'll rejoin later. Highway 50 winds its way westward across the Delmarva Peninsula all the way to the Chesapeake Bay near Annapolis. It's possible to follow Highway 50 all the way into Washington, D.C., right past the National Mall and the Lincoln Memorial as Constitution Avenue.

Before venturing into Washington by car, though, be aware that traffic is often horrendous, and street parking is difficult to find. Parking garages are expensive near popular tourist attractions. You may be better off driving around Washington on the Capital Beltway – Interstate 495 – and finding a spot at one of the Park-and-Ride complexes in the suburbs. From there catch a ride on the Washington Metro into town. The city's subway system is efficient and beats the stress and expense of trying to find a parking space near the museums or attractions downtown.

Into the Mountains

Leaving the Washington metro area on I-66 traveling west, you'll eventually arrive at the town of Front Royal. This town marks the entrance to one of the most beautiful driving tours in the Eastern United States: Shenandoah National Park's Skyline Drive. Although it costs ten dollars per car to drive the 100-mile long trail, it's well worth the cost. (See Chapter 18 for more details.)

Washington makes for a perfect stop on our cross-country trek

Once south of Interstate 64, you leave Shenandoah and begin traveling on the famous Blue Ridge Parkway. This scenic, sometimes winding mountain road gives some spectacular views of the Blue Ridge and Smoky Mountains as it winds its way nearly 400 miles through Virginia and North Carolina, almost to the Tennessee border. (More details in Chapter 18.)

Our journey along the Blue Ridge Parkway, though, takes us only as far as Roanoke, about 100 miles from where it begins. Roanoke, the largest city along the Blue Ridge Parkway and the largest city for the next 350 miles along our route, is worth a visit of its own. The city's historic downtown area boasts a popular farmer's market, a science museum, and numerous local shops.

From Roanoke, our route continues west along U.S. 460, paralleling the interstate before turning north to cross the Brush Mountains near Blacksburg. After a short jaunt through the southern tip of West Virginia, Highway 460 turns back into

Roanoke's 88-foot Mill Mountain Star can be seen from all over the city every evening.

Virginia as a scenic four-lane highway that continues almost all the way to the Kentucky state line.

Highway 460 continues as a mountain road through the Appalachians into Kentucky. The first town of consequence in Kentucky is Pikeville, home to one of the largest land-removal projects in America. In fact, U.S. 460 passes through the so-called Pikeville Cut-Through, which essentially sliced through a mountain to alleviate flooding in town, increase the amount of usable land in the town's center, and provide a more convenient transportation route. Pikeville is also home to a small university, located atop a steep hill in the mountain town.

Destination: Washington, DC

Our nation's capital is a fun place to visit, especially if you're a history buff. You may be surprised, though, that it's also an inexpensive destination. The most popular museums and sites offer free admission. Lodging can be inexpensive, too, if you're willing to stay in the suburbs.

First of all, getting around Washington is *most* difficult in your own car. If possible, try to park at your hotel or in a lot outside the city – there are plenty of Park-and-Ride facilities in the suburbs near major Metro stations. Take the efficient Metrorail into the city center; most major attractions are within walking distance of a subway station. Remember, it's cheaper to take the subway during non-rush hours.

Some of the most popular destinations are government sites; the Capitol building and Supreme Court both welcome visitors. The White House is open, too, but tickets must be obtained well in advance from your member of Congress. See the Constitution, Declaration of Independence, and Bill of Rights at the National Archives. The Library of Congress is also an interesting destination; look for Thomas Jefferson's first draft of the Declaration of Independence. Admission is free to all these sites.

If you're a museum buff, you won't be disappointed here. The granddaddy of all museum complexes, the Smithsonian, is a collection of over a dozen individual museums, each dedicated to a different facet of American life and culture. Some favorites include the National Air and Space Museum, the National Museum of Natural History, the National Museum of American History, and the National Zoo. The most popular museums are adjacent to the National Mall, within walking distance of numerous monuments, memorials, and government buildings. Once again, admission is free to all Smithsonian museums in the Washington area.

Monuments and memorials abound in the area, as well. The Lincoln Memorial, Vietnam Veterans Memorial, and World War II Memorial are all located on the National Mall, a pedestrian-only park located almost exactly in the middle of the city. If you want to ascend to the top of the Washington Monument, a 555-foot stone obelisk also found on the Mall, you'll need to obtain a free ticket at the lodge on 15th Street. Other monuments worth a visit include the Jefferson Memorial, located alongside the Potomac River, and Arlington National Cemetery, found across the Potomac in Virginia.

Although Washington is best navigated by foot and public transportation, there's enough to do in this city to keep travelers of any budget satisfied for a week or more. So plan a stop in our nation's capital and discover one of America's most interesting destinations.

Pikeville is in the middle of coal mining country, and mining has shaped the fortunes of many of the area's residents. This prosperity is in stark contrast to the abundant poverty of the region, though, as cramped trailer parks and run-down housing are common throughout this part of Appalachia.

Keep following U.S. 460 west until nearing the town of Prestonsburg, where you'll turn left onto State Route 114. This highway eventually becomes the Bert T. Combs Mountain Parkway, which winds through the last 50 miles of the Appalachian Mountains, first as a two-lane highway, then widening to a four-lane freeway.

Kentucky's Bluegrass Region

The central part of Kentucky is called the Bluegrass region, so called because of the light green grass that grows here; it's not really blue. Interstate 64 takes you into the Lexington area, which is known for the two H's: higher education and horses. From the east side of the city, follow U.S. Highway 60; it runs straight through downtown Lexington and is an easy way to get through town. Staying on the interstate only shuttles motorists to the north and east of Lexington; highway 60 takes you past the University of Kentucky campus and the famous Keeneland racetrack, where much of the movie *Seabiscuit* was filmed.

West of Lexington, continue on U.S. 60; look for the castle on the right side of the highway as you leave town. It was built in the 1970's and can now be rented for private events.

West of Versailles (pronounced ver-SALES), keep traveling west on U.S. 62. This road features rolling hills across nearly the rest of the state. Bardstown, a town along this route, is known for the My Old Kentucky Home Dinner Train, one of the few dinner trains of its type in this part of the country.

Past Elizabethtown, Highway 62 flattens out a little, but remains scenic as it crosses an increasingly green – not blue – region of Kentucky. Passing towns such as Beaver Dam, Central City, and Dawson Springs, you'll see that we've returned to coal country, with a land of rivers and lakes soon to follow. (See Chapter 18 for more details on this region.)

The Land of Rivers and Lakes

U.S. 62 eventually takes drivers over gargantuan Kentucky Dam along the Tennessee River, which impounds Kentucky Lake. At over 180 miles in length, it's one of the largest artificial lakes in the country. Nearby is Land Between the Lakes, a federal recreation area with hiking paths, camping facilities, horseback riding, and even a planetarium.

If you keep driving west on Highway 62, you'll end up along the Ohio River in Paducah, the largest town in westernmost Kentucky. It's home to the National Quilt Museum and a thriving art community near the downtown area.

Past Paducah, follow U.S. 60 toward the little town of Wickliffe and a small archeological site called Wickliffe Mounds. Here you'll see what life was like for Native Americans who lived in this area hundreds of years ago.

As you drive past Wickliffe, U.S. 60 turns north briefly to cross the Ohio River. If you look carefully to your left as you cross the river, you'll see the exact confluence of the Ohio and Mississippi Rivers. As soon as you cross into Illinois, turn left to cross the Mississippi River and head into Missouri.

Although U.S. 60 passes through Illinois for only nine-tenths of a mile, there are a couple of interesting places to see along this short segment. Right before crossing into Missouri is the scruffy Fort Defiance Park, located at the confluence of the Mississippi and

Ohio Rivers. It was used as a strategic fort during the Civil War, and there's archeological evidence to suggest that the site has been used for warfare for as much as 1000 years. And yes, it's possible to stand at the point where the two rivers converge, which also happens to be at the lowest elevation in the state of Illinois.

About a mile to the north is the town of Cairo (pronounced CAY-ro). The historic significance of this town is highlighted in books such as Mark Twain's *Huckleberry Finn*. Today, the town is only a shadow of its former glory, but the historic downtown still contains some of the old mansions that exemplify late Victorian era architecture. (See Chapter 17 for more information about this area.)

The Ozarks

Once crossing into Missouri, keep motoring west on U.S. 60. Although the highway does its best to mimic an interstate well past Sikeston, the flat farmland of the Mississippi River valley gives way to rolling hills – and eventually the rugged mountains – of the Ozarks. During the summer, this area comes alive as tourists from all over the Midwest flock to towns like Van Buren to enjoy some of the best whitewater rafting and camping in this part of the country.

As U.S. 60 nears Springfield, our route emerges from the curves and hills of the Ozarks in favor of the flat, humid plains that await us for the next several hundred miles. Springfield is the largest city in southwest Missouri and is a popular gateway for tourists headed to Branson, or a stop for travelers along old Route 66.

For our route, though, we'll bypass most of Springfield along U.S. 60, which grazes the southern edge of the city as a four-lane freeway. Eventually, you'll follow Interstate 44 westbound for a few miles before veering onto Missouri Route 96, which intersects old Route 66, mentioned in Chapter 15. Just past Webb City, head north on Route 171 for a few miles before crossing into Kansas.

Driving the Kansas Plains

Many casual drivers complain about how boring it is to drive across Kansas, especially if they've seen nothing other than Interstate 70. Much of the state, though, features a tranquil beauty that simply can't be appreciated from the interstate. Most of our trek across Kansas will be on U.S. Route 400 in the southern half of the state through the quiet, rural countryside. Be aware, though, that the first 150 miles of our trip through Kansas will have few services. Fill up the gas tank before getting onto Highway 400, and plan to spend the night back in Springfield or ahead in Wichita.

Wichita, with a population of over a third of a million, is the largest city on this route since Washington, D.C., and the largest you'll see until Denver. It's been rated as one of the most livable cities in the country, and boasts several art museums, a zoo, as well as a few other places of interest to roadtrippers. If you're interested in notable pieces of roadside history, you can visit the site of the first Pizza Hut, as well as the first White Castle; both were founded right here in Wichita.

West of Kansas' largest city on U.S. 400, you'll pass a few small towns, mostly farming communities. Kingman, Pratt, and Greensburg are all agricultural towns. Of interest is the town of Greensburg, known as the home of the world's largest hand-dug well. However, one of the most powerful tornadoes ever measured ripped through the community in May 2007, destroying practically the entire town. Shortly after the tragedy, though, the city resolved to rebuild all structures in Greensburg to the highest of all environmental standards.

A little farther down the road is Dodge City, the setting for the 1950's western television series *Gunsmoke*. Today, Dodge City is the meat packing capital of America, with one of the largest beef processing plants in the country. Check out the historic downtown, where you'll catch a glimpse of what life was like in the Wild West.

Ascending into the High Plains

Although the last 300 miles may have seemed excessively flat, the elevation has actually increased by 2000 feet from Joplin to Garden City. And the elevation will increase another 2000 feet over the next 250 miles. From Garden City, turn north onto U.S. 83. Traveling northbound toward Interstate 70, you'll sample much of the beauty of the high plains. Many visitors to Kansas expect flat-lands; you may be surprised that this area is somewhat hilly. In fact, rocky hills and cliffs are visible in the distance throughout much of this area. (See Chapter 17 for more information on U.S. 83 between Garden City and Oakley.)

From Oakley, keep driving west on Interstate 70 to make the quiet three-and-a-half hour trip to Denver. Highway 70 crosses into Colorado at an elevation of just over 4000 feet near Burlington. If you need to grab a bite to eat or fill up the gas tank, stop now, because Burlington is the last town of consequence until Limon, almost a hundred miles away. The Colorado state welcome center, located near Exit 438, is a good place to stop for maps and tourist information.

Most travelers expect Colorado to be mountainous, but the eastern two-fifths of the state is actually flat, almost an extension of the wild high plains of western Kansas. From Burlington to the

At the Colorado state line, the terrain is high but flat

edge of Denver, expect little traffic, a generally straight and flat road, the occasional hill, and a 75 mile-per-hour speed limit. If you'd rather a somewhat slower drive through the Colorado high plains, take Highway 50 west from Garden City to Pueblo, then head north on I-25 through Colorado Springs.

Denver, the 'Mile High City', is surprisingly flat to the first-time visitor. The city lies at the foot of the Rocky Mountains, which are visible from nearly anywhere in the city. Colorado's largest city is a modern oasis boasting fine dining, some of the best museums in the country, major league sports, and plenty of lodging options. You could easily spend a week here, but if you're just passing through, consider a trip to the state capitol, which marks the exact elevation of 5,280 feet above sea level. The Museum of Nature and Science, Colorado History Museum, and Denver Art Museum are also located within easy access to U.S. 40, called Colfax Avenue as it passes through town.

Into the Rockies

The next hundred miles are some of the most-feared stretches of interstate highway in the entire country. Thousands of motorists drive hundreds of miles out of their way to avoid crossing the Front Range of the Rocky Mountains in Colorado. There's very little to fear though, as Interstate 70 is one of the best built and safest – not to mention one of the most beautiful – mountain freeways in the country. Heading west out of Denver on I-70, you'll rise quickly into the mountains. It took nearly 2000 miles from Ocean City to Denver to ascend the first mile in elevation, but you'll climb another mile in less than 70.

As the road rises, the terrain changes, too. Well into the summer, you'll see remnants of winter snow alongside the interstate. Several rest areas and scenic overlooks have been built along this stretch of road, making it easy to check out the surroundings at this elevation. You'll

Even in June, you'll find snow at higher elevations in the Rockies

pass major ski resort towns such as Breckinridge, Vail, and Avon. Take note: near milepost 211, you'll go through the Eisenhower Memorial Tunnel, which at an altitude of over 11,000 feet, is the highest point on the U.S. interstate system. From here at the Continental Divide, on average it's downhill until you reach the Pacific Ocean near San Diego.

Glenwood Canyon: Jewel of the Highway

Shortly after passing Avon, the road flattens a bit for a few miles, and you may think you've finished crossing the mountains. However, you're about to drive through Glenwood Canyon, one of the last sections of the interstate to be built through Colorado. Due to the fragile ecosystem surrounding the canyon, there was intense public opposition to building a freeway here. Well into the 1980's, this stretch of the interstate was still in jeopardy, as legal battles and engineering challenges threatened its construction.

Eventually, the interstate was completed, but under the condition that the environment be protected in the process. As a result, the Glenwood Canyon crossing showcases its region's natural, rugged beauty like few other interstates do. Be sure to enjoy the scenic overlook rest areas – there are four of them – to admire the majesty of the canyon from outside your vehicle. The canyon really is a sight to see, as the rocky walls around you tower 1300 feet straight into the air. It's been called one of the most scenic natural formations on the entire interstate system, so don't miss it!

Into Utah: Canyons, National Parks, and Desert

From Glenwood Springs to Grand Junction, the interstate generally parallels the Colorado River, often passing right next to it. From here west, the interstate levels off at just under 5000 feet in elevation, with deep-red tinted mountains off in the distance. Once you reach Grand Junction – named for the Grand River, the original name of the Colorado River – your trip through the mountains is essentially complete. Traffic gets very light west of Grand Junction. Fill up in Grand Junction or Fruita, because you're nearly 100 miles from the next small town: Green River, Utah, population 900.

As Interstate 70 crosses into Utah, the scenery is still majestic, yet subdued due to the lack of traffic, as mountains give way to desert. The scenic overlooks here are not to be missed. Along the way, you'll pass massive geologic formations with names such as Ghost Rock, Book Cliffs, and Goblin Valley, with sweeping vistas that live up to their names.

This area of eastern Utah between Salina and the Colorado state line is nearly uninhabited except for the little town of Green River. In fact, the interstate was the first modern road to be built through here. Cell phone signals may be weak or even nonexistent through this area, but its grandiose beauty is well worth any lack of conveniences.

Eastern Utah is also dinosaur country. This stretch of interstate is part of the Dinosaur Diamond Prehistoric Highway, and dinosaur remains have been unearthed through much of this area, as well as northwest Colorado. Eastern Utah, especially turning south on U.S. 131 at the Moab exit, is a popular gateway for vacationers headed to Utah's numerous national parks. Arches National Park, Canyonlands National Park, Capitol Reef National Park, and Bryce Canyon National Park are all within easy reach of I-70.

Near Salina, we continue west, rejoining U.S. 50. Through this part of central Utah, the terrain flattens considerably, and the road becomes arid and dusty. Highway 50 joins Interstate 15 for a few miles before heading west again through the little town of Delta. Then, towns and villages become a rarity for the next few hundred miles along our route, especially as we cross into Nevada.

Lonely Highways of the Great Basin

U.S. 50 through Nevada has been called the 'Loneliest Road in America' due to the lack of traffic. The drive from Ely to Reno is over 300 miles long and crosses nine mountain ranges. At times, the view along this highway in the Great Basin is so straight that you can see thirty miles or more of road ahead. For more information about this exceptional highway, see Chapter 19.

The Great Basin in Nevada is one of the loneliest places in America

For our journey, though, we'll be turning left onto U.S. 93 shortly before getting to Ely. Route 93 is almost a 'Loneliest Road' of its own, with so little traffic that one wonders if it will eventually lead anywhere. Off in the distance, you'll see snowcapped Wheeler Peak, one of Nevada's highest mountains. This route through the

Great Basin curves up and over numerous mountains and hills down the eastern spine of the state of Nevada before descending upon the towns of Pioche, Panaca, and Caliente.

As you travel the final stretch of Highway 93 before touching the interstate, notice the straight, level road ahead of you. The road runs for nearly 50 miles with little more than a slight curve or two. Eventually, U.S. 93 runs into Interstate 15 and continues south to Las Vegas.

Interstate 15 parallels the Las Vegas Strip, so you'll have a great view of the gargantuan hotel-casinos for which the city is famous – from the Stratosphere at the north end to Mandalay Bay at the south end. Although Las Vegas is built around the gaming industry, there's still much to see and do, even if you're not a gambler. The spectacle of the city's architecture is worth a visit, and the shopping and dining options are endless.

The Desert

The California state line through here sits squarely in the desert

Leaving Las Vegas for the south, take I-215 east until you reach I-515 east. Once you've left the city, continue south on U.S. Highway 95. And all of a sudden, you're back in the quiet, barren desert, on the straight-as-an-arrow dusty road. As you drive south on U.S. 95, you're about 60 miles from the California state line. You cross into California not far from Needles, a small town named for the needle-like mountains visible here. Our route crosses Old Route 66 one last time along what's now Interstate 40. South of the interstate, the desert continues as a seemingly endless backdrop of scrub brush and dry land. As the road keeps going south, we eventually hit Interstate 10, and our route backtracks to the east for nearly 20 miles, entering the state of Arizona.

Here, you're squarely in the desert, and the elements were inhospitable to travelers passing through these parts back in the Old West. Today, though, our drive is quick and relatively easy, and we're left to admire the tranquil grandeur of the western desert.

Eventually, U.S. 95 meets the city of Yuma, Arizona, right on the California state line. Yuma is the sunniest city in the world; the sun shines for over 90% of all daylight hours here, according to the Guinness Book of World Records. It's also one of the hottest towns in the United States, as average high temperatures for the month of July average a scorching 107 degrees Fahrenheit!

From Yuma, our route enters its homestretch, continuing west on Interstate 8. This freeway through southern California just about has it all: deserts, mountains, and cities, eventually reaching the San Diego beach.

Interstate 8 parallels the Mexican border through nearly its entire journey through California; through Imperial County, the road is as little as a mile or two from the border in places. You'll pass the Imperial Sand Dunes, an unmistakable sign that you're still in the desert.

Of note along this route is the town of El Centro. The name would suggest that the town is located in the center of California, but it's actually one of the southernmost – and actually most remote – cities in the state. Interstate 8 near El Centro also holds the honor of having the lowest elevation on the entire Interstate Highway System, around 50 feet *below* sea level.

> For more details on what to see along I-8, see Chapter 19 – Road Trip Ideas for the West

Destination: Las Vegas

In a word, Las Vegas, Nevada, can be described as a *spectacle*. It's a city known for extravagant excesses and one of the few places of the world most famous for architecture inspired by – or more accurately, copied from – other cities. Most hotel-resorts are based on other places: Paris, New York New York, Mandalay Bay, Rio, Luxor; the list goes on and on. It's the only place in the world where you can see the Eiffel Tower on one side of the street, the Empire State Building on the other, with an Egyptian pyramid in the distance.

Of course, this city is built on gambling, and those extravagant casinos weren't built on the backs of winners. Casinos will do everything they can to lure potential players into their properties. That's why they've traditionally been willing to offer dinner specials or buffets at low prices.

Although Las Vegas doesn't cater to 'cheapskates' anymore, there are still a few inexpensive meals to be had, mainly at off-Strip locations. Some off-Strip casinos feature lunch buffets for as little as $8. Most of the higher-quality buffets are found at Center Strip and South Strip properties. One of the best is the Bellagio Buffet, which at about $24 for lunch and $35 for dinner, is actually quite reasonable, considering the quality and quantity of food available.

After dinner, enjoy a stroll down the Strip – South Las Vegas Boulevard – and gawk at the larger-than-life hotels and architecture that's sometimes even more fun than the originals on which they're based. Walk through the streets of Venice – town square, gondolas, canals, and all. Meander the streets of Paris and New York. Enjoy the surroundings and walk the indoor 'streets' of the hotels, most of which are lined with shops akin to an upscale shopping mall.

Once you're tired of the glitz and glamour of the Strip, get out of town and head south – either to the Grand Canyon or to Hoover Dam. Both are wonders that have to been seen to be believed – one natural and the other man-made – and they're within an easy drive of the city. Las Vegas is a town that's easy to explore, and you don't have to risk a dime!

After driving through the desert for several hundred miles, you're probably ready for a change of scenery. And I-8 fluctuates dramatically over its final hundred miles. The elevation rises – and then falls – a few thousand feet to cross the mountain pass a few miles before ploughing through scenic Cleveland National Forest. The wooded terrain and alpine greenery belie the fact that you're so close to the desert.

Descending Toward the Pacific

Leaving the forest near the town of Alpine, it's downhill all the way into the San Diego suburbs. If you choose to continue on Interstate 8 all the way through San Diego, you'll be able to see the Pacific Ocean in the distance just as the freeway ends. At this point, you're within easy access of Sea World, numerous oceanfront parks, and of course, the beach itself.

If you've followed the route described in these pages, you'll have driven nearly 3,500 miles from coast to coast. You'll probably be a bit tired, but you will have seen a little of everything America has to offer – from desert to forest, from mountains to plains, from ski resorts to beaches, from rivers to lakes to oceans.

Most Americans have never experienced this type of coast-to-coast adventure; to enjoy it to the fullest would take at least two weeks, likely more. It could be the road trip of a lifetime for many people. But how about another type of ultimate trip – one to the top of the world? I'll cover that journey – north to Alaska – in the next chapter.

21

North to Alaska

One of the most fascinating adventures you can take in North America is a trip to Alaska. Over the years, the trip along the famed Alaska Highway has gotten a reputation for being one of the longest, most difficult, and most isolated trips in North America. Although that reputation may have been well-deserved in decades past, today's Alaska Highway is well-maintained and paved the entire way. And even though the highway itself is a long 1,400 miles, it passes through some of the most amazing scenery in the world. For that reason, the drive north to Alaska is often considered the trip of a lifetime.

The Alaska Highway officially begins in Dawson Creek, British Columbia, which is already nearly 750 miles north of the U.S./Canadian border at Sweet Grass, Montana. When planning your trip to Alaska, keep in mind the huge distances involved. For most travelers from the Lower 48, driving to Alaska involves a round-trip distance of well over 8,000 miles. You'll need to allow, at the very minimum, a month to savor your time in Canada and Alaska.

The budget for this journey should be bigger than a typical road trip of the same distance. Gas prices in Canada and Alaska are much higher than what you'll find in the lower 48 -- expect to pay at least a dollar more per gallon, even more in the most remote sections of the road. Motels are relatively few and far between, and they'll be expensive. Expect prices of $120 a night and up for even the simplest accommodations.

Contrary to what you may have heard, fuel is fairly easy to find along the Alaska Highway. Gas stations, though expensive, are found at least every 50 miles along the way. The longest stretch of highway without any fuel services is about 100 miles in northern British Columbia. So don't worry about having to carry an extra fuel tank to make the trip.

The highway is in relatively good shape, much better than 30 or 40 years ago, when much of the road was unpaved gravel. Still, the severe winters up here do damage the road. and you will find potholes and breaks in the pavement. During the summer, road construction is an ongoing project, and you'll be slowed by road crews from time to time.

Although the Alaska Highway is now paved, there are still narrow stretches of road where you won't find a center line. And there are still a few blind curves, especially in the more mountainous stretches. But there's no denying that the breathtaking scenery and abundant wildlife you'll find along this route are well worth any minor inconveniences.

Gearing Up for Alaska

In addition to any specialized equipment you may want for your trip, there are a few items every Alaska traveler should have. A good full-size spare tire -- not just a doughnut -- is a good idea, especially if you plan to go off-road. Gravel roads are the rule off the main highway, and you'll need to be prepared. Bring a good jack, as well as some simple tools and an emergency road kit. As long as you drive sensibly, you likely won't need any specialized vehicle equipment, other than the emergency supplies you'd take on any long trek.

Even in the summer, prepare for cool weather, especially at night. It's not unheard of to see near-freezing temperatures even in July at northern latitudes, particularly in the mountains. Bring long-sleeved shirts and a jacket. Of course, temperatures can also soar as high as 90 during the summer, so be flexible.

Staying connected can be a challenge on the Alaska Highway. Cell service is spotty in northern Canada, and international roaming charges can be exorbitant. Think seriously about installing a CB radio before leaving home. In some areas, it may be your only way to call for help.

It's a wise idea to invest in a motor club membership that includes long-distance towing. Tow trucks and mechanics can be very expensive in remote areas; expect to pay about $5 a mile to get your vehicle towed. And don't forget to carry some cash or traveler's checks for repairs; many mechanics up here don't take credit cards.

Make sure to schedule enough time to enjoy the drive to Alaska. Allow 7 - 10 days to drive from the central U.S. to Fairbanks. Allow more time if starting from the East Coast. If your plans include hiking or fishing along the way, or side trips into more remote parts of the North country, allow for double that time.

Along the Route

The Alaska Highway officially begins about 700 miles north of the Canadian border. The absolute best route guide for the Alaska Highway is *The Milepost*, which is published annually and contains a mile-by-mile guide to attractions, stops, and scenery available at every turn along the way. If you plan on driving to Alaska, you owe it to yourself to pick up this essential guide. However, I'm glad to share some attractions that come highly recommended by many travelers of the Alaska Highway.

Head-Smashed-In Buffalo Jump. Not located on the Alaska Highway, but about 2 ½ hours past the Canadian border just west of Lethbridge, Alberta. This UNESCO World Heritage Site marks the location where Native Americans hunted buffalo for thousands of years by chasing them over a cliff, then prepared their carcasses on the land below. Museum open daily 10 - 5; CAD$10.00.

Calgary, Alberta. This major city is located about four hours north of the border and has a population of 1.2 million. Although it was famous for hosting the 1988 Winter Olympics, Calgary is best known as the gateway to the Canadian Rockies. From high atop Calgary Tower, you can look east and see the seemingly endless prairies. Look west and see the majestic Rockies. The city is also famous for a 10-day festival in July celebrating its western cowboy roots, the Calgary Stampede.

Dawson Creek, BC marks Mile 0
of the Alaska Highway

Edmonton, Alberta. Located about four hours north of Calgary, with a population of 1.1 million, Edmonton is Canada's "Festival City." It's the capital of the province of Alberta and holds many fascinating cultural gems such as the Royal Alberta Museum. One of the most popular attractions in the city is West Edmonton Mall, the largest shopping mall on the continent. It has over 800 stores, as well as the world's largest indoor water park.

Dawson Creek, British Columbia. Population 12,000. When you get to the official southern terminus of the Alaska Highway, you've likely already been on the road for a few days. The excitement is just beginning, though. Check out the exhibits at Walter Wright Pioneer Village depicting the Alaska Highway's construction during the 1940s. Gardens North is a fascinating botanical garden that makes for an enjoyable stroll on a summer afternoon.

Watson Lake, Yukon. Population 1,500.If you've made it this far, you've just crossed the 60th parallel and entered the Yukon Territory. You're also halfway from Dawson Creek to Alaska. Watson Lake has the only outdoor water slide in the Yukon, and yes, it does get warm enough in the summer to use it. Travelers from all over the world pass through here, so it's appropriate to see the Sign Post Forest, a site with nearly 80,000 road signs and license plates from around the world, some dating back as far as the 1940s, when the road was under construction.

Whitehorse, Yukon. Population 23,000. Whitehorse is the capital of the Yukon, with all the amenities of a bigger town. In fact, this is the largest 'city' on the Alaska Highway. If you choose to stay here for a couple days, you'll find several museums, interesting architecture, good food, and abundant hiking and fishing to keep you busy. Summer daylight up here lasts over 19 hours, but you still have another 350 miles before you get to Alaska.

Haines Junction, Yukon. This small town, population 600, is the gateway to Kluane National Park, where you'll find Mount Logan, Canada's tallest mountain. This is one of the best places along the Alaska Highway for spotting wildlife, such as moose, grizzly bears, mountain goats, and Dall sheep. This is a site you won't want to miss.

Tok, Alaska. Population 1,200. The stunning subarctic mountain vistas keep on coming as you drive the next stretch of highway past Haines Junction through Kluane National Park. Just under 300

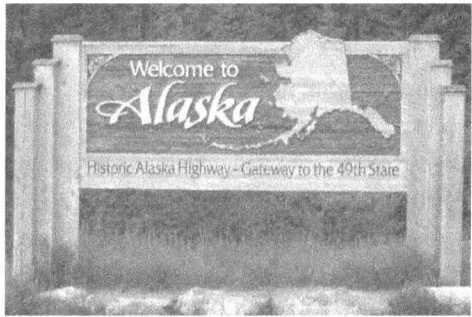

After driving through Canada for 1900 miles, you're finally welcomed to Alaska.

miles after leaving Haines, you finally cross back into the United States and into Alaska. Tok is the first town on Alaska on this route. Enjoy some good food and hospitality; the people here are friendly, and you'll be ready to celebrate your crossing into Alaska. This is the "Dog Capital of Alaska," where dog breeding is a major industry.

Delta Junction, Alaska. Population 1,000. About 110 miles past Tok, you've reached the official end of the Alaska Highway. After passing historic milepost 1422, you'll have a chance to reflect on the unforgettable scenery you've seen. Most roadtrippers will continue on to Fairbanks, which is another 100 miles past Delta. From Fairbanks, you can continue further into the interior of Alaska, which guarantees adventure at every turn.

Want to Go to the Top of the World?

For a few ambitious roadtrippers, it's not enough just to reach Alaska; they want to drive across the Arctic Circle and see the Arctic Ocean. If your vehicle is in good shape, and you're willing to endure bumpy gravel roads for several hundred miles, it's possible to drive within just a few miles of the Arctic Ocean. From there, you can take a tour of the beach and even dip your feet in the frigid ocean waters. This route is not for the faint of heart; it's called the Dalton Highway, and it literally takes you as far north as you can drive on the planet.

The Dalton Highway, also known as Alaska Highway 11, is primarily a haul road used by truckers ferrying supplies to the oil fields. The road passes through some of the coldest territory in the country, where temperatures in the wintertime routinely drop to −50°F, and wind chills can be as low as −100°F. Conditions that cold can be fatal in a matter of minutes. This drive *should not be attempted in the wintertime* by anyone other than professional drivers, such as those featured in the series Ice Road Truckers, which actually featured the Dalton Highway for three seasons.

The summer is a different matter, though. Between mid-June and Labor Day, the ice on the road melts and the temperatures rise enough to make the journey between Fairbanks and the Arctic an attainable yet difficult drive. Although the temperatures this far north never get much higher than 70°F, even on the warmest days, snowfall is possible at any time of the year. Although this is primarily a road for truckers, passenger vehicles and even motorcycles can be found here. I recommend a vehicle with higher clearance, such as an SUV or pickup, due to the rough gravel surface and frequent potholes.

Driving the Dalton

About 84 miles north of Fairbanks, the Dalton Highway begins at a place called Livengood (Mile 0). I recommend filling your gas tank in Fairbanks, because filling stations after that will be rare. At the Yukon River Bridge (Mile 56), you'll cross the widest river on this route. This bridge has a wooden deck, and it's best to drive slowly. Don't stop on the bridge though, especially in wet weather, because you're apt to slide on the slick surface.

At Mile 115, you'll cross the Arctic Circle. Stop to take a picture, as it's one of only two places in North America where roads cross into the Arctic. North of here, the sun never sets for at least one day during the summer. During the winter, the sun never rises for at least one day. Many visitors travel here in late June to experience the 'midnight sun.'

The Dalton Highway is the only road in the U.S. to cross the Arctic Circle

Coldfoot (Mile 175), pop. 10, is a small but important stop, sometimes called the "world's northernmost truck stop." Many travelers spend the night here at the Slate Creek Inn. This is the last place you'll find services for the next 240 miles. Unless you have an unusually large gas tank, fueling up here is just about mandatory. The town developed over 100 years ago, but experienced a small revival in the 1970's during the construction of the Alaska Pipeline. It remains an important stop both for truckers and tourists traveling the Dalton.

For the next hundred miles, you'll be crossing the rugged mountains of the Brooks Range. Even in July, snow is possible from here on up to Deadhorse. Grades reach up to 12 percent, especially nearing Atigun Pass (Mile 244) and the Continental Divide. North of the pass, all water drains into the Arctic Ocean, while to the south, streams eventually drain to the Pacific. This is also the highest point on the Dalton, at over 4700 feet.

North of the Brooks Range, the vegetation changes considerably. You'll find few trees this far north, just grasses and small shrubs. The last 100 miles or so are increasingly flat and filled with wetlands and marsh in the summer. Still, this area of the North Slope is permafrost. Even in the warmer months, the ground is permanently frozen just a few inches below the surface.

After traversing the flat marshland, you'll finally arrive at Deadhorse (Mile 414). Here, the Dalton Highway ends, and you won't be allowed to drive onto the private roads that lead to the Arctic Ocean, about ten miles away. However, the hotels in town can help you book tours of the Prudhoe Bay oil facilities for about $50 a person, which will also take you to the Arctic Ocean. Con-

Coldfoot marks the last services for 240 miles.

---

gratulations! You've driven to the top of the world!

Driving Tips for the Dalton

The Dalton Highway is one of the most challenging long-distance highways in North America. Remember the following tips to make your trip safe and enjoyable:

- The speed limit on the Dalton is 50 mph. Since most of the road is gravel, you probably won't be able to go that fast for most of the route.

- Go very slowly when meeting oncoming trucks, no faster than 10 mph, to avoid flying gravel. When trucks come up from behind and want to pass, pull over and let them by. Remember, the Dalton is a haul road primarily for trucks. Let them have priority.

- Visibility is often low, so drive with your headlights on at all times.

- Make sure your vehicle is in excellent shape before leaving Fairbanks. Check your tire condition and pressure often. You don't want to get stranded up here; in a worst-case scenario, you'd be hundreds of miles from a mechanic.

- Install a CB radio for this trip and keep it tuned to Channel 19. Forget about cell phone service up here; it's too remote.

- Most of the Dalton is covered in gravel. Pavement this far north tends to get cratered with potholes, so gravel is actually a more reliable surface choice. Just take it slow, and allow a *minimum* of 3 full days for the trip from Fairbanks to Deadhorse and back.

- 🐾 Bring cash and major credit cards for expenses. Debit cards have not always been accepted at stations along this route.

- 🐾 When you see a gas station, fill up! There are only *four gas stations along the entire route*: two near the Yukon River (Mile 56), one at Coldfoot (Mile 175), and one at Deadhorse (Mile 414). Gasoline will be extremely expensive, but you do not want to run out up here. Between Coldfoot and Deadhorse is a 240-mile stretch of highway with no fuel services, the longest such stretch in the nation.

- 🐾 The Dalton Highway comes relatively close to the Alaska Pipeline. Enjoy the view from a distance. For security reasons, no one is allowed near the pipeline.

- 🐾 Enjoy the wildlife, but from a distance. Bears are common up here, so learn as much as you can about them, and don't leave food containers in the open.

When you get home, you may wish you'd have spent more time on your Alaska trip. Budget at least a month for a trip from the Lower 48 up to Alaska, more if you can be away that long. There's a reason Alaska is called the Last Frontier; much of it is practically untouched by human hands and has a pristine beauty that can be found in few other places on the planet. Your drive north will definitely give you memories you'll want to share; savor every moment of a trip you'll never forget!

22

South to Mexico

Y ears ago, before I starting taking long trips by car, my impression of driving in Mexico was one that had been shaped by legends and rumors instead of reality. That impression, as it turned out, was a myth. Mexico is a modern country, and although driving down south is different from the U.S.A., it simply requires a little more preparation and vigilance.

This route is adventurous, especially if you've never driven south of the border before. During early spring – February, March, and April to be specific – you'll go from a cold, wintry climate to a tropical paradise where you're surrounded by palm trees and warm sand. Although the trip can easily be made in three days – or even two, in the case of an ambitious speed run – this route is best enjoyed over the course of at least a week, or even more.

Our eventual destination is the picturesque Emerald Coast – *Costa Esmeralda*, as it's called in Spanish – located on the Gulf of Mexico in the central part of Veracruz state. It's a good twelve hours of solid driving from the United States border, but those twelve hours would wisely be divided into two or three days, to best enjoy the scenery that few Americans ever get to see.

Signs of a Border

The route we've chosen begins in Robstown, Texas, nearly 150 miles from the Mexican border. For hundreds of years, the Hispanic influence on the region has always been immense. Many of the towns and counties in this part of Texas have names derived from the Spanish language, like Refugio, Nueces, and Sarita. Turn on the FM radio near here, and you'll likely hear popular Tejano music. Family-owned taco stands dot the side of the road in little communities throughout this area. Instead of the rolling hills found in East Texas, the land here is flat and dry. Instead of tall pines, scrub brush is the common foliage. Further south, you even start to see small cactus line the side of the road.

The Rio Grande Valley and Tropical Texas

Continuing south on Highway 77, the highway enters Willacy County, and the first thing you'll notice will be the palm trees lining the median of the expressway. From this point, it's no more than a half hour to Harlingen, the first big town in the Rio Grande Valley. Although it's called a valley, there are no mountains to be seen within 100 miles of here. And contrary to what the name implies, the Rio Grande isn't really that big. At this point along its riverbed, the river separating the two countries is really not much more than a wide stream. (For more information about the Rio Grande Valley, see Chapter 18.)

The Queen Isabella Causeway leads to the beaches and resorts of South Padre Island

If you're planning on continuing into Mexico, you can cross the Rio Grande on any one of several toll bridges. Nearly a dozen international bridges throughout the Valley carry thousands of people – not to mention cargo – across the border in both directions every day.

Your trip will be less stressful – and safer – if you avoid the downtown bridges, that is, any bridge in downtown Brownsville or

McAllen. The bridges at Los Indios, Nuevo Progreso, and Pharr make for the easiest border crossings, in that order.

Walking into Mexico

If you're just planning to explore a border town instead of continuing to the interior of Mexico, don't even bother driving across the Rio Grande. Find one of the numerous parking lots on the U.S. side; most of them charge just a couple of dollars to leave your car all day. Walking into Mexico is less stressful and lets you see the border towns much more easily; the bridge toll for pedestrians is about 50 cents.

Probably the best border town for those who have never visited Mexico is Nuevo Progreso. Located within easy walking distance of Highway FM 1015 south of Weslaco, Nuevo Progreso provides a little bit of everything. Shopping, restaurants, bars, and hotels are located all along the main street as soon as you walk across the bridge into Mexico. You'll find an abundance of dentists and pharmacies here, too; thousands of Americans cross the border every year to fill prescriptions or have dental work done. Since the price is often a fraction of that in the U.S., it's an attractive option, especially for those on a limited income.

It's possible to buy almost any Mexican product in Nuevo Progreso, from clay pottery to porcelain dolls representing cultures of every state in the country. And don't worry about exchanging your money;

Crossing the Mexican border over the Rio Grande at Nuevo Progreso

American dollars are actually preferred here.

If you decide to walk through town, be aware that Nuevo Progreso is very compact and designed for pedestrians, but not so much for drivers. From the International Bridge to the farthest edge of town is about seven blocks. And since most businesses for the tourist are on the main street, there's little reason to stray much from the main thoroughfare.

Once you've reached the border, this trip is just beginning. The most spectacular parts are yet to come. If you're nervous about driving in Mexico, though, read on. The next section will give you tips on legal requirements for driving your car in Mexico, as well as tips on driving safely south of the border.

Passport

Driver's License

Credit Card

Title to Your Car

Before Crossing the Border

Important Documents. Well before you drive to Mexico, you'll need to take several steps to ensure a smooth entry into the country. Plan on the taking the following documents with you:

If you're still making payments on your car, the border authorities *may* ask to see a letter from the lienholder, leasing company, or bank granting permission for the car to be driven into Mexico.

If you don't yet have a passport, get one. Mexico now requires *all* U.S. citizens to present a passport or a passport card at all entry points, even land crossings. Apply at least two months before your trip; sometimes there are delays, especially before busy travel periods.

Buy insurance. Think seriously about buying auto insurance for your trip to Mexico. Regardless of what your friends may say, your liability coverage from home *does not* cover you once you cross the border. To have coverage, you must buy a special policy from a company licensed to do business in Mexico. Not to worry, though, as most border crossings will sell policies on the spot, and it's even possible to buy insurance by the day.

Buying insurance at the border will usually cost much more than buying a good policy online. Do an online search for "Mexico Insurance," and you'll find dozens of options. When buying, make sure that the policy includes legal assistance in the event of an accident. As a comparison, the liability policy I purchased on my last trip to Mexico cost less than $160 for an entire year. Shop around, and you'll find a good deal.

Although auto insurance is not mandatory for motorists in most parts of Mexico, it's wise to obtain a good policy before making the trip. Normally, drivers without insurance who get into an accident automatically go to jail – regardless of fault – until the details are sorted out. With liability insurance, though, an accident is treated much as it is in the United States, and insurance companies handle matters.

If your car has full coverage back home in the U.S., it's normally easy to add full coverage to your Mexican policy, as well. Be aware, though, that you normally can't add comprehensive or collision coverage to your policy in Mexico unless you're already covered back in the States.

At the Border

It's really quite easy to take your car to Mexico. However, you'll need to follow a few steps at the border to register your vehicle to be able to drive past the border region into Mexico's interior.

On a good day – and at a non-congested border crossing – it may take as little as 20 minutes to complete this process. When there's a line, though, it can be up to two hours. Plan ahead, take all your documents, and you won't have a problem. Be aware that the least congested times at most border stations are early morning and mid-afternoon – from 9:00 to 10:00 and 1:00 to 3:00.

Step One: Tourist Card. As soon as you cross the border, you'll see a customs station marked "Car Permits", "Banjercito", "Tourist Permits", or something similar. Pull into the parking lot and go inside. The first step will be to obtain a *tourist card*, sometimes called a *tourist visa* or *F.M.T.* From this point onward, it will help if you can speak at least a little Spanish, since the government workers at the border stations usually speak little English.

At larger border crossings, you'll wait in line at a window similar to those at a bank. At smaller crossings, you may actually step into a small office. Whatever the case, present your passport, and then you'll be asked to fill out the actual visa form. Return it to the officer, who will then stamp it. He or she might also stamp your passport. The border officer will grant you a stay of up to 180 days.

Step Two: Pay the Tourist Fee. Mexico

Children Traveling to Mexico

If any minors traveling to Mexico with you are not accompanied by both parents, he or she must bring a notarized letter from the parent(s) not traveling with the child. The letter needs to state that the child has permission to travel to Mexico, and it needs to give the names of the adults who *will* be accompanying the child. If one or both of the child's parents are deceased, the appropriate death certificate should be presented.

charges a fee of about 25 dollars to process a tourist card. Most border crossings will have a bank where you can pay this fee. You can pay either in dollars or pesos, so don't worry about exchanging your money yet. After you pay the fee, the bank teller will stamp the tourist card, showing proof of payment.

Is there no bank at this crossing? Or is it closed? If so, don't worry about paying the fee now. You're allowed to pay it at any time before leaving Mexico. Find a bank in a small town a couple hours down the road and pay it there.

Step Three: Make Copies. To register your car temporarily in Mexico, you'll have to present your tourist card, passport, vehicle title, driver's license, and credit card. You'll be required to present copies of the first four documents during step four. You can save time by making copies of your license, title, and passport identification page before leaving home. There will be someone, likely in a little office, offering to make copies for a fee, likely between 50 cents and a dollar.

Step Four: Banjercito. *Banjercito* is the official bank of the Mexican army, and one of their jobs is to register cars driven by foreigners into the country. You may have to wait in a slow-moving line at this step, but when you finish, you'll be done! Make sure that *Banjercito* is open when you plan to cross. Although larger, downtown border crossings operate 24 hours a day, smaller crossings, such as Los Indios and Nuevo Progreso, tend to keep 'banker's hours,' and may close as early as 4:00 p.m.

At the Banjercito window, present your tourist card, passport, vehicle title, license, credit card, and all copies to the clerk. Make sure the names on all five of these documents are yours; if they don't match, getting a car permit will become much more difficult, if not impossible. After a few minutes, you'll sign an agreement stat-

What You Can Take Into Mexico

Vacationers can generally take personal belongings into Mexico without any problems. Mexican customs provides an exhaustive list of exactly what can and cannot be taken into the country. Instead of memorizing a list, though, simply be reasonable. Anything that resembles commercial goods will raise suspicions, if you're traveling as a tourist. Anything that resembles an illegal drug, a weapon, or ammunition will disrupt your trip and *will* likely land you into prison. Although pets can be brought into Mexico under certain circumstances, the hassle may be more than it's worth; animals may be better off staying home.

ing you won't sell the car while in Mexico. You'll also sign a credit card slip authorizing a charge of about $44, the current fee for car permits. Your credit card will also be charged a deposit of several hundred dollars, *which will be refunded* when you cancel your car permit before it expires upon leaving Mexico.

It's important to note that only the owner may import his or her own car into Mexico; you won't be allowed to import someone else's car – whether borrowed or rented. Also, the credit card must be issued to the same person whose name is on the vehicle's title. If you don't have a major credit card, you'll still be able to get a car permit; you'll just have to leave a bond, or deposit, of several hundred dollars *in cash* as a guarantee that you'll take the car back to the States before your permit expires.

When the clerk is finished processing your papers, he or she will present you with a registration certificate and a hologram. The certificate – which serves as the actual permit – should be kept in the car *at all times* when driving in Mexico. Your car could be impounded if you do not carry the permit when driving. The hologram, which has a small microchip, should be placed on the windshield just below the rearview mirror; it serves as visible evidence that your car has been brought into the country legally.

One of the conditions of your car permit is that you will not let anyone else drive your car while in Mexico, unless you are physically present in the vehicle at the time. So, you can't lend your car to a friend or relative. If you do, the authorities will assume the car is stolen and impound it. There are a few specific instances in which someone else *can* drive the car; they're specifically listed on the back of the car permit certificate.

Step Five: You're Done! Now that you have the car permit and hologram attached to the windshield, you're free to drive all over Mexico. About 25 miles past the border, you'll pass a Mexican border patrol checkpoint. You'll probably be asked to show your papers. If so, present the officer your car permit. You may also be asked for your tourist card or passport.

Step Six: Cancel the Permit. When you leave Mexico, make sure to stop by the *Banjercito* branch at the border and cancel your car permit. Larger border crossings will have a drive-thru window where you can cancel; smaller crossings may require you to get out of the car and stand in line to cancel your permit. Either way, don't forget this step!

Visitors who forget to cancel their car permits before they expire will forfeit their credit card deposit, costing them several hundred dollars. This can only be done at the border, so by all means, cancel the car permit on your way home!

Currency in Mexico. There's no need to obtain Mexican pesos before your trip. You'll find currency exchanges near the border and within the interior of Mexico; in fact, nearly every bank in the country will be happy to exchange currency if you present a passport or other identification.

At most crossings, there will be at least one currency exchange just north of the border. These usually offer a fair exchange rate, normally much better than what you'd find at an airport, or even at your hometown bank. Very few currency exchanges at the border charge a commission on top of the rate; those that do should be avoided.

One of the best ways to obtain local currency is via ATM. The ATM card from your local bank should work just fine in Mexico, and the same PIN number will be valid. Although most banks charge a few dollars for an international transaction, you'll likely get a better exchange rate. To come out ahead, withdraw a few hundred dollars worth at a time, instead of just a little.

Mexico's unit of currency is the peso. The symbol for the peso is $, which is the same as our dollar sign. So when you see a meal at a restaurant that costs $90.00, that's 90 pesos, which is a little less than seven dollars. Bills are available in 20, 50, 100, 200, 500, and 1,000 peso denominations. Coins are issued in 10, 5, 2, and 1 peso values, as well as 10, 20, and 50 cents.

A Primer on Driving in Mexico

After you get your car permit, you'll be ready to embark on an exciting journey few Americans ever take. Before charging forward, though, review a few tips on driving in Mexico that will make your trip more enjoyable.

Look out for the speed bumps. They're called *topes* (pronounced TOA-pays) in Mexico, and they're giant speed bumps designed to slow you down to almost a halt when approaching a town or major intersection. Hit one of these *topes* at anything more than about five miles per hour, and you're likely to throw your front end out of alignment or do serious damage to your muffler.

Most of the time, *topes* are announced ahead of time with a sign reading "Zona de Topes" or a yellow sign with two or three bumps. In many small communities, *topes* are used in lieu of traffic signals to slow down vehicles near intersections. You'll also find them when approaching a town or a school crossing. Be careful; some of these *topes* are hidden and may take you by surprise!

Obtain a good map. Quality road maps in Mexico are hard to come by. Most road atlases sold in the U.S. relegate Mexico to one page in the back. Those maps are practically useless as road maps, except perhaps for locating major cities or states. Unlike in the United States, good road maps are not handed out freely at rest areas; you'll have to buy one.

My favorite is the comprehensive *Guía Roji* road atlas. It covers the entire Mexican republic, as well as much of Guatemala and Belize. They can be bought online or special-ordered through a bookstore. However, you'll frequently find them sold at gas stations in Mexico, so keep your eyes open for one. The basic atlas runs just under 200 pesos (about 15 dollars), which may seem expensive, but it's money well spent.

Buying gasoline. Fuel, called *gasolina*, is easily available throughout Mexico. Don't bother shopping around for the best price, though, as only one brand – government-controlled *Pemex* – is available. *Pemex* stations don't post their prices, but they don't need to, since the price is set by the government and is the same across the republic. And all stations are full service.

Gas stations accept cash only, as is the case with most roadside businesses in Mexico. They don't accept dollars either, so make sure you have a reserve of pesos on hand. Diesel fuel is also found at most stations, and unleaded fuel can be bought in two

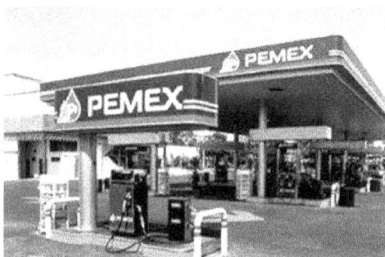

Pemex is the only brand of gasoline available in Mexico

grades: *Magna* and *Premium*. *Magna* is the equivalent of regular unleaded gas in the U.S. and is rated 87 octane. *Premium* is high-grade gasoline, rated at 93 octane. I've purchased dozens of tanks of gas in Mexico, and I've had virtually no problems with fuel quality, contrary to what many might expect.

If you need a fillup, just tell the attendant *Lleno con Magna, por favor*. Make sure the gas pump is reset to zero, instead of adding your total to the last customer's – an old scam. Some attendants may wash your windshield, others may not; give a small tip if you feel it's appropriate. Don't be surprised to be approached by vendors selling everything from chewing gum to pirated CD's while waiting for your gas to be dispensed. Most of the merchandise they sell are convenience items; take a look if you feel like it. If you don't, just say *No, gracias*.

Most *Pemex* stations offer public restroom facilities, but they may not be free, even to customers. Don't be surprised to be charged a couple of pesos to use the gas station restroom. And sadly, my experience is that price is not proportional to cleanliness.

Don't drive at night. During the day, driving in Mexico is about as safe as driving back home. But at night, things change rapidly. Few highways have reflectors or even reflective paint to mark the lanes. *Topes* are harder to see at night. Some of the locals drive without taillights or even headlights, foolishly thinking it will save gas. Instead of forging ahead at night, plan on getting a hotel. You'll enjoy the drive much more during daylight hours.

Toll roads and free roads. Most two-lane highways are free of charge. However, heavily-trafficked routes, especially those connecting major cities, have an alternate four-lane toll road that parallels the two-lane road. The two-lane free road is called the *libre* (pronounced LEE-bray), and the toll road is called the *cuota*. These toll roads are similar to our interstate highways, except that exits are few and far between. Likewise, gas stations and restaurants are a rarity on rural stretches of the *cuota*.

Toll roads are expensive even by American standards; they seem to average about one peso – or almost 10 cents U.S. – per mile. Your toll does include insurance and free towing services, though, should you break down or have an accident while on the expressway. And nearly every toll booth will be adjacent to the Mexican equivalent of a rest area, complete with free restroom services and a convenience store.

If you really want to see towns and villages along the way, though, skip the *cuota*. The slower, two-lane *libre* passes through every town and village along the route. However, I recommend taking the *cuota* under two circumstances. First, when you're getting a little tired of following slow trucks and winding around curves and hills, driving on the fast, four-lane *cuota* can be a relief. Second, when bypassing major cities, definitely opt for the *cuota*. Small towns in Mexico are charming and peaceful; large cities are stressful and generally to be avoided. Be aware, though, that even the *libre* may have an occasional toll bridge; most of those are unavoidable.

Military check-points. One of the main jobs of the Mexican army is to confiscate drugs and guns, both of which are generally illegal in the country. On highways throughout the republic, the army operates checkpoints. You will be expected to slow down and come to a complete stop. They may ask where you're coming from or where you're going. Respond with *Vengo de...* (I'm coming from...) or *Voy a...* (I'm going to...)

The men, most of whom are teenagers or in their early twenties, may ask you to pull over for a routine search. There's no reason to fear; they are normally very professional and polite, and they usually treat foreigners with the utmost respect. For your own protection, never bring illegal drugs, a gun, or even as much as a single bullet into Mexico; doing so will send you to prison.

Calling Home from Mexico

Calling a U.S. number from Mexico is easy, but expensive. Making a phone call home may still cost eight pesos per minute (about 70¢ U.S.) or even more. Nearly every town will have a *caseta telefónica* – a payphone center – where it's easy to make phone calls to anywhere in the world. Just give the number to the attendant, who will dial it, then direct you to a private booth where you'll have your conversation. At most *casetas*, payment is made after the call. To dial a U.S. number from Mexico, dial 001, followed by the area code and telephone number.

Of course, e-mail, text messaging, and Skype are cheaper and often more convenient ways to stay in touch while south of the border.

Speed limits in Mexico. Speed limits are indicated by a number with a red circle around it, measured in kilometers per hour. On the open road, speed limits are disregarded by most vehicles. For example, on a wide two-lane straight highway, the speed limit may be 80 kph (about 50 mph), but you may see buses and cars driving at least 70 miles per hour, which is over 110 kph! Very little speed enforcement is seen on the open highway.

In towns, though, it's completely different. Local traffic cops often look for speeders and write them tickets. Even without enforcement, though, it may be difficult to speed when a series of *topes* slow traffic to a crawl. Bottom line: use good judgment and common sense when driving in Mexico.

Restaurants. Typical restaurants along the side of the road are plentiful and reasonably priced. With the equivalent of ten dollars per meal, you'll eat very well in all but the most expensive tourist areas. Since few servers speak English, a little Spanish goes a long way. You won't get the check until you ask for it – *La cuenta, por favor* – and there are no free refills on drinks at most diners in Mexico. A 10% tip for good service is well appreciated and considered generous.

Lodging. All but the smallest of towns will have at least one hotel. Unless you're in a resort area, forget the free breakfast, Wi-Fi, and swimming pool. Most hotel rooms will be simply furnished and have a television, free parking, private bath, hot water, and possibly a phone. Air conditioning *may* cost extra. The prices will usually be posted at the front desk, but may be negotiable. It's common to let the guest see a room before sealing the deal.

Look for hotels with an enclosed parking lot. Many will actually lock your car in their secure lot overnight.

Remember the classes of lodging from Chapter 11? The situation is similar in Mexico. At the high end are **American-style Hotels**. Many of these are the chains you've heard of from the

States, such as Holiday Inn, Best Western, Howard Johnson, and so forth. These hotels, found in only the largest cities, will give you the surroundings you're used to, but the prices are also the highest.

The mid-tier hotels are **Roadside Hotels**. These are not chains, but locally-owned places. The prices usually range from 300 to 600 pesos a night (about 25 to 50 dollars). You'll usually get a clean, comfortable room at these places. Most of them have a restaurant attached or nearby.

Then there are the **Auto Hotels**. Often found at the edge of towns, their prices are usually very cheap, with an enclosed curtain to conceal your car. However, these motels tend to appeal to shady characters and those who have something to hide. Several of these places charge by the hour, if you get the idea.

Credit cards. In most of Mexico, credit cards are not yet widely accepted. They may be accepted at large department stores and in tourist areas frequented by foreigners, but for the most part, cash is king. Although credit cards are uncommon, ATM machines are found at every bank and nearly every chain convenience store – the most common of which is *Oxxo* – in the country.

Local driving customs. Some two-lane roads, especially in the northern half of Mexico, are especially wide. Here, you are expected to slide over to the right when being passed. Likewise, if you see an oncoming vehicle passing a car, you're also expected to slide over to the right. This system

Many two-lane roads in Mexico can actually accommodate three lanes of traffic

Using the Internet in Mexico

Hotels in Mexico rarely offer free wireless internet – or internet service of any type, for that matter. The easiest way to get online is to visit an internet shop – usually signed *Internet* or *Renta de Computadoras* – and pay by the hour. Most of the time, renting a computer costs less than two dollars an hour, occasionally a little more. I've paid as little as five pesos an hour (about 50¢) and as much as 25 pesos an hour. Of course, printing costs extra.

actually works quite well and serves to accommodate *three* lanes of traffic on a two-lane road.

In some places, especially the North, if you're following a vehicle displaying a left turn signal, that means it's safe to pass. This custom seems to be fading, especially in the South, and isn't seen as often as in years past. Also, motorists in construction zones are expected to drive *much* slower than Americans are used to – 20 to 30 miles per hour maximum.

If your car breaks down. Mexico's tourism agency supports the Green Angels, who patrol major highways helping motorists. If you break down or run out of gas, pull over to the side of the road, open the hood, and wait for help. *Los Ángeles Verdes*, as they are called in Spanish, provide free repairs, charging only for parts and gasoline. Many of these *Ángeles* speak at least some English.

Staying out of trouble. For the most part, use the same common sense you do at home. Stay out of questionable areas, especially at night. Avoid bars and cantinas, especially on the weekends. Never drink and drive. Be friendly and polite, and most people will treat you accordingly. The Mexican people are known for their hospitality and friendliness, especially to strangers.

Traffic cops, or *tránsito*, as their uniforms say, may be paid very little. Some of them live off the bribes they manage to pluck from unsuspecting motorists. To avoid them, try to blend in with other vehicles. Don't give them a reason to stop you. Although they may stop you just to perform a routine check of your paperwork – car permit and license – be polite and don't give them a reason to bother you. Even better, bypass major cities if possible, where most of these *tránsito* cops lurk, and stick to smaller towns.

If you live in a state which issues only one license plate, affix a spare license plate to the front of your car after crossing into Mexico. Traffic police may view the lack of a front plate as suspicious, or at least as a reason to stop you. Putting a temporary plate on the front can keep from drawing attention to yourself. Of course, remove the spare plate before crossing back into the U.S.

Really, with only a few exceptions, driving in Mexico is very similar to driving stateside. Although some customs may be different, the same basic rules apply: Know your surroundings, be a courteous driver, and use common sense.

Heading South

The least congested border crossing in the Rio Grande Valley is located at Los Indios, just to the southwest of Harlingen. It's in a rural area with few businesses nearby, so traffic is practically nonexistent. This road continues straight to the first small city on our route: Valle Hermoso. With all the comforts of a prosperous town, it makes for a convenient first stop before continuing to the interior of Mexico; it's also the last town before leaving the border zone.

Shortly after Valle Hermoso, the road merges south onto Highway 101, the major thoroughfare leading toward Tampico on the coast and Victoria, the capital of the state of Tamaulipas. After skirting the edge of San Fernando, the roadway quickly leaves the Rio Grande Valley behind in favor of the highest hills we've seen on this trip. The elevation rises several hundred feet, relatively high considering our proximity to the Gulf.

Eventually, we get to a major intersection where we can head to Victoria or to Tampico. We turn left, taking us almost due south, in the direction of Tampico. This route, Highway 180, is the route

Good Places to Spend the Night

The following towns offer inexpensive, convenient lodging options near the main highway. In order from north to south.

Nuevo Progreso – Look for the Las Flores Inn on the south side of town. Restaurant, convenient parking, in a relatively quiet area of this border town.

Valle Hermoso – Several hotels, but the less expensive ones tend to be on the north side of town, before getting to the central business district.

Highway 101 – Look for the large hotel on the right, next to the Pemex station, at the intersection of Highways 101 and 97 – exactly 47 miles south of Valle Hermoso.

Tampico Alto – Just south of Tampico on Highway 180. Two hotels are located across the street from one another. Both have enclosed parking and are within walking distance of several small restaurants.

Cerro Azul – About 80 miles south of Tampico. The Hotel San Carlos sits on a steep hill, but has protected parking and a couple of restaurants nearby.

we will generally follow all the way to the Emerald Coast. But first, we must traverse the flat savannah leading up to the town of Soto La Marina and the river sharing its name.

Soon, the road starts to wind around hills and mountains, passing through the most hauntingly desolate stretch of highway we'll pass this side of the Rio Grande. Although several cars and buses take this road, towns are few and far between. All of a sudden, you've crossed a major milestone; twenty-eight miles after leaving Soto La Marina, you cross the Tropic of Cancer.

As we travel farther into the tropics, the climate slowly becomes warmer and more humid. The town of Aldama, the first town we pass in the tropics, is known for fishing and subterranean rivers that attract cave divers from around the world.

Nearing Tampico

Arriving at the town of Manuel, we turn left and continue toward Tampico. Driving along the first four lane rural highway we've seen south of the border, the route passes more villages and settlements, especially nearing Tampico. The highway flattens out, though, signaling our nearness to the Gulf coast. We pass the edges of Altamira, a suburb of Tampico, and the once rural highway becomes a bustling, urban thoroughfare. Instead of heading straight into Tampico, though, we take a bypass around the city's worst congestion. Signaling the bypass is a large fishing boat permanently parked to the right of the highway.

The bypass starts as a two-lane highway, curving around homes and settlements. The terrain through here is swampy, as our elevation is no higher than 30 feet. As the two-lane bypass ends, we take the ramp to the right, crossing a large river that carries us into the state of Veracruz. This part of the Tampico area is filled with small businesses and industry. After a few miles on this four-lane street, take the exit ramp marked for "Tuxpan".

This new road shifts back down to two lanes as you cross another bridge and pay another toll. You'll quickly pass through another little town, Anahuac. It's slow going through here, as trucks and buses clog this little highway to avoid the city, too. At the fork in the road, veer to the left, climbing a steep hill. Soon, you come to the main road – Highway 180 – turn right, heading south again.

The Hills of Northern Veracruz

Shortly, we hit the southern edge of the Tampico metropolitan area, passing through the town of Tampico Alto. It's a good place to spend the night, there are several hotels and restaurants here within easy access of the highway. Continuing south for the next 80 miles, the terrain transitions from a flat coastal plain to rolling hills. Once you reach Cerro Azul, about 80 miles south of Tampico, we're clearly in a mountainous area. You can look to your left and see practically the whole town, nestled in the valley below. All the while, though, we're no more than a few miles from the Gulf coast.

Coastal Veracruz is surprisingly hilly in places

About eight miles past Cerro Azul, we turn right, then turn left less than a mile later, avoiding the city of Tuxpan in favor of the smaller town of Alamo. Officially, this 'shortcut' is labeled Highway 131, and it traverses both tropical plains and steep hills. Several miles after passing Alamo, you'll see a sign that reads "Veracruz Cuota". This is the road to take that bypasses the congested oil town of Poza Rica. It's quite a scenic highway, too, as we speed around the steepest mountains in the region at nearly 70 miles per hour.

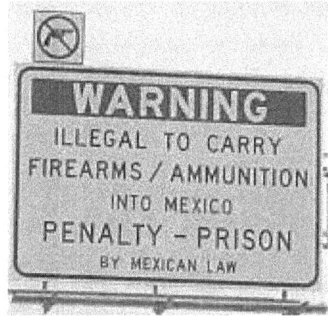

This sign is not a joke

Follow this two-lane *cuota* bypass until it ends, shortly after the toll booth. Then turn left, returning to Mexico 180. You're back in the mountains, and you'll cross several rivers, hills, and streams before getting to the town of Tecolutla and the toll bridge that shares its name. Then, almost exactly ten miles after crossing the bridge, we see a welcome sight on our left – the Gulf of Mexico.

Costa Esmeralda

The plentiful palms you see all around the highway and the hotels you see on both sides of the road are a sure sign the beach is near. You've reached *Costa Esmeralda*, the Emerald Coast, as it's called in English. Highway 180 stays within sight of the beach for the next several miles, all the way to the town of Casitas.

Beachside hotels in this area are inexpensive and range in level from the most basic of roadside inns to the more comfortable and modern. Many of the managers speak English, and a room can sometimes be had for as little as 300 pesos (25 dollars). The little town of Casitas is also a great place to try local seafood – caught that very morning – at reasonable prices. It's here where our journey into Mexico ends. But this is really only the beginning, for the possibilities are endless if you decide to continue your tropical trek even further.

Returning to the U.S.A.

When you drive your car across the Rio Grande back into the United States, you'll have to wait in line at the border station – anywhere from five minutes up to three hours, depending on traffic that day. The border patrol agent will ask for your passports and may ask where you were born and if you're bringing anything back. The agent may also ask about the purpose of your trip and want to know where you've been. Answer honestly. Your car and luggage may be searched. Remember that you're generally not allowed to bring fresh fruits, vegetables, or meats back into the United States. Even if your vehicle is searched, you'll likely be detained only a few minutes during the actual inspection.

The Cold, Hard Facts About Traveling in Mexico

Every serious road traveler should consider driving down to Mexico at least once. In the interest of full disclosure, though, you should know that it's not always a carefree ride south of the border. There are some key differences you should be aware of:

1. Most roads in Mexico, especially two-lane *libre* highways, are not up to the quality of American highways. Many rural highways are in poor condition and marked by potholes and ruts. Drive much slower on these roads. Although the four-lane *cuotas* are better, some of those aren't that great, either.

2. Under no circumstances should you ever take illegal drugs, guns, or even a single bullet into Mexico. If caught, you *will* go to prison.

3. If you think public restrooms are bad in the United States, just wait until you get to Mexico! Hand sanitizer is a must, as is your own roll of toilet paper. Taking your own paper towels isn't a bad idea, either. Don't throw paper into the toilet, as it may clog the plumbing.

4. Water systems are not very reliable in Mexico, especially in rural areas. It's not unusual for water towers to be shut off at night or at other times. I've known of areas being without running water for weeks at a time. And, of course, don't drink the tap water; bottled water is plentiful and cheap.

5. Most importantly, use common sense. Travelers who stay out of questionable situations rarely experience any serious problems in Mexico. Although it's very different from what most Americans are used to, a visit to our southern neighbor is filled with treasures at every turn of the road and is well worth any minor inconveniences you may encounter.

Spanish Primer

Although it's not obligatory to speak Spanish to take a road trip to Mexico, it certainly helps. Even if you don't, though, here are a few words and phrases to help you get by:

Basics

por favor [por fah-VOHR]	please
gracias [GRAH-see-ahs]	Thank you
baño [BAH-nyoh]	bathroom, restroom
gratis [GRAH-tees]	free
pasaporte [pah-sah-POR-tay]	passport
un momento [oon moe-MEHN-toe]	one moment

Eating Out

almuerzo [al-MWER-soe]	lunch
desayuno [day-cye-OO-noe]	breakfast
cena [SAY-nah]	dinner
¿Cuánto cuesta? [KWAHN-toe KWAYS-tah]	How much does it cost?
La cuenta [lah KWEN-tah]	the bill, the check
abierto [ah-bee-AIR-toe]	open
cerrado [say-RAH-doe]	closed

On the Road

despacio [des-PAH-see-oe]	slow
cuota [KWOE-tah]	toll, fee, toll road
libre [LEE-bray]	free road
topes [TOE-pays]	speed bumps
la carretera a [la car-reh-TEHR-ah ah]	The highway to
Dónde está… [DOHN-day es-TAH]	Where is…?
mecánico [meh-KAHN-ee-koe]	mechanic
No sirve [no SEER-vay]	It doesn't work.

Lodging

hotel [oh-TELL] hotel	
una habitación [oo-nah ah-bee-tah-see-OHN]	A hotel room
dos camas [dohs KAH-mahs]	two beds
clima [KLEE-mah]	climate, air conditioner

23

Road Trip Resources

Each U.S. state and Canadian province operates a tourism department which provides free vacation guides and maps. These free guides highlight places of interest and popular tourist destinations. To request free information by mail, visit the following websites, and click on the link that directs you to 'more information', 'vacation guide', or 'free travel guide.' For most states, you can also download information directly from the web or request information by phone.

State Tourism Information

Alabama	www.alabama.travel
Alaska	www.travelalaska.com
Arizona	www.arizonaguide.com

Arkansas	www.arkansas.com
California	www.visitcalifornia.com
Colorado	www.colorado.com
Connecticut	www.ctvisit.com
Delaware	www.visitdelaware.com
D.C.	washington.org
Florida	www.visitflorida.com
Georgia	www.exploregeorgia.org
Hawaii	www.hawaiitourismauthority.org
Idaho	www.visitidaho.org
Illinois	www.enjoyillinois.com
Indiana	www.in.gov/visitindiana
Iowa	www.traveliowa.com
Kansas	www.travelks.com
Kentucky	www.kentuckytourism.com
Louisiana	www.louisianatravel.com
Maine	www.visitmaine.com
Maryland	www.visitmaryland.org
Massachusetts	www.massvacation.com
Michigan	www.michigan.org
Minnesota	www.exploreminnesota.com
Mississippi	www.visitmississippi.org
Missouri	www.visitmo.com
Montana	www.visitmt.com
Nebraska	www.visitnebraska.com
Nevada	travelnevada.com
New Hampshire	www.visitnh.gov
New Jersey	www.visitnj.org

New Mexico	www.newmexico.org
New York	www.iloveny.com
North Carolina	www.visitnc.com
North Dakota	www.ndtourism.com
Ohio	consumer.discoverohio.com
Oklahoma	www.travelok.com
Oregon	www.traveloregon.com
Pennsylvania	www.visitpa.com
Rhode Island	www.visitrhodeisland.com
South Carolina	www.discoversouthcarolina.com
South Dakota	www.travelsd.com
Tennessee	www.tnvacation.com
Texas	www.traveltex.com
Utah	www.utah.com
Vermont	www.vermontvacation.com
Virginia	www.virginia.org
Washington	www.experiencewa.com
West Virginia	www.wvtourism.com
Wisconsin	www.travelwisconsin.com
Wyoming	www.wyomingtourism.org

Canadian Provinces

Alberta	www.travelalberta.us
British Columbia	www.hellobc.com
Manitoba	www.travelmanitoba.com
New Brunswick	www.tourismnewbrunswick.ca
Northwest Territories	www.spectacularnwt.com

Newfoundland & Labrador	www.newfoundlandlabrador.com
Nova Scotia	www.novascotia.com
Nunavut	www.nunavuttourism.com
Ontario	www.ontariotravel.net
Prince Edward Island	www.tourismpei.com
Quebec	www.bonjourquebec.com
Saskatchewan	www.sasktourism.com
Yukon	travelyukon.com

Mexico

Mexico Tourism	www.visitmexico.com

Packing

In addition to the packing list in Chapter 7, the following websites are excellent resources for travelers looking to pack light.

www.onebag.com - Learn to put everything in one bag.

www.ricksteves.com/plan/tips/packlist.htm - Although this list is tailored to European travel, most of the principles apply to road trips, too.

Dining on the Road

www.roadfood.com - The best website for finding local diners on the road. Complemented by the book *Roadfood*, also available for purchase on the site and at bookstores.

www.restaurant.com - A good resource for finding discount gift certificates for independently-owned restaurants across the country. Most $25 gift certificates can be bought for $10 on the site, saving you more than 50%.

www.fatwallet.com - A series of discussion boards for sharing restaurant coupons and other deals. This site directs you to sales, coupons, and other travel deals available both on the web and in traditional stores.

Road Trip Planning

www.roadtripamerica.com - The country's best discussion board for planning a route. Includes great road trip ideas and dozens of experienced roadtrippers sharing advice.

www.roadsideamerica.com – The best source for odd or unusual roadside tourist attractions. Here the authors have catalogued over 10,000 kitschy roadside spots and have even designed an app listing them all.

maps.google.com – One of the easiest-to-use online mapping services. Also integrates satellite imagery from Google Earth. Changing a route is as easy as dragging a line to a different road you wish to take.

www.mapquest.com - The granddaddy of mapping services on the web. Mapquest integrates local business information and makes it easy to get door-to-door directions to your next destination.

www.randmcnally.com - Complete with features that integrate seamlessly with Rand McNally's printed road atlas. Also includes turn-by-turn directions and ideas for road trips.

Weather Conditions

www.weather.gov - Complete forecasts, current conditions, and meteorological data for anywhere in America. Enter any city and state combination in the country, and complete radar, satellite, and forecast information will be shown immediately.

www.weather.com - The Weather Channel's website. Special links for travel weather. Includes tips for driving in various types of weather.

www.weather.com/outlook/driving/interstate/regional?reg=us – This link at the Weather Channel deserves its own link. At a glance, determine which parts of the country's roads are dangerous for travel.

Unconventional Road Travel

www.cheaprvliving.com – Details on creating your own camper van. See Chapter 14 for details.

www.rvforum.net – A forum dedicated to RV living, with sections dedicated to smaller RV's (Classes B and C) and van conversions.

Gas Prices

www.gasbuddy.com - The most thorough information on gas prices available on the web, submitted by thousands of volunteer participants. Find the cheapest gas prices in a region with an interactive color-coded map.

Comparing Hotel Prices and Quality

www.priceline.com - Usually the cheapest avenue for booking a hotel room. Granted, when 'naming your own price' you won't get to choose your hotel; it will be assigned to you based on your chosen star level and price. You'll also have to wait to see if the hotel accepts your price. Still, the savings can be as much as 50% off the lowest published rate.

www.hotwire.com - Usually a few dollars more expensive than Priceline, but you get to choose the amenities the hotel will have. And there's no waiting to see if your offer is accepted; the price you see *always* gets accepted. Often the best choice when you need a discount hotel room the same day and need to book it quickly.

www.betterbidding.com - Web message board where people share their winning bids for Priceline and Hotwire. It takes much of the guesswork out of booking a room on these two websites.

biddingfortravel.yuku.com - Similar to BetterBidding, except this site covers only Priceline.

www.expedia.com - Book hotels, car rentals, and plane tickets.

www.orbitz.com - This site makes it easy to compare prices for plane tickets, as well as hotels and cars.

www.travelocity.com - Another good source for comparing hotel rates and reserving a room online.

www.hotels.com - A useful site for comparing hotel prices in a city and making your reservation.

www.skyauction.com - An auction site for travelers. Bid on stays at resort properties and hotels across the world. There are some excellent deals to be had on this site, if you're willing to do some research and be *very* flexible.

www.tripadvisor.com - The most comprehensive site for user-generated hotel reviews. Practically every hotel, motel, and inn in the United States is reviewed on this site. Some reviews should be taken with a grain of salt, but if a location's negative reviews outnumber its positive ones, beware.

Hotel Chains by Classification

High-end Hotels – These hotels cater to business travelers and higher-budget travelers. Expect more luxurious furnishings and public areas. Most of these hotels have a pool and gym. You'll probably pay extra for breakfast and internet at these properties.

Clarion Hotels   www.clarionhotel.com
Crowne Plaza   www.crowneplaza.com

Doubletree	doubletree.hilton.com
Embassy Suites	embassysuites.hilton.com
Four Points by Sheraton	www.fourpoints.com
Hilton	www.hilton.com
Holiday Inn	www.holidayinn.com
Hyatt	www.hyatt.com
Hyatt Place	www.hyatt.com/hyatt/place
Marriott	www.marriott.com
Omni	www.omnihotels.com
Radisson	www.radisson.com
Renaissance	www.renaissancehotels.com
Sheraton Hotels	www.sheraton.com

Roadside Chains – These hotels/motels cater to leisure travelers, roadtrippers, and those on a budget. Expect modest, comfortable furnishings. A continental breakfast and internet service are usually complimentary at these properties.

AmericInn	www.americinn.com
America's Best Value Inn	www.americasbestvalueinn.com
Baymont Inn & Suites	www.baymontinns.com
Best Western	www.bestwestern.com
Comfort Inn	www.comfortinn.com
Comfort Suites	www.comfortsuites.com
Country Inns & Suites	www.countryinns.com
Courtyard by Marriott	www.courtyard.com
Days Inn	www.daysinn.com
Drury Inn	www.druryhotels.com

Econo Lodge	www.econolodge.com
Fairfield Inn (Marriott)	www.fairfieldinn.com
Hampton Inn (Hilton)	hamptoninn.hilton.com
Hilton Garden Inn	hiltongardeninn.hilton.com
Howard Johnson	www.hojo.com
Jameson Inn	www.jamesoninns.com
Knights Inn	www.knightsinn.com
La Quinta Inn & Suites	www.lq.com
Microtel	www.microtelinn.com
Motel 6	www.motel6.com
Ramada Inn	www.ramada.com
Red Roof Inn	www.redroof.com
Rodeway Inn	www.rodewayinn.com
Sleep Inn	www.sleepinn.com
Travelodge	www.travelodge.com
Wingate Inn	www.wingatehotels.com

Extended-Stay Properties – Lodging at this level usually won't provide a free breakfast, but you will have access to an in-room kitchen complete with refrigerator and stove, where you can prepare your own meals. Internet access will be available, but you *may* have to pay extra.

Candlewood Suites	www.candlewoodsuites.com
Extended Stay America	www.extendedstayamerica.com
Hawthorn Suites	www.hawthorn.com
Homestead Studio Suites	www.homesteadhotels.com
Homewood Suites	homewoodsuites.hilton.com

Mainstay Suites	www.mainstaysuites.com
Residence Inn by Marriott	www.residenceinn.com
Staybridge Suites	www.staybridgesuites.com
Studio 6	www.staystudio6.com

Speed Limits and Key Laws by State

Each state's speed limits for passenger vehicles on rural interstate highways are as follows:

Alabama	70	
Alaska	65	(on major two-lane highways)
Arizona	75	
Arkansas	70	
California	70	(Handheld phone use prohibited)
Colorado	75	
Connecticut	65	(Handheld phone use prohibited)
Delaware	65	(Handheld phone use prohibited)
D.C.	55	(No Handheld phones; radar detectors illegal)
Florida	70	
Georgia	70	
Hawaii	60	(Handheld phone use prohibited)
Idaho	80	
Illinois	70	(Handheld phone use prohibited)
Indiana	70	
Iowa	70	
Kansas	75	
Kentucky	70	
Louisiana	70	(75 on rural parts of I-49)
Maine	65	(75 on I-95 north of Bangor)

Maryland	65	(Handheld phone use prohibited)
Massachusetts	65	
Michigan	70	
Minnesota	70	
Mississippi	70	
Missouri	70	
Montana	75	
Nebraska	75	
Nevada	75	(Handheld phone use prohibited)
New Hamp.	65	(70 on I-93 north of Concord)
New Jersey	65	(Handheld phone use prohibited)
New Mexico	75	
New York	65	(Handheld phone use prohibited)
N. Carolina	70	
N. Dakota	75	
Ohio	70	
Oklahoma	70	(75 on turnpikes)
Oregon	65	(Handheld phone use prohibited)
Pennsylvania	70	
Rhode Island	65	
S. Carolina	70	
S. Dakota	75	
Tennessee	70	
Texas	75	(as high as 80 in parts of rural West Texas and 85 on specified toll roads)
Utah	80	
Vermont	65	
Virginia	70	(Radar detectors illegal)

Washington	70	(Handheld phone use prohibited)
W. Virginia	70	(Handheld phone use prohibited)
Wisconsin	65	
Wyoming	80	

In addition, radar detectors may not be mounted on a vehicle's windshield in California, Florida, Pennsylvania, New Jersey, or Minnesota.

Visit the author on the web at

www.roadtripradiousa.com